Montenegro

THIS EDITION WRITTEN AND RESEARCHED BY

Peter Dragičević

Vesna Marić

PLAN YOUR TRIP

ON THE ROAD

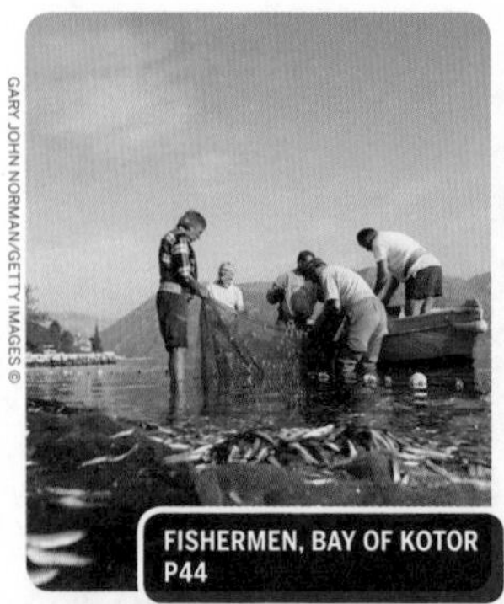

GARY JOHN NORMAN/GETTY IMAGES ©

FISHERMEN, BAY OF KOTOR P44

ALDO PAVAN/GETTY IMAGES ©

BULJARICA BEACH P74

GREG HAHN/GETTY IMAGES ©

Contents

KOTOR P44

SPECIAL FEATURES

Welcome to Montenegro

Montenegro, Crna Gora, Black Mountain: the very name conjures up images of romance and drama – and this fascinating land doesn't disappoint on either front.

Small but Perfectly Formed

Imagine a place with sapphire beaches as spectacular as Croatia's, rugged peaks as dramatic as Switzerland's, canyons nearly as deep as Colorado's, palazzos as elegant as Venice's and towns as old as Greece's and then wrap it up in a Mediterranean climate and squish it into an area two-thirds of the size of Wales and you start to get a picture of Montenegro. You could easily drive clear across the country in a day – or spend a month and be left wanting more. Ironically, this tiny place is populated by giants – arguably the tallest people in the world.

Where Land & Sea Embrace

There's not a lot of it – barely 100km from tip to toe – but Montenegro's coast is quite extraordinary. Mountains jut sharply from crystal-clear waters in such a way that the word 'looming' is unavoidable. As if that wasn't picturesque enough, ancient walled towns cling to the rocks and dip their feet in the water like they're the ones on holiday. In summer the whole scene is bathed in the scent of wild herbs, conifers and Mediterranean blossoms. The word 'magical' is similarly impossible to avoid.

Go Wild

When the beaches fill up with Eastern European sunseekers, intrepid travellers can easily sidestep the hordes in the rugged mountains of Durmitor and Prokletije, the primeval forest of Biogradska Gora or in the many towns and villages where ordinary Montenegrins go about their daily lives. Hike, mountain bike or kayak yourself to somewhere obscure and chances are you'll have it all to yourself. This is, after all, a country where wolves and bears still lurk in forgotten corners.

Living on the Edge

Ever since the Roman Empire split in two 1600 years ago, this land has sat on the borderline between east and west – and it's all the more interesting for its turbulent past. The richness of its cultural history can be seen in the mosaic floors of Roman villas, flamboyantly painted Orthodox monasteries, ornate Catholic churches, the elegant minarets of mosques, and the sturdy fortresses built by the numerous powers that have fought over these lands. Then there's the legacy of 50 years as a communist state, independent of both the Eastern Bloc and the West. For those with even a passing interest in European history, it's a fascinating place.

Why I Love Montenegro

By Peter Dragičević, Author

I still remember the sheer thrill I felt when confronted with the extraordinary beauty of the Bay of Kotor for the first time – and each time I visit, that thrill returns. For me, Montenegro is at its most magical on long summer evenings when the streets fill up with people, young and old, heading out for a slow, social stroll – a scene that's repeated in every city, town and village throughout the country. Sit me somewhere with a glass of local wine, a plate of grilled squid and a view of the passing parade, and I'm in heaven.

For more about our author, see page 192

Above: Bay of Kotor (p32)

Montenegro

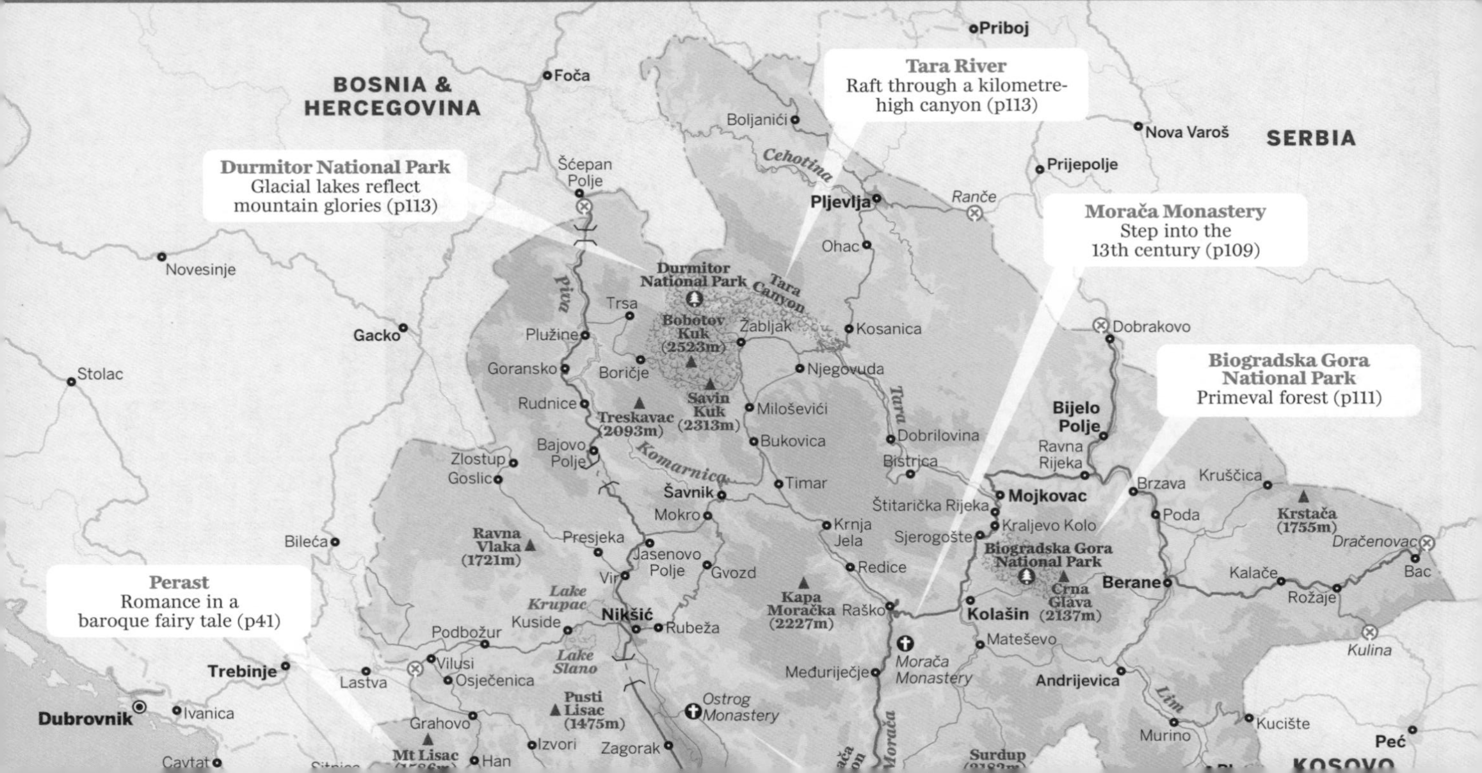

0 — 50 km
0 — 25 miles

Durmitor National Park
Glacial lakes reflect mountain glories (p113)

Tara River
Raft through a kilometre-high canyon (p113)

Morača Monastery
Step into the 13th century (p109)

Biogradska Gora National Park
Primeval forest (p111)

Perast
Romance in a baroque fairy tale (p41)

BOSNIA & HERCEGOVINA
SERBIA
KOSOVO
Priboj
Foča
Boljanići
Nova Varoš
Prijepolje
Šćepan Polje
Cehotina
Pljevlja
Ranče
Novesinje
Ohac
Durmitor National Park
Tara Canyon
Trsa
Bobotov Kuk (2523m)
Žabljak
Kosanica
Dobrakovo
Piva
Plužine
Gacko
Goransko
Boričje
Njegovuda
Stolac
Rudnice
Savin Kuk (2313m)
Miloševići
Tara
Treskavac (2093m)
Bijelo Polje
Bajovo Polje
Bukovica
Dobrilovina
Zlostup
Komarnica
Bistrica
Ravna Rijeka
Goslic
Timar
Brzava
Kruščica
Šavnik
Mojkovac
Štitarička Rijeka
Poda
Krstača (1755m)
Mokro
Krnja Jela
Kraljevo Kolo
Ravna Vlaka (1721m)
Presjeka
Sjerogošte
Dračenovac
Bileća
Jasenovo Polje
Biogradska Gora National Park
Redice
Bac
Vir
Gvozd
Kalače
Lake Krupac
Kapa Moračka (2227m)
Berane
Crna Glava (2137m)
Rožaje
Nikšić
Raško
Kolašin
Kuside
Rubeža
Podbožur
Mateševo
Kulina
Vilusi
Morača Monastery
Trebinje
Lake Slano
Lastva
Osječenica
Međuriječje
Andrijevica
Lim
Ostrog Monastery
Pusti Lisac (1475m)
Dubrovnik
Ivanica
Grahovo
Morača
Murino
Kučište
Izvori
Zagorak
Peć
Mt Lisac
Cavtat
Han
Surdup

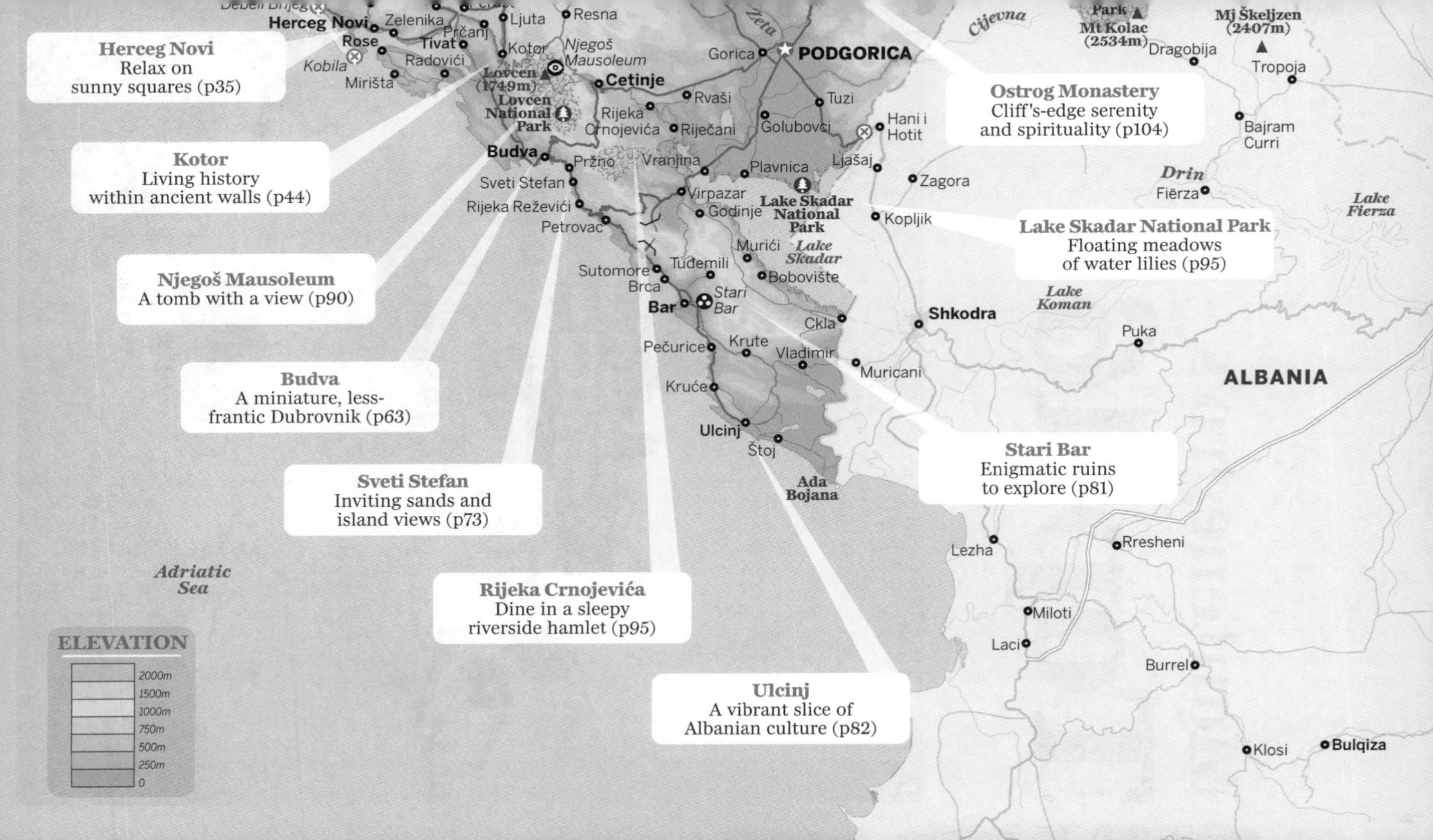
Herceg Novi
Relax on sunny squares (p35)
Kotor
Living history within ancient walls (p44)
Njegoš Mausoleum
A tomb with a view (p90)
Budva
A miniature, less-frantic Dubrovnik (p63)
Sveti Stefan
Inviting sands and island views (p73)
Rijeka Crnojevića
Dine in a sleepy riverside hamlet (p95)
Ulcinj
A vibrant slice of Albanian culture (p82)
Stari Bar
Enigmatic ruins to explore (p81)
Lake Skadar National Park
Floating meadows of water lilies (p95)
Ostrog Monastery
Cliff's-edge serenity and spirituality (p104)
Adriatic Sea
ELEVATION
2000m
1500m
1000m
750m
500m
250m
0
Herceg Novi
Zelenika
Rose
Kobila
Mirišta
Tivat
Prčanj
Radovići
Ljuta
Kotor
Resna
Njegoš Mausoleum
Lovcen (1749m)
Lovcen National Park
Cetinje
Budva
Pržno
Sveti Stefan
Rijeka Reževići
Petrovac
Rijeka Crnojevića
Rvaši
Riječani
Vranjina
Virpazar
Godinje
Sutomore
Brca
Tuđemili
Bar
Stari Bar
Murići
Lake Skadar
Bobovište
Pečurice
Krute
Vladimir
Kruće
Ulcinj
Štoj
Ada Bojana
Zeta
Gorica
PODGORICA
Tuzi
Golubovci
Plavnica
Lake Skadar National Park
Hani i Hotit
Ljašaj
Zagora
Kopljik
Ckla
Muricani
Shkodra
Cijevna
Mt Kolac (2534m)
Dragobija
Mj Škeljzen (2407m)
Tropoja
Bajram Curri
Drin
Fiërza
Lake Fierza
Lake Koman
Puka
ALBANIA
Lezha
Rresheni
Miloti
Laci
Burrel
Klosi
Bulqiza

Montenegro's Top 16

1

Sveti Stefan

1 The postcard-perfect walled island village of Sveti Stefan (p73) is a wonder to behold. It's a little slice of Mediterranean heaven, with oleanders, pines and olive trees peeking between the terracotta roofs of pink stone dwellings. Content yourself with the views, as access to the island is limited to guests of the exclusive resort that owns it. Laze on the beach, take a stroll through the woods to Pržno, and go crazy taking photographs – it's hard to get a bad shot.

Njegoš Mausoleum

2 Once upon a time there was a Black Mountain. And on top of that mountain there was a tomb guarded by two granite giantesses. And inside the tomb, under a canopy of gold, there rests a great hero, lying in the arms of a giant eagle... This fairy-tale location is the final resting place for the very real 19th-century Vladika (bishop-prince) Petar II Petrović Njegoš. The simple but affecting structure (p90) and monumental statuary do little to distract from the remarkable views over all of Old Montenegro.

GREG HAHN / GETTY IMAGES ©

PAUL BRIRS / GETTY IMAGES ©

Kotor

3 Time-travel back to a Europe of moated walled towns with shadowy lanes and stone churches on every square. It may not be as impressive as Dubrovnik's or as shiny as Budva's, but Kotor's Stari Grad (Old Town; p44) feels much more lived in and ever-so dramatic. The way it seems to grow out of the sheer grey mountains surrounding it adds a thrill of foreboding to the experience – as if they could at any point choose to squeeze the little town in a rocky embrace.

Ostrog Monastery

4 No photo can do justice to the wonder that is Ostrog Monastery (p104). Set in a seemingly sheer mountain wall, it's impossible to frame a photo to reveal its great height without reducing the luminous white monastery to little more than a speck. Orthodox Christians consider this Montenegro's holiest site and, whether you're a believer or not, it's an affecting place. The complex includes several stone churches, but none are more atmospheric than the cave chapels of the Upper Monastery, their rock walls covered in centuries-old frescoes.

3

4

MARTIN CHILD / GETTY IMAGES ©

MILIVOJE MISA MARIC /ALAMY ©

Biogradska Gora National Park

5 Nestled within the folds of the Bjelasica Mountains, Biogradska Gora (p111) has such a peaceful, solitary, untouched-by-the-world feel to it that you might not want to leave. The national park's showcase is pretty Lake Biograd, but further enchantments await on the hiking tracks through one of Europe's most significant remaining tracts of virgin forest. This green world is quite unlike the rocky terrain that characterises most of the country's mountains, and in autumn it kicks up its heels and turns on a colourful show. Lake Biograd (p111)

Perast

6 An oversized village consisting almost entirely of elegant baroque palaces and churches, romantic Perast (p41) forms a worthy centrepiece to the entire Bay of Kotor. The positioning is perfect, sitting at the apex of the inner bay, looking straight down the narrow channel leading to the outer section. Catch a boat to Gospa od Škrpjela (Our-Lady-of-the-Rocks), one of two tiny islands sitting just offshore, where a sky-blue dome covers a church filled with votive offerings left by grateful sailors.

Morača Monastery

7 A location like the Morača Canyon (p109) is guaranteed to set the spirits soaring, making it the ideal place for medieval monastery builders to set to work. Great masters of Serbian Orthodox art added the finishing touches, and here it still stands... The frescoes may have faded but otherwise it's barely unchanged since the 13th century. The highway that now whizzes above does little to dent the tranquility of this peaceful place. Suddenly a life in black robes tending beehives seems almost appealing.

GAVIN HELLIER / GETTY IMAGES ©

Stari Grad, Budva

8 Budva's walled Old Town (p64) is simply gorgeous, rising from the Adriatic like a miniature, less-frantic Dubrovnik. There's an atmosphere of romance and a typically Mediterranean love of life on every corner. While away the hours exploring the labyrinth of narrow cobbled streets, visiting tiny churches and charming galleries, drinking in al fresco cafe-bars, snacking on pizza slices, and being inspired by the sea views from the Citadela. When it's time to relax, there's a beach on either side.

Rafting the Tara River

9 It's hard to get a decent view of the beautiful Tara Canyon – its tree-lined walls, up to 1300m high, tend to get in the way. The effect is most impressive from the water, which goes some way to explaining why rafting is one of the country's most popular tourist activities (p114). You'll hit a few rapids but outside of April and May it's a relatively gentle experience, gliding over crystalline waters through a landscape untouched by human hands.

Mountain Eyes, Durmitor National Park

10 Reflecting the beauty of the imposing grey peaks of the Durmitor range are 18 glacial lakes, known locally as *gorske oči* (mountain eyes). The largest and most beautiful of them is the Black Lake (p113), its inky appearance caused by the black pines that surround it and the peak known as the Bear (Međed) rearing above it. The Black Lake is a breeze to get to and a delight to walk around, but other, more remote lakes await discovery further up, along the park's hiking trails.
Black Lake

Ulcinj

11 There's a special buzz to Ulcinj (p82), Montenegro's southernmost town – an indefinable excitement that's particularly apparent on summer nights, when the beachfront thrums with Eastern-tinged pop and a constant parade of holidaymakers. Looking up to the skyline, minarets compete with an oversized socialist sculpture and the imposing walls of the Old Town, set high up on the cliff. Continuing along the coast, rocky coves give way to the long sandy expanses of Velika Plaža (Big Beach) and the clothing-optional island, Ada Bojana. Mala Plaza Beach (p82)

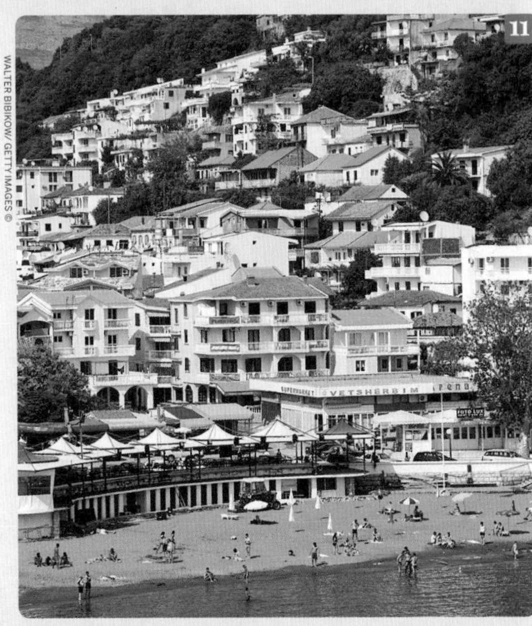

WALTER BIBIKOW/ GETTY IMAGES ©

12

13

O-CHE / GETTY IMAGES ©

14

Lake Skadar National Park

12 Shared between Montenegro and Albania, the Balkans' largest lake (p95) is home to an extraordinary array of birdlife. On the Montenegrin side, a national park encompasses island monasteries, old stone villages famous for their wine and the serpentine loops of the Crnojević River. Descending from the mountains, the river winds sluggishly through the water lilies on its journey to the lake and the conical pair of mountains that the locals affectionately call Sofia Loren. No Italian actress ever looked so sublime.

Stari Bar

13 While there's not much to recommend the modern industrial town of Bar, there's a real gem hidden in the hinterland. The ancient city of Stari Bar (Old Bar; p81) sits in enigmatic ruins atop a bluff surrounded by gnarled olive trees, many of which are over a thousand years old. The city itself has been here for around 2800 years but its current state of dilapidation dates from a thorough bombardment in 1878. Now the whole place is laid bare for you to explore.

Herceg Novi

14 Between the bustling waterfront promenade and the busy highway lies an unassuming Old Town and it's here that the very essence of Herceg Novi (p35) hides. Catholic and Orthodox churches abound in equal profusion, cafe-bars set up their tables on sunny squares, and hulking fortresses huddle in silent menace. Order a glass of wine and soak it all in. The town beaches may not be great, but some of Montenegro's very best are only a short boat ride away.

Rijeka Crnojevića

15 Clinging to the banks of the Crnojević River, this little village (p95) was a favourite of Montenegro's ruling Petrović-Njegoš dynasty, and some of the relatively humble stone houses were once royal dwellings. A picturesque stone bridge spans the river and a marble promenade extends along one bank, providing a launching point for boat and kayak tours heading towards Lake Skadar. The peace and quiet is just as appealing today, but the village now also has one of Montenegro's best seafood restaurants.

The Kotor–Lovćen Road

16 One of the great highlights of Montenegro is the simple joy of travelling along its many scenic routes and taking in the beauty and power of the landscape. The back road connecting Kotor with Cetinje (p48) is one of the very best – looping up and up, and providing ever more jaw-dropping views of the Bay of Kotor and the Adriatic Sea beyond. Any white-knuckle moments caused by the narrowness of the road and its sheer drops are compensated by vistas of lavender-grey mountains and glassy green water.

15

16

Need to Know

For more information see Survival Guide (p159)

Currency
Euro (€)

Language
Montenegrin (extremely similar to Bosnian, Croatian and Serbian)

Visas
Many nationalities are entitled to a stay of up to 90 days without a visa.

Money
ATMs widely available. Credit cards are accepted in larger hotels but aren't widely accepted elsewhere.

Mobile Phones
Montenegrin SIM cards can be used in most unlocked handsets. Rates are relatively expensive.

Time
Central European Time (GMT plus one hour)

When to Go

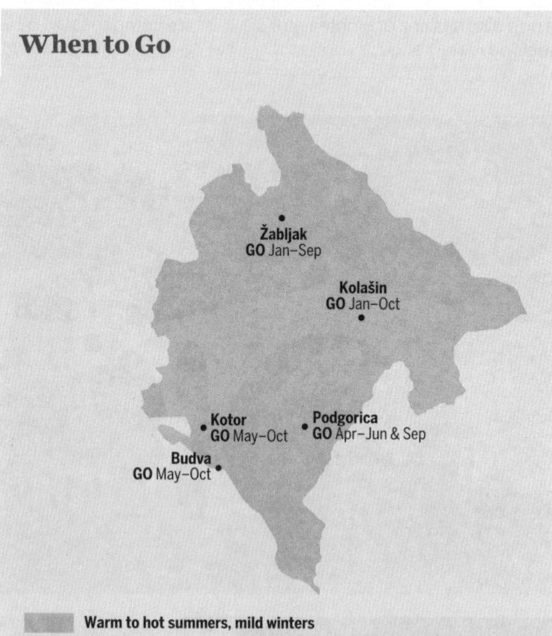

High Season (Jul–Aug)

- The warmest, driest, busiest and most expensive time to visit.
- Accommodation should be booked well in advance; some places enforce three-day minimum stays.

Shoulder (May–Jun & Sep–Oct)

- The best time to come, with plenty of sunshine and average water temperatures over 20°C.
- Some beach bars and restaurants are closed and activities can be harder to arrange.

Low Season (Dec–Mar)

- The ski season kicks in, with peak prices in Kolašin and Žabljak.
- Many hotels, restaurants and bars on the coast close their doors and prices plummet.

Useful Websites

Montenegrin National Tourist Organisation (www.montenegro.travel) Packed full of information, photos and some downloadable resources.

National Parks of Montenegro (www.nparkovi.me) All five national parks are covered, with info about activities and park fees.

Explore Montenegro (www.exploremontenegro.com) Specialises in apartment rentals, especially at the top end, as well as flights and tours.

Visit Montenegro (www.visit-montenegro.com) The most informative of the commercial sites, although some of the information is very out of date.

Destination Montenegro (www.destination-montenegro.com) Has interesting sections on Montenegrin cuisine and *gusle* music, amongst other things.

Lonely Planet (www.lonelyplanet.com/montenegro) Destination information, hotel bookings, traveller forum and more.

Important Numbers

International access code	☎ 00
Country code	☎ 382
Police	☎ 122
Ambulance	☎ 124
Roadside Assistance	☎ 9807

Exchange Rates

Australia	A$1	€0.80
Canada	C$1	€0.77
Croatia	1KN	€0.13
Japan	¥100	€0.90
NewZealand	NZ$1	€0.64
Serbia	100DIN	€0.88
UK	£1	€1.23
US	US$1	€0.76

For current exchange rates see www.xe.com

Daily Costs

Budget: Less than €80

- Dorms or shared room in private accommodation: €10-15
- Pizza slice: €2

Midrange: €80–180

- Single room with bathroom in midrange hotel: €25–80; double room: €40–100
- Apartment rental: €50–150
- Sit-down meal in a traditional restaurant: €10–30

Top End: More than €180

- Single room in an upmarket hotel: €80–360; double room €100–500
- Fish meals that stare back at you while they're served: €30–50

Opening Hours

Montenegrins have a flexible approach to opening times. Even if hours are posted on the door of an establishment, don't be surprised if they're not heeded. Many tourist-orientated businesses close between November and March.

Post offices 7am-8pm Monday to Friday, sometimes Saturday. In smaller towns they may close midafternoon, or close at noon and reopen at 5pm.

Banks 8am-5pm Monday to Friday, 8am-noon Saturday

Shops 9am-8pm. Sometimes they'll close for a few hours in the late afternoon.

Restaurants, Cafes & Bars 8am-midnight

Arriving in Montenegro

Podgorica Airport (p168)Taxis charge a standard €15 fare for the 9km to central Podgorica. There are no buses.

Tivat Airport (p168) Taxis charge €5 to €7 for the 3km to Tivat, €10 for Kotor and €25 for Budva. There are no buses.

Dubrovnik Airport (Croatia; p169) There are no buses directly to Montenegro, but buses to Dubrovnik Bus Station (24km in the wrong direction) are timed around flights (35KN). From Dubrovnik there are only two buses a day to Herceg Novi (€10) and Kotor (€14), one of which continues to Podgorica (€19). Herceg Novi travel agencies and accommodation providers can usually pre-arrange a transfer for €40.

Getting Around

Bus Buses link all major towns and are affordable, reliable and reasonably comfortable.

Car While you can get to most places by bus, hiring a car will give you freedom to explore some of Montenegro's scenic back roads. Some of these are extremely narrow and cling to the sides of canyons, so it may not suit the inexperienced or faint-hearted.

Train Trains are cheap but the network is limited and the carriages are old and can get hot. The main line links Bar, Virpazar, Podgorica, Kolašin, Mojkovac and Bijelo Polje, and there's a second line from Podgorica to Danilovgrad and Nikšić.

For much more on transport, see p168.

What's New

Hostels
From out of nowhere, a hostel scene has finally blossomed in Montenegro. Granted, it's in its infancy and mainly concentrated on Kotor and Budva, but it's off to a very good start. Old Town Hostel is our favourite. (p48)

Prokletije National Park
Montenegro's newest national park was born in 2009, protecting the mountainous stretch bordering Albania and Kosovo. Here's hoping that improved, non-intrusive visitor infrastructure will follow. (p121)

Ethnic Eating
Variety is the spice of life, and spicy variety has finally come to Podgorica with the opening of the country's first Indian restaurant (Mantra, p103), while Tivat now has Japanese (Mitsu, p54).

Miodrag Dado Đurić Gallery
The 2010 death of Montenegro's most acclaimed artist was a blow to the country's artistic fraternity, but the opening of this gallery in his honour has been a wonderful boon. (p91)

Green Boats
A new association of small private boat operators has made life much easier for travellers seeking to cruise Lake Skadar, with set prices and coordinated departure times. (p96)

Virpazar Tourist Office
This new visitor centre showcases both Lake Skadar National Park and the region's winemakers. It's made it much easier for independent travellers to access both. (p97)

Porto Montenegro
Tivat has been completely transformed by the opening of this ritzy superyacht marina, complete with a naval museum, glamorous beach club, day spa, restaurants, bars and, soon, a Regent Hotel. (p51)

New Hotels in the Northwest
Until recently, Žabljak's hotels were fair to middling at best and Nikšić's not even that good. Newcomers Hotel Soa and Hotel Marshal have raised the bar for both towns. (p117) (p105)

Za Vratlom Mountain Hut
Both the hut itself and its website have been completely reconstructed, making it the most comfortable, environmentally conscious and easy-to-access of all of Montenegro's mountain huts. (p39)

Kitesurfing
Sure, people have been kitesurfing on Velika Plaža for years, but things have stepped up a notch, with excellent operators whizzing thrillseekers over the waters from here and neighbouring Ada Bojana. (p87)

Dobrota Waterfront
In the last five years the potholes have gone, the public beach has been tidied up, a boardwalk has been added and many of the crumbling palazzos have been restored. (p43)

Formore recommendations and reviews, see **lonelyplanet.com/montenegro**

If You Like...

Historic Towns

Kotor Frozen in time behind its walls, Kotor may look like a movie set but it's still very much a living town. (p44)

Perast Baroque buildings line the water's edge in Montenegro's prettiest little town. (p41)

Budva's Stari Grad Like a mini-Dubrovnik, Budva's walled Old Town juts out over the blue Adriatic waters. (p64)

Ulcinj's Stari Grad Set high on a bluff above the beach, the uneven cobbled lanes within Ulcinj's walls ooze antiquity. (p83)

Herceg Novi's Stari Grad It doesn't have all its walls, but the marbled heart of Herceg Novi has plenty of sunny squares. (p35)

Cetinje The dinky old royal capital is crammed full of 19th-century buildings and interesting churches. (p91)

Beaches

Kraljičina Plaža Near Čanj, this pretty stretch of pink sand can only be reached by boat. (p78)

Drobni Pijesak Green hills and turquoise waters frame this secluded cove, hidden from view below the coastal road. (p77)

Žanjic & Mirišta These beaches gaze out to sea from their remote perch near the end of the Luštica Peninsula. (p55)

Lučice Lined with cypress trees and oleanders and with picturesque church-topped islets offshore, Lučice is a Mediterranean dream. (p74)

Sveti Stefan The island view from the pink sands is sublime; neighbouring Miločer Beach is even better, but the day-use fee is exorbitant. (p73)

Amazing Views

Njegoš Mausoleum Perched on one of the Black Mountain's peaks, this tomb offers views over all of Old Montenegro. (p90)

Kotor–Lovćen road The entire Bay of Kotor is laid out before you as you negotiate the old Austrian road to Lovćen. (p48)

Sveti Stefan Pull into viewing bays on the highway for grand views over the walled island village turned resort. (p73)

Kotor's Town Walls Sublime views are the reward for the gruelling 1350-step climb up Kotor's ancient fortifications. (p45)

Kolašin–Andrijevica road This minor road through the mountains opens up to breathtaking views of the Komovi and Prokletije mountains and the Lim valley. (p109)

Hiking

Durmitor National Park Walks can be as easy as a stroll around the Black Lake or as challenging as an assault on Bobotov Kuk. (p115)

Bjelasica Massif More forgiving than Montenegro's other mountains; hit the tracks through the virgin forest of Biogradska Gora National Park. (p111)

Orjen Massif The local mountain club is to thank for the well-maintained trails and excellent huts on this rugged mountain. (p39)

Prokletije National Park This challenging area offers a true wilderness for experienced hikers to explore. (p121)

Lovćen National Park Hiking tracks criss-cross the mountain vastness of Old Montenegro. (p90)

IF YOU LIKE... WINE

Producing varietals you've almost certainly never heard of before, Montenegro's smaller winemakers are under-represented in the nation's restaurants. Taste some at Kotor's Mon Ami Wine House. (p49)

Local Cuisine

Njeguši Producing the country's best *pršut* (prosciutto) and cheese, this village is synonymous with traditional Montenegrin cooking. (p90)

Konoba Ćatovića Mlini Adriatic coastal cuisine is well represented by this atmospheric family-run restaurant, hidden in a fold of the Bay of Kotor. (p41)

Kolašin Montenegrin mountain food is at its stodgy best in Kolašin's traditional restaurants. (p110)

Religious Art & Architecture

Ostrog Monastery Set on a mountainside and visible for many miles, this gleaming white monastery is Montenegro's most significant Orthodox site. (p104)

Morača Monastery The country's most beautiful monastery, filled with highly acclaimed frescoes and icons. (p109)

St Tryphon's Cathedral Kotor's Catholic cathedral is a masterpiece of Romanesque architecture and is home to many lovingly crafted religious objects. (p45)

Hussein Pasha Mosque A soaring minaret, elegant domes and elaborate frescoes, inside and out, make this Montenegro's most impressive mosque. (p117)

Gospa od Škrpjela The gorgeous blue-domed Catholic church on Our-Lady-of-the-Rocks island is filled with devotional treasures. (p42)

(Above) A market in Kotor (p44)

(Below) Religious icons at Cetinje Monastery (p93)

Month by Month

TOP EVENTS

Carnival, February and April

Adventure Race Montenegro, September

Fašinada, July

Kotor Art, July–August

Petrovac Night, August

January

New Year's celebrations are quickly followed by Orthodox Christmas on 7 January. The ski season kicks off, heralding peak prices in Kolašin and Žabljak; it's low season everywhere else.

February

The ski season is in full swing in the north. Despite chilly temperatures in the Bay of Kotor (average highs of around 12°C), residents find reasons to celebrate.

Mimosa Festival

Herceg Novi gets a jump on spring with this festival, which has been held, perhaps coincidentally, since the Flower Power era of the late 1960s. Expect concerts, sports events, majorettes and lots of yellow blooms.

Carnival

The traditional pre-Lent festivities continue to be held in the once predominantly Catholic towns of Kotor and Tivat. Expect Venetian-style masked balls (for adults and for children), concerts, theatre performances and parades.

March

The ski season continues up north but spring arrives elsewhere, with average highs jumping above 10°C in Podgorica and hitting around 15°C on the coast.

Camellia Day

Not to be outdone by mimosa, the camellia gets its moment in the sun with this festival held in both Kotor and Stoliv in mid-March.

April

You might get a few skiing days at the beginning of the month before the rising temperature melts the snow and speeds up the flow of the Tara River – leading to the start of the rafting season.

Carnival of Budva

Bucking tradition in favour of warmer weather, Budva gets into the Venetian swing of things in late April, with parades, folk music, concerts and DJs.

May

Late spring is a great time to visit Montenegro, with average high temperatures in the 20s everywhere except the mountains. Rafting is at its most thrilling; accommodation moves into shoulder season price brackets.

Water Polo Championship

Montenegro's top teams (Herceg Novi, Kotor and Budva) slug it out as the season comes to an end for one of the country's most popular sports. The final is held in either May or June.

June

Summer brings with it warm, dry days and rising accommodation prices on the coast, but not yet peak

rates. Tourist-orientated businesses reopen, including beach bars and restaurants.

Theatre City

Budva turns thespian for six weeks from mid-June, with performances held in such dramatic spots as the Citadela and in front of the Stari Grad (Old Town) walls.

July

The official start of 'The Season'. Peak rates kick in, temperatures soar, beach clubs crank into life and tourists flood the beaches. The weather is perfect for mountain hiking.

Kotor Art

Continuing to August, Kotor's summer arts umbrella shelters several well-established festivals, such as Don Branko's Music Days (classical music) and Perast's International Klapa Festival (traditional Dalmatian unaccompanied singing). International companies head to the Children's Theatre Festival in early July. (p47)

Purgatorije

Also known as the International Festival of Mediterranean Theatre, this event runs to September, attracting touring theatre companies to Tivat's summer stage.

Fašinada

On 22 July Perast men row decorated boats laden with stones to Gospa od Škrpjela in a centuries-old tradition, adding to the artificial island created by their ancestors. The event is now accompanied by the Perast to Tivat yacht regatta.

August

August is the hottest and driest month, sometimes resulting in wildfires. The party continues on the coast and Lake Skadar is at its very best, but in Podgorica it gets unbearably hot.

River Zeta Festival

Sleepy Danilovgrad wakes up near the end of the month for this three-day festival. River-based competitions include diving, fishing and wooden raft and kayak races. Less obviously related are the beauty contest and organic food festival.

Petrovac Night

Actually held over two nights – the last Friday and Saturday of the month – this beachside town offers majorette parades, pop performances and, as if that wasn't enough of an inducement, free fish, wine and beer.

September

Temperatures drop back to the 20s and 'The Season' comes to an abrupt halt, with prices dropping and some beach businesses disappearing – despite the weather remaining lovely. It's a great time to visit.

Adventure Race Montenegro

Held in late September or early October, this multidisciplinary event (including trekking, kayaking and mountain-biking) has two strands: the one-day Coastal Challenge in the Bay of Kotor, and the gruelling two-day Expedition Challenge in the northern mountains. (p114)

October

On the coast, sea and water temperatures remain in the 20s but rainfall increases. Rafting comes to an end. The autumn leaves put on a show in Biogradska Gora National Park.

November

Wrap up warm and bring a raincoat. November is the wettest month and temperatures drop to the low teens, with average lows falling below freezing level in the mountains.

Culture Days

Art exhibitions, theatre performances and concerts attempt to tempt the good burghers of Tivat out into the late-autumn chill.

December

Rainfall remains high. On the coast, many businesses remain completely closed. Towards the end of the month you might get some days on the ski slopes.

Festival of Wine & Bleak

Any bleak winter mood can be dispelled by heading to Virpazar and consuming the two things the area is known for: locally produced wine and the lake fish called bleak.

Itineraries

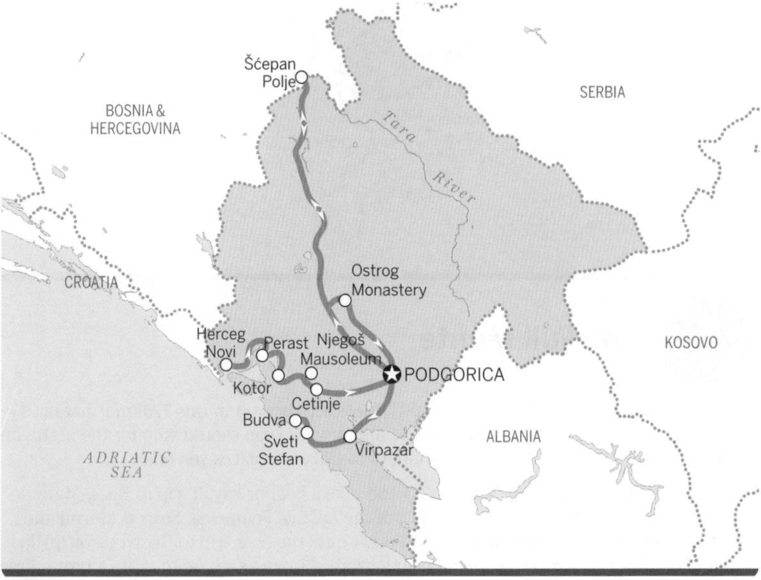

Essential Montenegro

Taking in the country's most emblematic sights, this 425km trip requires a car. Montenegro is teensy-weensy, so a short journey clear across the country is suggested, giving a taste of the mountains and a day's rafting. Note, rafting is only possible between April and October.

Start in **Herceg Novi** (p35) and slowly wind your way towards **Kotor** (p44), allowing at least an hour in **Perast** (p41) en route. All three are ancient bayside towns filled with old churches and marbled squares. The next morning, take the dazzling drive to the former Montenegrin capital **Cetinje** (p91) through Lovćen National Park, stopping to visit the **Njegoš Mausoleum** (p90) on the way. Continue north through the Piva Canyon to **Šćepan Polje** (p114), the main staging point for one-day rafts of the river, and stay the night at one of the rafting camps.

Hit the Tara River the next morning on a half-day's rafting trip, then drive to the dramatically positioned **Ostrog Monastery** (p104). Continue on to **Podgorica** (p99) and celebrate the day's achievements in the capital's bars. On day four, continue to **Virpazar** (p95) for a chilled-out cruise on Lake Skadar. Carry on down to **Sveti Stefan** (p73), check into somewhere with an island view and head to the beach. Spend your last day in **Budva** (p63), exploring the Stari Grad (Old Town) and lazing on the sand.

The Full Monte

Most of Montenegro's big-hitting beauty spots are covered in this 770km itinerary. We haven't attempted to be too prescriptive about where you should stop for the night, and the schedule has room for a couple of days to linger in places you enjoy.

Base yourself in **Herceg Novi** (p35) and take a boat or kayak trip to Rose, Mamula Island, the Blue Grotto and the beaches of the Luštica Peninsula. Stop at Morinj and Risan on your way to **Perast** (p41), and don't miss the boat trip to Gospa od Škrpjela island. Continue to **Kotor** (p44) and use the walled town as a base to visit Dobrota, Prčanj and Stoliv. Then head through Lovćen National Park to **Cetinje** (p91), stopping in **Ostrog Monastery** (p104) on the way to a rafting trip at **Šćepan Polje** (p114). Instead of heading straight back to Podgorica after the rafting trip, take the scenic road east from Plužine through Durmitor National Park to **Žabljak** (p113). Allow some time to enjoy the park and, at a minimum, make sure you hike around the Black Lake.

Follow the road along the Tara River to the isolated Dobrilovina Monastery then continue on to **Biogradska Gora National Park** (p111) – you can stay in the cabins here or continue on to the upmarket hotels in **Kolašin** (p109). Stop at the Morača Monastery on your way to **Podgorica** (p99), then hang out in the capital for a day. Continue down to **Virpazar** (p95) for a morning's cruise on Lake Skadar, then head on to Murići. Skirt the Rumija Mountains until the road shies away from the Albanian border and hooks down to the buzzy beachside town of **Ulcinj** (p82). Be sure to visit Velika Plaža before continuing back up the coast. Stop to check out the charming ruins of **Stari Bar** (p81) before heading on to the family-friendly beach town of **Petrovac** (p74). Continue along the coast, stopping at the beaches of **Sveti Stefan** (p73) and **Pržno** (p72) before finishing up in **Budva** (p63), with its walled Old Town and busy beachfront promenade

If you're travelling by bus, you'll need to pare back the itinerary a little. From Kotor, the easiest way to Cetinje, Ostrog or rafting is on a day-tour. Swap the Plužine–Žabljak road for a Nikšić–Žabljak bus. To get from Žabljak to Kolašin you'll need to go via Pljevlja or Podgorica. From Virpazar take a train to Bar followed by a bus to Ulcinj.

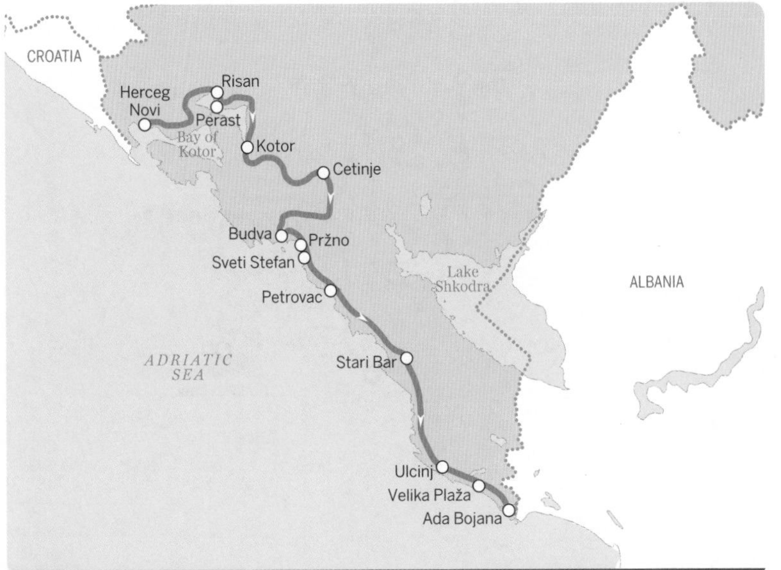

The Coast

Spend a day in **Herceg Novi** (p35) and consider taking a kayak tour or a boat to the beaches on the Luštica Peninsula. The following day, make your way slowly to Kotor, stopping to view the Roman mosaics at **Risan** (p41) and the Baroque beauty of **Perast** (p41). Base yourself in **Kotor** (p44) on day three; consider climbing the fortifications, hiking the Vrmac Ridge, exploring the neighbouring coastal villages or just hanging out in the fascinating Old Town.

If you've got a car, take the serpentine road up to Lovćen National Park, ascend the steps to the Njegoš Mausoleum and spend the rest of the day exploring the museums and galleries of **Cetinje** (p91) before heading on to **Budva** (p63) for the night. If you're travelling by bus, head straight to Budva and save Cetinje for another day.

For the following two days base yourself anywhere on the 20km stretch of coast between Budva and Petrovac. The advantages of Budva include its old walled town and its nightlife, and it's the easiest place to arrange day tours to Ostrog Monastery and Lake Skadar, or a Tara River rafting trip. **Petrovac** (p74) is more family-friendly, with a more relaxed vibe and great beaches nearby. Close neighbours **Pržno** (p72) and **Sveti Stefan** (p73) have excellent accommodation at every price level, great restaurants, and striking coastal views.

No matter where you put down roots, make sure you take the walk through the woods from Sveti Stefan to Pržno. A car or bike will get you to hidden bays such as Drobni Pijesak and Rijeka Reževići, and there are several monasteries to explore, including Podmaine and Podostrog, near Budva, and Reževići and Gradište, near Petrovac.

Continuing southeast along the coast, visit the ruins of **Stari Bar** (p81) on your way to **Ulcinj** (p82). The atmosphere of this largely Albanian town is quite different from anywhere else in Montenegro and there's a palpable buzz on the streets at night. It too has an interesting Old Town and the succession of rocky coves heading east from the crowded town beach are great for snorkelling. Nearby is the 12km continuous stretch of sand known as **Velika Plaža** (Big Beach; p86) and just across the Bojana River there's a further 3km of beach on the nudist island **Ada Bojana** (p86).

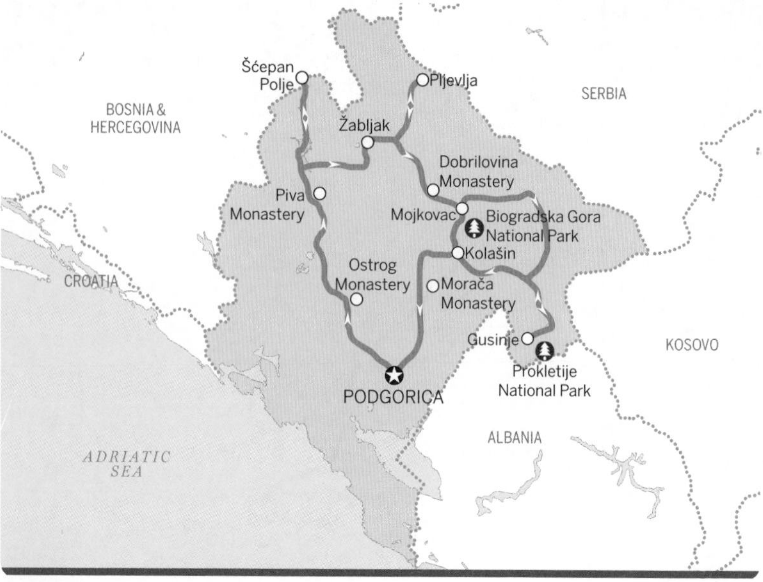

1 WEEK The Hidden North

This mountainous 650km loop combines some of Europe's most beautiful drives with visits to isolated monasteries and opportunities for wilderness hiking. You won't be able to tackle this route in winter, as snows close the Plužine–Žabljak road, and rafting stops in October.

Spend the morning exploring the nation's capital and biggest city, **Podgorica** (p99), then head through Danilovgrad to the extraordinary **Ostrog Monastery** (p104). Continue on through Nikšić where the highway passes through farmland before reaching **Piva Monastery** (p116), and the start of the Piva Canyon. From here the road passes through numerous tunnels cut into the canyon walls until you reach the Bosnian border at **Šćepan Polje** (p114), the main rafting base. Check yourself into one of the rafting camps for the night.

Start day two with a half-day's rafting on the Tara River and then jump in the car and double back through the canyon as far as Plužine. From here, take the scenic mountain road through Durmitor National Park to **Žabljak** (p113). Spend the rest of today and tomorrow hitting the park's hiking tracks.

On day four, drive east to the Tara Bridge and head north to **Pljevlja** (p117) to visit Montenegro's most beautiful mosque and a picturesque Orthodox monastery. Double back to the Tara Bridge and continue southeast along the river road. Consider making Eko-Oaza Suza Evrope your pitstop for this leg. From here you can walk to the secluded **Dobrilovina Monastery** (p113) and to a swimming hole on the river.

Continue to Mojkovac and then head north around the Bjelasica Massif and back down through Berane to Plav. Base yourself nearby for a day's hiking in **Prokletije National Park** (p121); make sure you fit in a quick visit to the old Ottoman town of **Gusinje** (p121). The next day, take the awe-inspiring back road through Andrijevica to the mountain resort of **Kolašin** (p109), and tackle the tracks in **Biogradska Gora National Park** (p111).

The road back to Podgorica follows the Morača Canyon and is just as extraordinary as any on this trip. At the start of the canyon, call in to admire the exquisite frescoes and icons at peaceful **Morača Monastery** (p109). You might also like to offer a prayer for your safety on the scenic but treacherous road ahead.

Plan Your Trip

Outdoor Activities

Montenegro's diverse landscape lends itself to so much more than simply lazing on the beach. Five national parks beckon, taunting nature buffs and adrenaline addicts with all of the myriad deeds that such mighty mountains, rivers and lakes can inspire. And when nature calls, why resist?

On the Water

Rafting

This is Montenegro's premier active drawcard. Commercial rafting is well established on the Tara River (p114) and once you've experienced the spectacular canyon you'll understand why.

Kayaking

The Bay of Kotor and Lake Skadar are both brilliant places for a paddle, and several operators specialise in day tours. Very experienced white-water kayakers can take on the rapids of some of Montenegro's rivers, but you're best to take local advice first as some stretches are dangerous.

Diving

Not all the landscape, wildlife and history is above ground. Montenegro's azure waters hide caves, shelves, springs and thousands of years' worth of shipwrecks – those Ulcinj pirates were busy chaps and WWII added to the collection. Visibility ranges from 10m to 25m but is usually around 15m. The main fauna you're likely to spot are swarms of young dentex, gilthead bream and the occasional lobster or sea turtle.

Need to Know

When to Go

The best time for a well-rounded roster of adventures is May and early June, when the melting ice adds thrills to a rafting trip and the wildflowers are bursting into bloom.

Sea and air temperatures are highest in July and August but you'll be battling the crowds on the beaches and there are sometimes wildfires during particularly hot summers. Otherwise, it's a good time to be in the mountains.

September and October are also good options, especially if you like your hikes accompanied by a blazing backdrop of autumn colour. This is also when the excellent Adventure Race Montenegro (p114) is held.

Ski-buffs should head north between January and March.

What to Pack

You'll need a pair of sturdy hiking boots and you should consider packing a compass, first aid kit and a torch (flashlight). If you're a serious rock-climber or mountaineer, you're best to bring any specialist gear you might need with you.

The best times to dive are from the middle of May until September, when the surface water is up to 25°C, dropping to 16°C under 30m (you'll need a 7mm neoprene wetsuit). You'll find diving operators in Budva, Pržno and Ulcinj.

Kitesurfing

At the far south of the coast, Velika Plaža and Ada Bojana have taken off as one of the Mediterranean's kitesurfing hubs. It's a great place to learn the sport.

On Land

Hiking

Thanks to the enthusiastic members of mountain clubs all over the country, Montenegro has an excellent network of hiking tracks – although they're not all well maintained or well marked.

Whether you're armed with a tent or just planning a day-walk, be well prepared for sudden changes in temperature and storms, and note that water supplies can be limited.

The main difficulty serious walkers and mountaineers will face is access to accommodation on longer expeditions. Mountain huts are available in some places but it isn't easy for the independent traveller to access them. Adventure-focused travel agencies can help with this, and can also arrange experienced guides from the local club.

Some of the best short hikes include the easy circuits of Biogradska Gora's Lake Biograd and Durmitor's Black Lake, and the Vrmac ridge in the Bay of Kotor.

EXPERT HELP

Rafting, kayaking and skiing can be easily organised when you get to Montenegro, but arranging mountain guides, access to huts, specialist equipment and logistical support for more difficult expeditions can be a nightmare. If you're planning an action-intensive holiday, it is well worth engaging the services of one of the agencies that specialise in such things. Options include the following:

- Black Mountain (p37)
- Montenegro Adventures (p101)
- Undiscovered Montenegro (p96)
- Montenegro Adventure Centre (p71)
- Explorer Tourist Agency (p110)
- Anitra Travel Agency (p105)
- Summit Travel Agency (p116)
- Active Travels Montenegro (p37)

Cycling

With so many mountains you'd expect that mountain biking would be on the agenda, and you'd be right. The National Tourist Office (www.montenegro.travel) has developed five 'top trails', outlined in a Wilderness Biking pamphlet (available from tourist offices). The 14-day, 1276km **Tour de Montenegro** circles the entire country and should only be attempted by those with thighs carved from granite, as 30km of climbing is involved.

For a single day's cycling, consider the Vrmac ridge (starting near Kotor), the loop track from Cetinje through Lovćen National Park or the loop from Virpazar through Crmnica field.

Skiing

Montenegro's ski season lasts from roughly January to March, with the peak time being around New Year. The best-equipped ski resort is near Kolašin, but the most reliable skiing is in Durmitor National Park, where there are slopes close to Žabljak with options for beginners or serious skiers. There's also a small ski centre near Nikšić. Cross-country skiing can be undertaken in Lovćen and Durmitor National Parks.

In the Air

Paragliding & Parasailing

Montenegro has plenty of precipices from which you can hurl yourself and while hang-gliding is yet to take off, paragliding (p71) is starting to soar. If you want the feeling of flying without having to jump off anything, consider trying the less vertigo-inducing option of parasailing. Both activities are offered from near Bečići.

Regions at a Glance

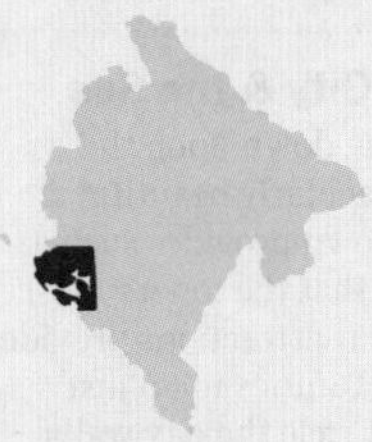

Bay of Kotor

Views
Architecture
Food

Vistas of the Bay
Whether gazing at it from water level or from high above on the Lovćen road, the bay's mountain ramparts and inky waters will take your breath away.

Echoes of Venice
Built to last out of gleaming stone, the Bay of Kotor's numerous palaces and churches owe much to the influence of its one-time taskmaster to the north. Nowhere is this more apparent than in Perast, a little town bathed in the baroque.

Coastal Cuisine
The seafood dishes of the coast represent the best of the country's traditional cuisines. Try specialties such as grilled squid, fish soup, squid-ink risotto or simply grilled fish, drizzled with olive oil, parsley and garlic.

p32

Adriatic Coast

Beaches
History
Entertainment

Beach Life
Clear waters, mountain backdrops and a sunny summer conspire to bring the Mediterranean fantasy into reality. Rows of umbrellas and recliners blanket the busier beaches, but you can escape the worst of the tourist hordes in secluded spots such as Kraljičina Plaža and Drobni Pijesak.

Walled Towns
From the marbled streets of Budva's Stari Grad (Old Town) to the cobbled lanes of Ulcinj's, to the ruins of Stari Bar, the coast's walled towns will transport you through time.

Beach Bars & Clubs
Come summer Budva becomes Montenegro's party capital. Up to 5000 people regularly dance the night away at the open-air Top Hill nightclub, while down by the water a string of al fresco bars and clubs pulls punters day and night.

p61

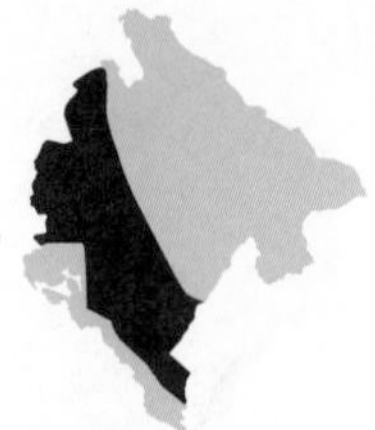

Central Montenegro

Nature
History
Monasteries

National Parks

From the depths of Lake Skadar to the heights of Lovćen, Central Montenegro's national parks protect a broad range of habitats. Birdwatchers will find plenty to twitch about, especially around Skadar, which is categorised as a wetland of international importance.

The Royal Capital

Much of Montenegro's history, culture and national identity is tied to Cetinje, its former capital. That story is told through the town's historic buildings and an array of museums.

Spiritual Outposts

The monastic life is integral to the Serbian Orthodox faith, and this region is blessed with the country's most significant shrine, Ostrog Monastery. Almost as affecting are the tiny island monasteries scattered around Lake Skadar.

p88

Northern Mountains

Nature
Activities
Monasteries

Mountain Majesty

Large areas of rugged wilderness blanket this region, from Durmitor in the northwest to Prokletije in the southeast and Bjelasica in between. It's an extraordinary landscape that never fails to astound.

Durmitor National Park

Durmitor is the activity capital of Montenegro. The big three are rafting, hiking and skiing, but there's also the potential for rock-climbing, canyoning and mountaineering.

Frescoes & Icons

Not only does Morača Monastery have an exquisite setting, it contains an extraordinary wealth of religious art. Morača may be the most beautiful of Montenegro's monasteries, but Piva, Dobrilovina and Pljevlja's Holy Trinity are no slackers on that front.

p107

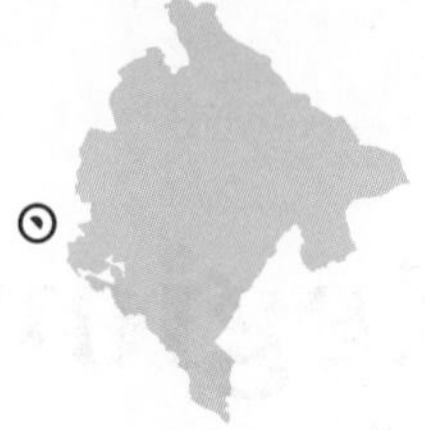

Dubrovnik (Croatia)

Views
Architecture
History

The City & the Sea

Gazing down upon the spectacularly beautiful Old Town provides such a thrill that the town's most popular attractions provide opportunities to do just that. Circle the city walls for an intimate perspective or take the cable car up Mt Srđ for the bird's-eye view.

Stone & Marble

Wandering amid the honey-coloured stone buildings of the Old Town is like walking through a *History of European Architecture* textbook. Everywhere you look there are impressive Romanesque, Gothic, baroque and Renaissance structures – still standing and still in use, despite the wartime battering.

Museums

Learn about the Republic of Ragusa in the Rector's Palace or brush up on more recent events at the Homeland War Museum and War Photo Limited.

p122

On the Road

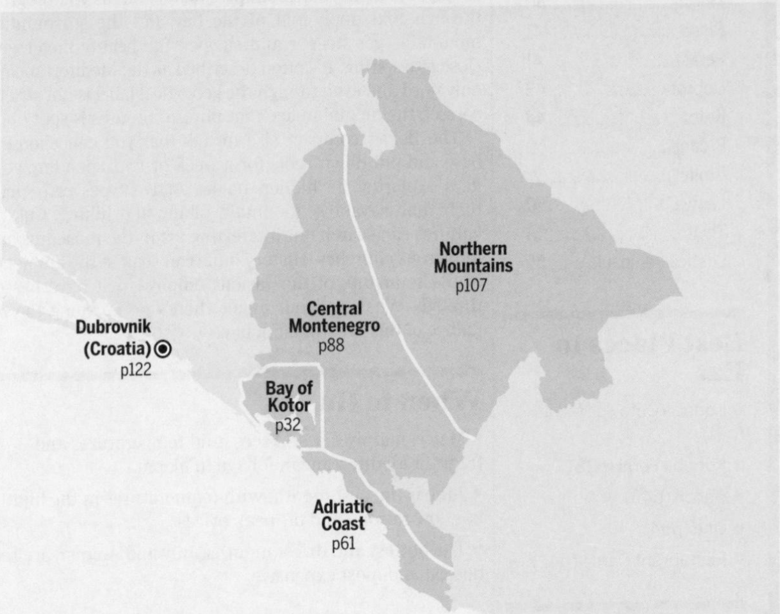

Northern Mountains
p107

Central Montenegro
p88

Dubrovnik (Croatia)
p122

Bay of Kotor
p32

Adriatic Coast
p61

Bay of Kotor

Includes ➡

Best Places to Eat

- Konoba Ćatovića Mlini (p41)
- Konoba Feral (p38)
- Galion (p49)
- One (p54)
- Restaurant Conte (p42)

Best Places to Sleep

- Old Town Hostel (p48)
- Camp Full Monte (p39)
- Palazzo Radomiri (p43)
- Forza Mare (p44)
- Villa Kristina (p56)

Why Go?

Coming from Croatia, the Bay of Kotor (Boka Kotorska, or simply 'the Boka') starts simply enough, but as you progress through fold upon fold of the bay and the surrounding mountains get steeper and steeper, the beauty meter gets close to bursting. It's often described as the Mediterranean's only fjord and even though the geological label is not strictly correct, the mental image that phrase conjures is spot on.

The Boka's compact size means that you can choose a base and put down roots for a week or two, spending your days exploring its hidden nooks. Active types can spend their time kayaking, mountain biking and hiking. Culture vultures can search out interesting art in the museums and numerous churches. History buffs can soak in the ambience of the remnants of the various empires that have passed through. Whatever your angle, there's no escaping the romance of this breathtaking bay.

When to Go

- May is mainly dry and sees mild temperatures and fragrant Mediterranean foliage in bloom.
- June is the best month, with temperatures in the high 20s, low rainfall and off-peak prices.
- The hottest and driest months, July and August, are the busiest and most expensive.

History

While it overlaps at times, this geographically compact area's history stands at a slight remove from that of the rest of Montenegro. Like most of the eastern Adriatic, the Boka was populated by the Illyrian tribes. The bay subsequently became part of the Roman province of Dalmatia and before long lavish Roman villas sprang up along Risan's waterfront. By the end of the 5th century, with the empire crumbling under barbarian incursions from the north, the Bay of Kotor briefly fell into the hands of the Ostrogoths and then the Slavic tribes.

The Slavic clans of the Boka lived in virtual city states, maintaining allegiances to both the west (Rome) and east (Byzantium). Kotor was eventually incorporated into the

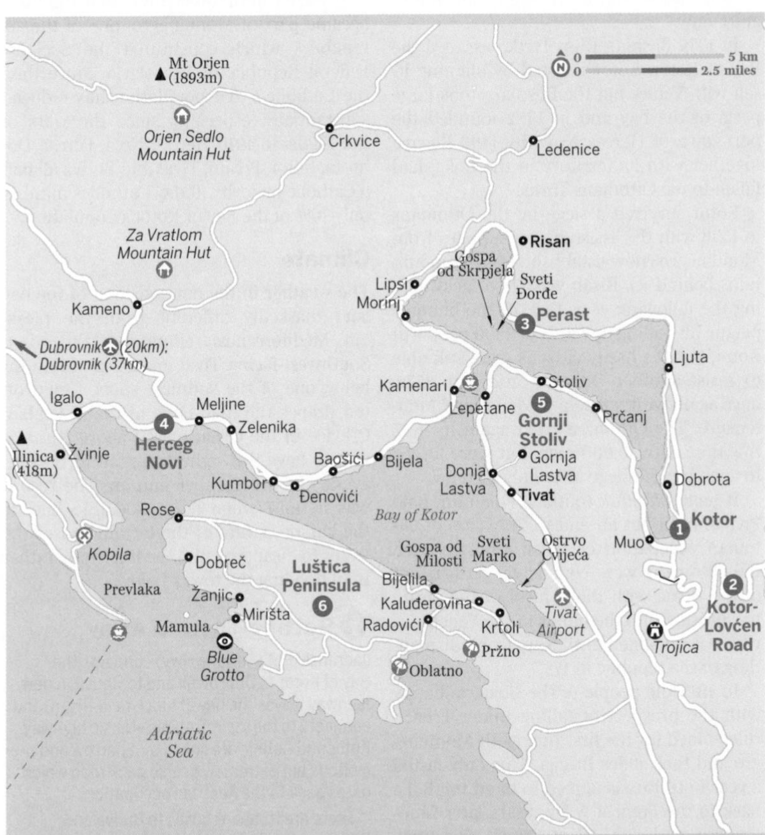

Bay of Kotor Highlights

1. Randomly roaming the atmospheric laneways of **Kotor's Stari Grad** (Old Town, p44) until you're at least a little lost
2. Winding your way to dizzying views on the snaking **back road from Kotor to Lovćen National Park** (p48)
3. Admiring the baroque beauty of historic **Perast's palazzos and churches** (p41)
4. Cooling off in the shade with an icy beverage on **Herceg Novi's Trg Herceg Stejpana** (p38)
5. Hiking up to peaceful views and heartbreaking ruins in the village of **Gornji Stoliv** (p50)
6. Losing yourself within the olive groves in the remote byways of the **Luštica Peninsula** (p55)
7. Paddling your way to island fortresses, remote beaches and sea caves on a **kayaking day tour** (p37)

principality of Duklja, considered a forerunner of modern Montenegro. At the time of the momentous split between the western (Catholic) and eastern (Orthodox) churches in 1054, Duklja was politically tied to Rome, but by 1190 was annexed by Raška (soon to be known as Serbia) and an Orthodox bishopric was established. Kotor and Perast, however, continued to have a largely Catholic population and to exercise a degree of autonomy.

In 1379 Bosnian King Tvrtko assailed the Bay of Kotor. Kotor resisted by aligning itself with Venice but the Bosnians took large parts of the bay and in 1382 founded the port town of Herceg Novi. By 1463 Bosnia, together with its territory in the Boka, had fallen to the Ottomans Turks.

Kotor survived a siege by the Ottomans in 1538 with the assistance of supplies from Montenegro (now established in the mountains behind it). Risan wasn't so lucky, falling the following year. In 1570 the bubonic plague hit, killing upwards of 3500 people in Kotor, but the hardy citizens were still able to resist another Ottoman attack in 1572, once again with the help of Venice and Montenegro. The Ottomans tried again in 1657, this time with 10,000 men, but were forced to abandon the siege after only 22 days.

It took a *hajduk* (outlaw) chieftain, Bajo Pivljanin, to put an end to 145 years of Ottoman occupation of Risan. Shortly after, the Ottomans were completely pushed out of the Boka, with the control of the entire bay passing into the hands of the Venetians, where it remained until Napoleon's dismantling of the republic in 1797.

In 1813 the people of the Boka, unhappy with the prospect of falling under French rule, joined for the first time with Montenegro and their allies Russia. This only lasted a year until Russia agreed to hand the Boka back to the French. A few years later Montenegro, with the aid of Britain this time, succeeded in wrestling the Boka off them but again Russia intervened, this time passing the control back to Austria.

Throughout the period of Venetian and Austrian rule the Boka was considered part of Dalmatia (a coastal province of today's Croatia), as it was in Roman times. However, before the advent of nationalism in the 19th century, the people of the bay were more likely to be described as 'Bokelj' than by terms such as Serb or Croat. Religion gradually became the defining factor of ethnicity, with Orthodox Christians identifying as Serbs and the Catholics as Croats. The Boka had always accommodated a mixed population – some churches even had dual Catholic and Orthodox altars – so the emerging pan-Slavic movement found fertile ground and the post-WWI formation of the Kingdom of Serbs, Croats and Slovenes (later Yugoslavia) was generally welcomed by the locals.

It wasn't until after WWII that the Boka became part of Montenegro, one of the six republics which constituted the Socialist Federal Republic of Yugoslavia. Since then the Catholic/Croat population has reduced substantially, especially since the wars of the 1990s. In 1910 Herceg Novi, Perast, Dobrota, Kotor, Prčanj, Tivat and Budva all had a Catholic majority. Today Catholics number only 10% of the Bay of Kotor's population.

Climate

The weather in the outer section of the bay isn't markedly different from the pleasant Mediterranean climate of the coast. Southwest-facing Tivat has a reputation for being one of the sunniest spots. Cloud often drapes the high cliffs of the inner bay. Crkvice in the Orjen massif above Risan is said to have the highest rainfall in Europe, averaging 5300mL per annum. The record was in 1937 when it hit 8065mL. Luckily the karstic nature of the terrain causes the water to disappear into the limestone rather than flooding the towns below.

Getting There & Away

Jadranski Put (Adriatic Hwy) connects the Bay of Kotor to Dubrovnik and to Budva. A new highway leaves the bay at Lipci, near Risan, and connects to the main Trebinje–Nikšić highway. Kotor and Cetinje are linked by a narrow and precipitous but extremely scenic back road which dates back to the Austrian occupation.

There are frequent buses to Budva and Podgorica from all around the bay, with some services heading as far as Sarajevo and Belgrade. Buses head between Kotor and Dubrovnik twice a day, via Herceg Novi.

Tivat airport welcomes domestic and international flights.

Getting Around

A road wends its way around the entire coast, narrowing considerably between Kotor and the car ferry and on the Luštica Peninsula. From Kotor the main road takes a tunnel and comes out near Tivat airport. A car ferry crosses backwards and forwards between Kamenari and Lepetane, at the bay's narrowest point.

There are three main bus routes in the Boka. Frequent services take the coastal road from Herceg Novi to Kotor, stopping at all the villages along the way. Buses also connect Herceg Novi to Tivat via the car ferry and Kotor to Tivat via the tunnel.

In summer, taxi boats are a useful form of transportation, particularly between Herceg Novi and the beaches on the Luštica Peninsula. They're easy enough to find in the busy marinas in July and August but more difficult at other times.

Herceg Novi Херцег Нови

POP 11,100

It's easy to drive straight through Herceg Novi without noticing anything worth stopping for, especially if you've just come from Croatia with visions of Dubrovnik dazzling your brain. However, just below the uninspiring roadside frontage hides an appealing Stari Grad (Old Town) with sunny squares and a lively atmosphere. The water's cleaner here near the mouth of the bay, so the pebbly beaches and concrete swimming terraces are popular. The town sprawls along the coast, absorbing former villages on either side, such as Igalo, which was once a health spa famed for its mineral-bearing mud.

Novi means 'new' and Herceg Novi is indeed one of the newer towns on the bay, but at 630-plus years it's no spring chicken. The Herceg (pronounced 'her·tseg') part refers to Herceg (Duke) Stjepan Vukčić of Hercegovina fame who fortified the town in the 15th century; the most dramatic of the remaining fortifications are a little younger.

Sights

Ulica Njegoševa STREET

Herceg Novi's Stari Grad is at its most impressive when approached from the pedestrian-only section of Ulica Njegoševa, which is paved in the same shiny marble as Dubrovnik and lined in elegant, mainly 19th-century buildings. The street terminates in cafe-ringed Trg Nikole Đurkovića, where steps lead up to an elegant crenulated **clock tower** (1667) that was once the main city gate.

Archangel Michael's Church CHURCH

(Crkva Sv Arhanđela Mihaila; 7am-midnight Jun-Aug, 7am-9pm Sep-May) Built between 1883 and 1905, this beautifully proportioned, domed Orthodox church sits flanked by palm trees at the centre of gleaming white Trg Herceg Stejpana (commonly called Belavista Sq). The archangel is pictured in a mosaic above the door under an elegant rose window.

Kanli-Kula FORTRESS

(Bloody Tower; admission €1; 8am-midnight) The big fort visible from the main road is the Kanli-Kula, a notorious prison during Turkish rule (roughly 1482–1687). You can walk around its sturdy walls and enjoy views over the town. In the dungeon below the lower set of flagpoles, former inmates have carved crosses and ships into the walls.

St Jerome's Church CHURCH

(Crkva Sv Jeronima) The Old Town's main Catholic church (1856) dominates Trg Mića Pavlovića. It is usually only open during services.

Fortemare FORTRESS

The bastion at the town's seaward edge was rebuilt by the Venetians during their 110-year stint as overlords (before the Austrians, French, Russians, Montenegrins, Austro-Hungarians, Serbs, Germans and Italians all had their turns). It's now used for film screenings on summer nights. In the sea below you can see the ruins of the **Citadella**, a victim of a major earthquake that hit the coast in 1979.

Šetalište Pet Danica WATERFRONT

Named after five young women, all called Danica, who died during WWII, this pedestrian promenade stretches along the waterfront for over 5km from Igalo to Meljine. It's lined with summer bars, shops, concrete swimming platforms and the odd rocky cove, and in places it ducks in and out of tunnels carved through headlands. This was once the route of a trainline linking Zelenika to Sarajevo via Herceg Novi and Dubrovnik. The old stone **railway station** still stands at the foot of the Old Town, although it's long since been converted into a cafe.

Regional Museum MUSEUM

(Zavičajni muzej; www.rastko.rs/rastko-bo/muzej/; Mirka Komnenovića 9; admission €1.50; 9am-6pm Mon-Sat) Apart from the building itself (which is a fab bougainvillea-shrouded baroque palace with absolute sea views), the highlight of this little museum is its impressive icon gallery.

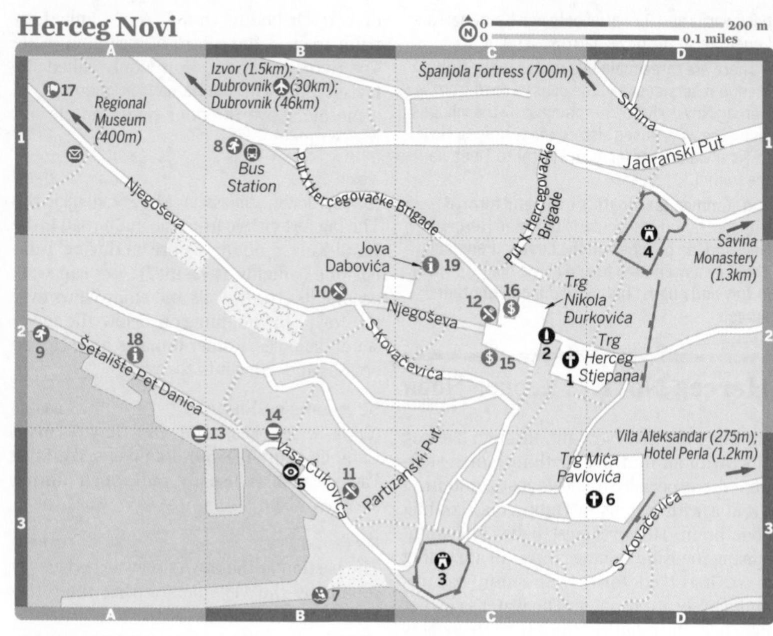

Herceg Novi

Sights

1 Archangel Michael's Church C2
2 Clock Tower C2
3 Fortemare C3
4 Kanli-Kula D1
5 Old Railway Station B3
6 St Jerome's Church D3

Activities, Courses & Tours

7 Kayak Montenegro B3
8 Trend Travel B1
9 Yachting Club 32 .... A2

Eating

10 Da Vinci B2
11 Konoba Feral B3
12 Market C2

Drinking & Nightlife

13 Jadran A3
14 Nautica B3

Information

15 CKB Bank C2
16 Opportunity Bank C2
17 Serbian Consulate A1
18 Tourist Information Kiosk A2
19 Tourist Office C2

Savina Monastery MONASTERY

(Braće Grakalić bb; ⌚6am-8pm) From its hillside location in the town's eastern fringes, this peaceful Orthodox monastery enjoys wonderful coastal views. It's dominated by the elegant 18th-century Church of the Dormition (Crkva Uspenja Bogorodice, literally 'the falling into sleep of the Mother of God'), carved from pinkish stone from the island of Korčula in Croatia. Inside there's a beautiful gilded iconostasis, but you'll need to be demurely dressed to enter (no shorts, singlets or bikinis). The smaller church beside it has the same name but is considerably older (possibly 14th century) and has the remains of frescoes.

The monastery is well signposted from the large roundabout on the highway at Meljine.

Španjola Fortress FORTRESS

Situated high above the town, this fortress was started and finished by the Turks but named after the Spanish (yep, in 1538 they had a brief stint here as well). If the graffiti and empty bottles are anything to go by, it's now regularly invaded by local teenagers. There's a signpost on the main road, but you'll need to take an unmarked left turn not far past Srbina 34.

Activities

Herceg Novi is arguably the country's best base for arranging active pursuits, largely due to a network of expats running professional, customer-focused, environmentally aware businesses.

Kayak Montenegro KAYAKING
(067-382 472; www.kayakmontenegro.com; hire per hr/4hr/8hr from €5/15/25) This excellent outfit offers paddling day tours across the bay to Rose and Dobreč or Mamula and Mirišta (€45 including equipment), as well as day trips to explore Lake Skadar. If you'd rather go it alone, single and double kayaks can be rented all year round, including from a stand near the marina from June to September.

Black Mountain ADVENTURE TOURS
(067-640 869; www.montenegroholiday.com) An excellent full-service agency that can arrange pretty much anything, anywhere in the country, including mountain biking, diving, rafting, hiking, paragliding, canyoning, boat trips and wine tasting. It can take care of the basics too, such as accommodation, car hire and transfers.

Active Travels Montenegro ADVENTURE TOURS
(068-658 285; www.activetravelsmontenegro.com) Local guys with excellent English lead rafting, hiking and canyoning trips, vineyard visits and sightseeing tours.

Trend Travel BUS TOURS
(031-321 639; www.trendtravelmontenegro.com; Bus Station, Jadranski Put) Day trips to Dubrovnik (€18), Ostrog (€20), Risan/Kotor/Budva/Sveti Stefan (€25), Trebinje (€30), Perast/Njeguši/Lovćen/Cetinje (€35) and Lake Skadar (€45), as well as rafting trips (€70) and accommodation services (rooms from €10 per person, apartments from €25).

Yachting Club 32 OUTDOORS
(www.yachtingclub32.com; Šetalište Pet Danica 32) Rents jet skis (€50 per 20 minutes), pedal boats (€8 per hour) and mountain bikes (€3/6/15 per one hour/three hours/day).

STEP BY STEP

Herceg Novi is extremely hilly and the fastest way from the highway to the beach is via one of the numerous sets of steps. Charming as the stairways (*stepenište*) are, they make Herceg Novi one of the most challenging towns in Montenegro for the mobility-impaired.

Festivals & Events

Mimosa Festival PARADE, MUSIC
(www.hercegfest.co.me; Feb-Mar) A mash of yellow blooms, marching majorettes, concerts and sports events.

Sunčane Skale MUSIC
(www.suncaneskale.org; Jul) Held in the first week of July, the three-day Sunčane Skale (Sunny Steps) music competition is a bit like a low-rent Eurovision.

Sinestezija Festival ART
(www.sinestezija.me; Jul) Turns Herceg Novi into a contemporary art space for 10 days at the end of July, with various exhibitions and events popping up around town.

International Book Fair LITERATURE
(late Jul) Herceg Novi has had a reputation as a magnet for writers ever since Yugoslav-era Nobel Prize for Literature winner Ivo Andrić moved into Njegoševa 65, and this annual book fair continues that legacy.

Herceg Novi Film Festival FILM
(www.ffhn.me; early Aug) A week-long festival showcasing movies from the region.

Sleeping

Private rooms start at about €15 per person. Either look for signs saying *'sobe'* or book through a local agency such as Trend Travel (p37).

Izvor HOSTEL €
(069-397 957; www.izvor.me; Jadranski Put bb, Igalo; dm €12; P) Hidden on the slopes above Igalo, this simple place consists of four basic shared rooms which open on to a terrace overlooking the bay. The charming young owner speaks excellent English and there's a traditional restaurant downstairs (mains €4 to €9). It's difficult to find; from the bus station head 1.5km in the direction of Igalo and look for a small wooden sign in Cyrillic

(Извор) pointing up a small road on the right, immediately before a red metal fence.

Vila Aleksandar HOTEL €€
(031-345 806; www.hotelvilaaleksandar.com; Save Kovačevića 64; s/d €51/82;) The decor's a little dated at this terracotta-roofed hotel but almost all of the rooms have balconies with sea views, and the blue-tiled pool on the sunny terrace is extremely enticing. The restaurant opens onto the waterfront promenade where stairs lead down to a pebbly beach.

Hotel Perla HOTEL €€€
(031-345 700; www.perla.me; Šetalište Pet Danica 98; s €84-112, d €104-140, apt €170-215;) It's a 15-minute stroll from the centre but if it's beach you're after, Perla's possie is perfect. The helpful staff speak excellent English and the front rooms of this medium-sized modern block have private terraces and sea views. Bikes are available for hire (per hour/day €2/10).

Eating

In the summer Herceg Novi offers dozens of eating options, although few are exceptional. Appealing places to linger over a bowl of pasta and a glass of wine include the waterfront promenade and Trg Herceg Stjepana.

Market MARKET €
(Trg Nikole Đurkovića; 6am-3pm Mon-Sat, 6am-noon Sun) If you want to take on the local women in a tussle for the best fresh fruit and vegetables, get to the little produce market by around 8am.

★**Konoba Feral** SEAFOOD €€
(Vasa Ćukovića 4; mains €7-17) A *feral* is a ship's lantern, so it's seafood, not wild cat, that takes pride of place on the menu. The grilled squid is excellent and comes with a massive serving of seasonal vegetables and salads.

Da Vinci ITALIAN, SEAFOOD €€
(Njegoševa bb; mains €5-15; breakfast, lunch & dinner) Gaze through the heads of the bay from the breezy terrace or ponder the Latin inscription in the small, smart dining room. On the menu, pasta and pizza rub shoulders with local seafood dishes.

Drinking

Nautica CAFE, BAR
(Vasa Ćukovića 24; 8am-1am;) Pull up a seat at the bar or at a table outside and sup on a coffee, cocktail or smoothie while you check your emails. Come nighttime there's sometimes live music.

Jadran CAFE, BAR
(322 018; Šetalište Pet Danica 34;) The cooked breakfasts are good (€3 to €5), but Jadran's smart waterside terrace, overlooking the water polo stadium, really comes into its own as an arena for competitive beverage quaffing.

Information

There's a cluster of banks with ATMs on Trg Nikole Đurkovića.

Tourist Information Kiosk (Šetalište Pet Danica bb; 9am-11pm May-Sep) There are further kiosks in Igalo (Sava Ilića bb), Kamenari (500m from the ferry) and near the big roundabout in Meljine.

Tourist Office (031-350 820; www.hercegnovi.travel; Jova Dabovića 12; 9am-10pm daily Jul & Aug, 9am-4pm Mon-Fri & 9am-2pm Sat Sep-Jun) The main tourist office is a little hard to find, above a house.

Getting There & Around

BOAT

Taxi boats ply the coast during summer, charging about €10 to €15 for a trip to the beaches on the Luštica Peninsula. You'll sometimes get a better rate in Igalo where there's more competition.

BUS

Buses stop at the **station** (031-321 225; Jadranski Put) just above the Old Town. There are frequent buses to Kotor (€4, one hour), which stop at all of the small towns around the bay. Buses to Budva (€5 to €6) either go via Kotor (1¾ hours) or on the ferry and through Tivat, which is usually quicker depending on the queues. Frequent services head to Cetinje (€7, 2½ hours) and Podgorica (€9, three hours), with some continuing as far as Rožaje (€18, four daily).

International destinations include Dubrovnik (€10, two hours depending on time at the border, two daily), Sarajevo (€24, seven hours, at least two daily) and Belgrade (€33, 13 hours, at least seven daily).

CAR

A torturous, often gridlocked, one-way system runs through the town, so you're best to park in the car park opposite the bus station if you're day-tripping. In the centre of town, street parks are divided into two zones charged at either 50c or 80c per hour, or €5 per day; purchase tickets from newsagents or kiosks, circle the time and date, and display them on your dashboard.

TAXI

Taxi More (☎19730; www.taximore.com; minimum fare €1.30, per km 70c) Advertises set fares to Dubrovnik Airport (€25), Tivat (€30), Kotor (€40), Budva (€55) and Podgorica Airport (€100). Add an extra €10 if there are queues for the Kamenari car ferry.

Around Herceg Novi

Herceg Novi's coastal sprawl starts at **Igalo** to the west, where the muddy silt from the sea floor is said to have therapeutic qualities. Heading east along the bay you'll pass beachside communities at **Zelenika**, **Kumbor**, **Đenovići** and **Baošići** before you reach **Bijela** with its dockyard – the largest industrial site on the bay.

Sights

Mamula ISLAND

Guarding the entrance to the bay, the circular splat of Mamula is only 200m in diameter. It's named after the Austro-Hungarian general who in the mid-19th century created the fort still standing on the island, which became an infamous Italian prison during WWII.

The island's a stop on one of the Kayak Montenegro day tours as well as many of the boat tours of the bay. Otherwise it's easily reached by taxi boat, or you can hire a kayak and paddle there in about one hour.

Mt Orjen MOUNTAIN

Hulking Mt Orjen (1893m) separates Herceg Novi from Hercegovina and is higher than the more famous Mt Lovćen, the 'black mountain' itself. Patches of evergreen maple and white oak can be found amongst the rugged limestone karst on the lower slopes, giving way to firs and beeches above the winter snowline.

It's a great landscape for hiking and mountain biking, but you'll need to be well stocked with water as any rain that falls here quickly disappears into the porous karst. For six months of the year there is snow on the mountain and even on a scorching summer's day you should be prepared for a storm.

A hiking trail commences near the bus station at Herceg Novi (look for the red and white painted markings); heading towards Kotor take the first road to the left, followed quickly by a right turn. This is the start of the mammoth Coastal Mountain Traversal hiking path, which leads all the way to the shores of Lake Skadar.

> **CYCLE THE SHORELINE**
>
> Cyclists should consider leaving the highway at Igalo and pedalling along the waterfront. In summer you'll be slowed by foot traffic but it's a much flatter, safer and more picturesque route than the highway. Apart from a few stretches where you'll be forced back on to the main road, you can travel most of the way to Kamenari alongside the water.

Planinarski Klub Subra (www.pksubra.me; guide per day €70), the local mountaineering club, operates two huts on the mountain and can arrange guides.

Sleeping

★**Camp Full Monte** CAMPGROUND €

(☎067-899 208; www.full-monte.com; campsites per person €10; ⊙May-Sep) Hidden in the mountains near the Croatian border, this small British-run camping ground offers solar-generated hot water, odourless composting toilets and a whole lot of seclusion. If you hadn't guessed already, clothing is optional. Tents (with full bedding) can be hired for an additional €5 to €15 per person and meals can be arranged (breakfast/lunch/dinner €3/4/7.50).

Za Vratlom Mountain Hut HUT €

(☎069-348 600; www.pksubra.me; adult/child dm incl linen €20/15, without linen €15/10, campsite €8/5) Situated at an altitude of 1160m, this stone lodge is a four-hour hike from Herceg Novi. Recent renovations have left it with solar power, a water recycling system, comfortable four-bed dorms with linen, a large bunkroom for those with their own sleeping bags and, of course, refurbished kitchen and toilets. Full board is offered for an additional €15.

Orjen Sedlo Mountain Hut HUT €

(☎067-829 519; www.pksubra.me; per person €10, minimum booking €50) Near the centre of the Orjen massif at a height of 1600m, the Orjen Saddle hut has a generator, toilets, a kitchen and 20 bunk beds. It's only opened by arrangement and you'll need to bring your own bedding, but meals can be booked.

Casa del Mare HOTEL €€

(☎031-673 706; www.casadelmare.me; Kamenari bb; r €90-100, apt €110-120; P ❄ 📶) Positioned

LOCAL KNOWLEDGE

MOUNTAIN MAGIC

We asked Marko Vučinić, a member of the Subra mountaineering club, about exploring the mountains around Herceg Novi.

Tackling Mt Orjen

You can walk straight up from the bus station to the Za Vratlom mountain hut, which is a tough four-hour walk. Or you can drive to the old Motel Borići [now defunct], where it's an hour's walk to the hut. You'll need good boots though – sports shoes aren't enough – and at least 3L of water on a hot day.

From the hut you can explore Orjen on day hikes as there are over 60km of marked tracks. Guides are available through the club. People should remember that this is a real wilderness: they're still discovering caves and unknown features on Orjen. And the weather can change suddenly, so you have to be prepared for all conditions.

You can also theoretically continue on the seven-day Coastal Mountain Traversal [a 150km hiking route from Herceg Novi to Lake Skadar], but logistics are the problem. There are only two huts and well-marked paths for the first two days. For the rest you'll need to carry everything: tents, food, water...

If You Don't Have Boots

One easier walk from Herceg Novi is the track up to Sv Ilija, an Orthodox church on Ilinica. It's great at sunset – you get views over Croatia and Montenegro. There's a communal grave for French soldiers there dating from Napoleonic times.

It's about a 16km loop walk from Herceg Novi. Follow the water's edge through Igalo and then either look for the marked walking trail heading up or continue on to the village of Žvinje and head up from there.

on the busy stretch of road leading to the car ferry, this attractive minihotel has spacious rooms with terraces and sea views. Across the highway, hammocks, loungers and day beds are arranged around the hotel's little white-pebble beach.

Tourist Complex Fanfani HOTEL €€
(☎031-676 103; www.fanfanimontenegro.me; Đenovići bb; s/d €40/50, bungalow €45, mains €7-18; P ❄ 📶) Facing over a tree-shaded garden to its own narrow stretch of pebbly beach, this complex has at its heart Hotel Milena, a traditional stone building with eight rooms above and a popular restaurant below. A collection of little white bungalows are scattered about outside.

Eating

Leut SEAFOOD €€
(Braće Pedišić 59-61, Meljine; mains €5-18) You'll need to make an effort to find this local favourite but the pay-off comes in the form of excellent Bokelj-style seafood served on a large terrace facing the water. To get here, follow the sign to Savina at the giant Meljine roundabout and then take the first left.

Al Posto Giusto ITALIAN €€
(www.harmonyoftaste.com; Nikole Kovačevića 6, Igalo; mains €6-19) With outposts in Tivat and Belgrade, this restaurant's expanding popularity is fuelled by its excellent woodfired pizza.

Morinj Моринь

POP 224

Secluded in the first bend of the inner bay, little Morinj is divided into *gornji* (upper) and *donji* (lower) sections, like many of the coastal villages. The silver dome of St Petka Church (Crkva Sv Petke) sparkles above, but the main attraction here is the pretty beach. It's a sheltered nook so you may see algae in places, but the water's mainly clear and the views down the bay are amazing.

In addition to a post office and store, this village harbours contenders for the titles of best camping ground and best restaurant in the country.

However, there is a darker side to this peaceful spot. Between 1991 and 1992 around 300 Croat prisoners of war were incarcerated here. Four former Yugoslav army reservists were subsequently imprisoned for war crimes relating to the inhumane treatment and torture of the prisoners.

Sleeping & Eating

Autocamp Naluka CAMPGROUND €
(032-373 101; www.naluka.montenegro.com; campsites per adult/child €4/1, per tent/car/campervan €3.50/3/8; May-Sep) Pitch your tent under the mandarin and olive trees and next to the stream that bubbles out of a spring at a constant 10°C – the water's too cold for mosquitoes but perfect for keeping your beer cold! There are only squat toilets but the site is kept immaculately by its English-speaking owner.

★**Konoba Ćatovića Mlini** SEAFOOD, MONTENEGRIN €€
(032-373 030; www.catovicamlini.me; mains €8-24; 11am-11pm) A crystalline stream flows around and under this rustic former mill which masquerades as a humble family-owned *konoba* but in reality is one of Montenegro's best restaurants. Watch the geese idle by as you sample the magical bread and olive oil, which appears unbidden at the table. Fish is the focus but traditional Njeguši specialities are also offered.

Getting There & Away

Morinj is a 30-minute bus ride from either Herceg Novi or Kotor.

Risan Рисан

POP 2040

While summer holidaymakers still head to its small beaches, Risan has a rundown feel, not helped by the port and large hotel hogging its sea frontage. You wouldn't think to look at it, but this is the oldest town on the bay, dating to at least the 3rd century BC when it was a fortified Illyrian town. Their queen Teuta is said to have retreated here during the Roman invasion and made it her capital. When the Romans inevitably took over, they erected sumptuous seaside mansions, one of which is now Risan's main claim to fame.

In 1930 the foundations of a grand villa were discovered, complete with wonderful **mosaics** (admission €2; 9am-7pm 15 May-15 Oct). A shelter has been erected over the site to protect it from the elements, and English-speaking staff are at hand to explain the building's layout. The dining-room floor is decorated with flowers, herbs, grapevines and squid, while other rooms have intricate geometric patterns. Best of all is the bedroom which features a wonderful depiction of Hypnos, the Greek god of sleep, reclining on a pillow.

After checking out the mosaics it's worth a short stroll through the leafy park, which hides the elegant Orthodox **Church of Sts Peter and Paul** (Crkva Sv Petra i Pavla; 9-11am), dating from 1796, and on to the central square, Trg 21 Novembra. Leading up the hill from here is **Gabela**, an atmospheric lane with interesting patterned cobbling dating from the Ottoman occupation.

Buses running between Herceg Novi and Kotor stop in Risan.

Perast Пераст

POP 270

Looking like a chunk of Venice that has floated down the Adriatic and anchored itself onto the bay, Perast hums with melancholy memories of the days when it was rich and powerful. Despite having only one main street, this tiny town boasts 16 churches and 17 formerly grand palazzos. While some are just enigmatic ruins sprouting bougainvillea and wild fig, others are caught up in the whirlwind of renovation that has hit the town. Michael Douglas and Catherine Zeta Jones are said to have paid €2 million for a house here.

The town slopes down from the highway to a narrow waterfront road (Obala Marka Martinovića) that runs along its length. At its heart is St Nicholas' Church, set on a small square lined with date palms and the bronze busts of famous citizens.

Sights

Perast Museum MUSEUM
(Muzej grada Perasta; 032-373 519; adult/child €2.50/1.50; 9am-7pm) The Bujović Palace, dating from 1694, has been lovingly preserved and converted into a museum showcasing the town's proud seafaring history. It's worth visiting for the building alone and for the wondrous photo opportunities afforded by its balcony.

St Nicholas' Church CHURCH
(Crkva Sv Nikole; museum admission €1; museum 10am-6pm) St Nicholas' Church has never been completed, and given that it was commenced in the 17th century and the bay's Catholic community has declined markedly

since then, one suspects it never will be. Its museum contains beautifully embroidered vestments and the remains of various saints. Climb the imposing 55m bell tower for views over the bay.

Sveti Đorđe & Gospa od Škrpjela ISLANDS
Just offshore from Perast are two peculiarly picturesque islands. The smaller, Sveti Đorđe (St George), rises from a natural reef and houses a Benedictine monastery shaded by cypresses.

Boats (€5 return) regularly head to its big sister, Gospa od Škrpjela (Our-Lady-of-the-Rocks), which was artificially created in the 15th century around a rock where an image of the Madonna was found. Every year on 22 July the locals row over with stones to continue the task. The magnificent church was erected in 1630 and has sumptuous paintings, hundreds of silver votive tablets and a small **museum** (admission €1; 10am-6pm). The most unusual exhibit is an embroidered icon of the Madonna and Child partly made with the hair of its maker.

Festivals & Events

Gađanje Kokota CULTURE
(Shooting a Cock; 15 May) Possibly even more distasteful than it sounds, this tradition commemorates a 1654 victory by the people of Perast over the Turks. A competition is held to shoot a rooster that is chained to a boat and floated out to sea. The festivities include a Catholic procession, solemn Mass and members of the Boka Navy dancing the *kolo* (wheel dance) in the square.

Fašinada CULTURE
(www.fasinada-cup.com; 22 Jul) In this traditional annual event, male descendents of Perast's leading families row a convoy of decorated and roped-together boats to deposit stones on Gospa od Škrpjela island. It's now accompanied by a two-day yachting regatta, the Fašinada Cup, with participants racing to Tivat and back.

International Klapa Festival MUSIC
(www.festivalklapaperast.com; Jul or Aug) Two days of traditional Dalmatian-style unaccompanied singing.

Sleeping

Perast makes an atmospheric and peaceful base from which to explore the bay. Look out for private rental signs in summer.

Boka Bay B&B APARTMENTS €€
(www.bokabay.com; apt €50-75;) There are only two cosy sloped-ceiling apartments here – a studio and a one-bedroom – but they both have water views, en suites and kitchenettes. Bookings must be made by email.

Hotel Conte APARTMENTS €€€
(032-373 687; www.hotel-conte.com; apt €100-160;) Conte is not so much a hotel as a series of deluxe studio to two-bedroom apartments in historic buildings scattered around St Nicholas' Church. The sense of age resonating from the stone walls is palpable, even with the distinctly nontraditional addition of a jacuzzi and sauna in the flashest apartment. It's worth paying €20 extra for a sea view.

Per Astra HOTEL €€€
(032-373 608; www.perastra.me; d from €139;) Located right at the top of the town (the stairs will get you fit, but they can be difficult at night), this old stone complex offers 11 suites with over-the-top decor, fine views and a small pool.

Eating & Drinking

Konoba Otok Bronza MONTENEGRIN, SEAFOOD €€
(032-373 607; mains €7-13) Dating from the 12th century (yes, you read that right), this memorable place has a cavelike interior with a spring spouting mountain water from its rock walls. Settle in for a reasonably priced traditional meal or just soak up the mood over a glass of local vino under the canopy of grapevines.

★ **Restaurant Conte** SEAFOOD €€€
(032-373 687; mains €9-20;) Meals come with lashings of romance on the flower-bedecked waterside terrace of the Hotel Conte. This close to the water, how could seafood not be the speciality? You'll be presented with platters of whole fish to select from; the chosen one will return, cooked and silver-served, to your table.

Piratebar BAR
(recliner/umbrella €2.50/1.50) Tucked under the road on the Risan edge of Perast, this little beach bar serves coffee, frappes and cocktails. It's also the best spot in Perast for a swim.

Information

The **post office** (8am-2.40pm Mon-Sat) faces the main square; there are no banks, ATMs or internet cafes.

KAMENARI–LEPETANE CAR FERRY

The Bay of Kotor is a very peculiar shape. The entrance is guarded by two peninsulas that shelter the first section of the bay incorporating Herceg Novi and Tivat. The waters then narrow into a thin channel before the spectacular inner bay opens up. **Car ferries** (car/motorcycle/passenger €4.50/1.50/free; 24hr) wend their way across the narrowest point from Kamenari (15km east of Herceg Novi) to Lepetane (5km north of Tivat). They depart roughly every 15 minutes (hourly after 10pm) and the journey only takes about five minutes.

The alternative, the coastal road along the bay to Kotor, is truly spectacular and should be travelled at least once, whether by car or bus. The distance between Herceg Novi and Kotor is only 43km but it can easily take an hour, longer if you get stuck behind a truck on the narrow winding road.

There's no doubt that the ferry is quicker for Tivat or Budva, but in the height of summer there can be horrendous queues, sometimes stretching for kilometres. For Kotor the benefit is more marginal. If there are no queues and you've already travelled the scenic route, you might consider catching the ferry and heading to Kotor via the tunnel south of the town. You're unlikely to gain more than about 10 minutes but you will save on petrol.

Buses from Herceg Novi to Budva take both routes.

Getting There & Away

Paid parking is available on either approach to town; car access into the town itself is restricted.

There's no bus station but buses stop at least hourly on the main road at the top of town. Expect to pay less than €3 for any journey within the bay between Kotor (25 minutes) and Herceg Novi (40 minutes).

Boat tours of the bay invariably stop here.

Dobrota Доброта

POP 8200

These days Dobrota is effectively a residential suburb of Kotor, starting north of Kotor's Old Town and stretching along the shoreline for 5km. Despite its close proximity to its famous neighbour, it retains a distinctive feel. While Kotor looks inwards from its walls, Dobrota gazes out to sea.

In recent years foreign investors have renovated many of the decaying palazzos, some of which are much grander than those you'll find in Perast or Kotor, and an elegant paved boardwalk has been constructed, tracing the water's edge.

Sights

St Matthew's & St Eustace's CHURCHES

Dobrota's most distinctive features are its two large Catholic churches. St Matthew's (Crkva Sv Mateja; 1670) is the older of the two and wears a baroque frontage, a well-proportioned dome and a tall steeple. Cavernous St Eustace's (Crkva Sv Eustahija) dates from 1773 but has a 19th-century steeple and a little walled graveyard. You'll rarely find either church open, which is a shame as St Matthew's apparently contains a painting by Bellini and St Eustace's has a Veronese.

Žuta Plaža BEACH

Dobrota is effectively Kotor's beach suburb. Private swimming platforms take up much of the waterline, but this pebbly stretch closest to Kotor is open to everybody. It's a beautiful spot for a swim, with the sheer mountain walls looming above, but it should be noted that there have been problems with water quality here.

Sleeping

Dobrota is a perfect base for exploring Kotor at arm's length from the noise and flurry of the Old Town.

★**Palazzo Radomiri** HISTORIC HOTEL €€€

(032-333 172; www.palazzoradomiri.com; s €80-90, d €120-130, ste €150-220; Mar-Oct; P) Exquisitely beautiful, this honey-coloured early-18th-century palazzo has been transformed into a first-rate boutique hotel. Some rooms are bigger and grander than others, but all 10 have sea views and luxurious furnishings. Guests can avail themselves of a small workout area, sauna, pool, private jetty, bar and restaurant.

★ **Forza Mare** BOUTIQUE HOTEL €€€
(☎032-333 500; www.forzamare.com; Kriva bb; r €180-252; ⊙Apr-Oct; P❄📶🏊) A bridge arches over a small pool lined in green tiles before you even reach the front door of this hotel, dripping in marble, slate and a general air of over-the-top opulence. There's enough bling, in fact, to have enticed Tina Turner, Jay-Z and Beyoncé through the doors. Downstairs there's a tiny private beach, an upmarket restaurant and a full spa centre.

Eating

Restoran Ellas SEAFOOD €€
(☎032-335 115; www.restoranelas.com; Dobrota 85; meals €8-20) Head upstairs to the rooftop terrace for lovely views of the bay and lots of Dalmatian-style seafood dishes, despite the name and the decor referencing Greece.

Restoran Stari Mlini SEAFOOD €€€
(☎032-333 555; www.starimlini.com; Jadranski Put; meals €12-20) It's well worth making the trip to Ljuta, just north of Dobrota, to this magical restaurant set in and around an 18th-century flour mill by the edge of the bay. It's pricier than most and the service is variable, but the food is excellent and the setting wonderfully romantic.

Information

Kotor Health Centre (Dom zdravlja; ☎032-334 533; www.dzkotor.me; Jadranski Put bb) Kotor's main clinic.

Apoteka Aesulap (☎032-334 699; Jadranski Put bb; ⊙7am-11pm) Pharmacy next to the health centre.

Getting There & Around

A one-way road runs along the waterfront heading south towards Kotor. This road can either be accessed from Jadranski Put at the top end or from a side road about halfway along. Expect an extremely slow crawl along here in summer.

Kotor Котор

POP 4800

Wedged between brooding mountains and a moody corner of the bay, this dramatically beautiful town is perfectly at one with its setting. Its sturdy walls – started in the 9th century and tweaked until the 18th – arch steeply up the slopes behind it. From a distance they're barely discernible from the mountain's grey hide, but at night they're spectacularly lit, reflecting in the water to give the town a golden halo. Within those walls lie labyrinthine marbled lanes where churches, shops, bars and restaurants surprise you on hidden piazzas.

In July and August people pour into Kotor and the yachts of the super-rich fill the marina, but this town never gets quite as Euro-trashy as some other parts of the coast – this sheltered arm of the bay just isn't as appealing for swimming. But anyone with a heart for romance, living history and architecture will find Kotor a highlight of their Montenegrin travels.

History

It's thought that Kotor began as Acruvium, part of the Roman province of Dalmatia. Its present look owes much to nearly 400 years of Venetian rule when it was known as Cattaro. In 1813 it briefly joined with Montenegro for the first time, but the Great Powers decided to hand it back to Austria, where it remained until after WWI. There's a strong history of Catholic and Orthodox cooperation in the area, although the number of Catholics has dropped from 51% in 1900 to 18% today. Nowadays only 11% of the population identify as Croats.

Sights

The best thing to do in Kotor is to let yourself get lost and found again in the maze of streets. You'll soon know every corner since the town is quite small, but there are plenty of old churches to pop into and many coffees to be drunk in the shady squares.

Sea Gate GATE
(Vrata od Mora) The main entrance to the town was constructed in 1555 when the town was under Venetian rule (1420–1797). Look out for the winged lion of St Mark, Venice's symbol, which is displayed prominently on the walls here and in several other spots around the town. Above the gate the date of the city's liberation from the Nazis is remembered with a communist star and a quote from Tito. As you pass through the gate, look for the 15th-century stone relief of the Madonna and Child flanked by St Tryphon and St Bernard. Stepping through onto Trg od Oružja (Weapons Sq) you'll see a strange stone pyramid in front of the **clock tower** (1602); it was once used as a pillory to shame wayward citizens.

St Tryphon's Cathedral CHURCH
(Katedrala Sv Tripuna; Trg Sv Tripuna; admission €2; ⏲8am-7pm) Kotor's most impressive building is its Catholic Cathedral, originally built in the 12th century but reconstructed after several earthquakes. When the entire frontage was destroyed in 1667, the baroque bell towers were added; the left one has never been finished. The cathedral's gently hued interior is a masterpiece of Romanesque architecture with slender Corinthian columns alternating with pillars of pink stone, thrusting upwards to support a series of vaulted roofs. Its gilded silver bas-relief altar screen is considered Kotor's most valuable treasure. Up in the reliquary chapel are some lovely icons, a spooky wooden crucifix (1288) and, behind the grill, assorted body parts of saints including St Tryphon. The early martyr's importance to both the Catholic and Orthodox churches makes him a fitting patron for the city.

Maritime Museum of Montenegro MUSEUM
(Pomorski muzej Crne Gore; www.museummaritimum.com; Trg Bokeljske Mornarice; adult/child €4/1; ⏲9am-6.30pm Mon-Sat, 9am-1pm Sun Apr-Oct, 9am-2pm daily Nov-Mar) Kotor's proud history as a naval power is celebrated in three storeys of displays housed in a wonderful early-18th-century palace. A free audioguide helps explain the collection of photographs, paintings, uniforms, exquisitely decorated weapons and models of ships.

St Luke's Church CHURCH
(Crkva Sv Luke; Trg Sv Luke) Sweet little St Luke's speaks volumes about the history of Croat-Serb relations in Kotor. It was built in 1195 as a Catholic church but from 1657 until 1812 a Catholic and Orthodox altar stood side by side, with each faith taking turns to hold services here. It was then gifted to the Orthodox Church. Fragments of 12th-century frescoes still survive along with two wonderfully painted iconostases: a 17th-century one in the main church and one from the 18th-century in the chapel of St Spiridon, another saint venerated by both faiths.

St Nicholas' Church CHURCH
(Crkva Sv Nikole; Trg Sv Luke) Breathe in the smell of incense and beeswax in this relatively unadorned Orthodox church (1909). The silence, the iconostasis with its silver bas-relief panels, the dark wood against bare grey walls, the filtered light through the dome and the simple stained glass conspire to create a mystical atmosphere.

St Mary's Collegiate Church CHURCH
(Crkva Sv Marije Koleđate; Trg od Drva) Built in 1221 on the site of a 6th-century basilica, this Catholic church is distinguished by impressive 20th-century bronze doors covered in bas-reliefs, a particularly gruesome larger-than-life crucifix, and a glass coffin containing the body of Blessed Osanna of Cattaro (1493–1565). She was what is known as an anchoress, choosing to be walled into a small cell attached to a church so as to devote her life to prayer.

River Gate GATE
(North Gate) Tucked in the quiet northern corner of town beside the parklike Trg od Drva (Wood Sq), this gate opens on to a moat formed by the clear mountain water of the bubbling Škurda River. It was built in 1540 to commemorate the attack on the city the previous year by the Ottoman navy.

Gurdić Gate GATE
(Vrata od Gurdića) Fewer tourists make it to the south end of town, where the houses narrow into a slim corridor leading to this bastion and gate (parts of which date from the 13th century) and the drawbridge over the Gurdić spring. Without the crowds you can easily imagine yourself transported through time here.

Town Walls FORTRESS
(admission €2; ⏲24hr, fees apply 8am-8pm May-Sep) Looming above Kotor is St John's Hill, one of the lower peaks of the Lovćen massif. The town's fortifications started to head up the hill in the 9th century and by the 14th century a protective loop was completed, which was added to right up until the 19th century. The energetic can make a 1200m ascent up the fortifications via 1350 steps to a height of 260m above sea level, for unforgettable views and a huge sense of achievement. There are entry points near the North Gate and behind Trg od Salate (Salad Sq); avoid the heat of the day and bring lots of water.

The truly vigorous can climb the ancient caravan trail known as the **Ladder of Cattaro**, which starts near the Škurda River and zigzags up the mountain to join the Coastal Mountain Traversal in Lovćen National Park.

Tours

Various tour boats leave from opposite the Old Town to explore the bay; expect to pay

Kotor

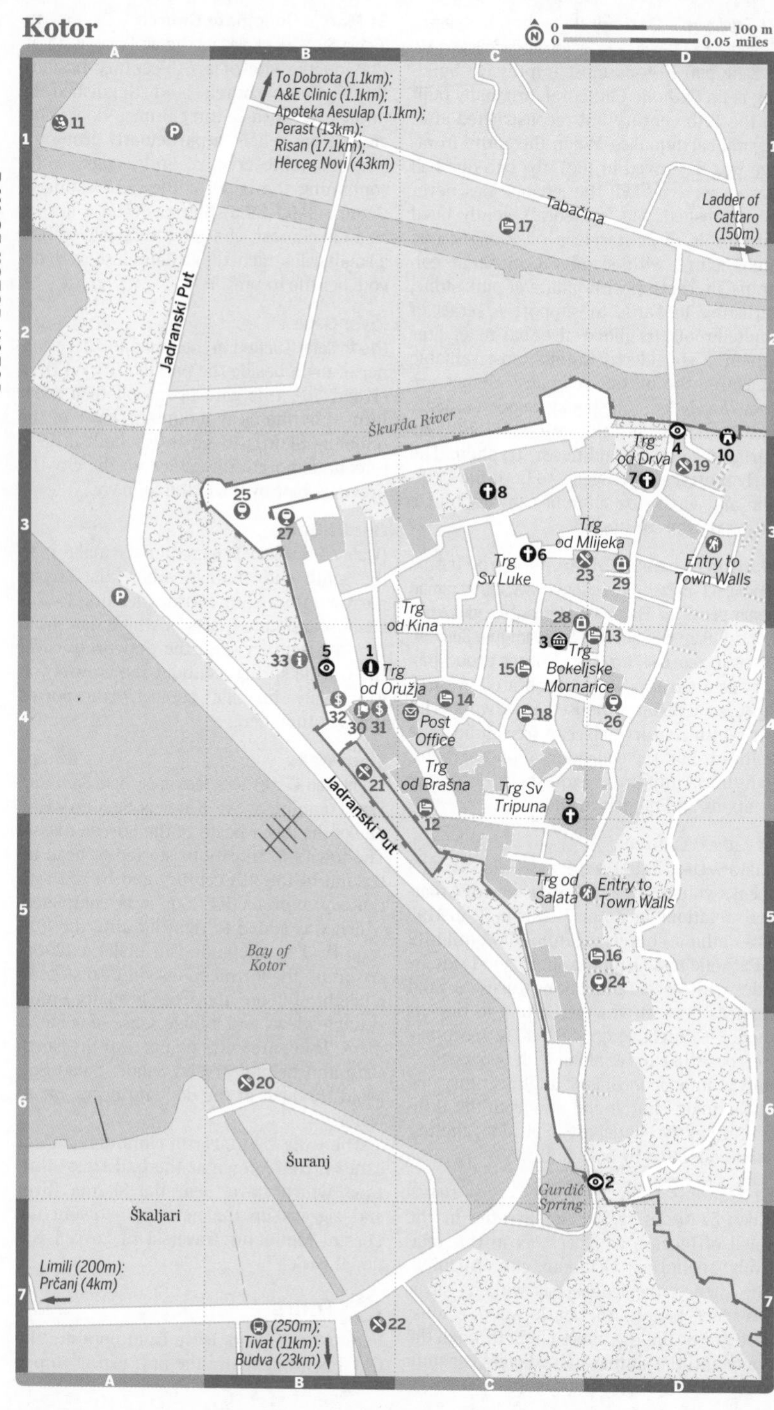
0
100 m
0
0.05 miles
To Dobrota (1.1km);
A&E Clinic (1.1km);
Apoteka Aesulap (1.1km);
Perast (13km);
Risan (17.1km);
Herceg Novi (43km)
Tabačina
Ladder of Cattaro (150m)
Jadranski Put
Škurda River
Trg od Drva
Trg od Mlijeka
Trg Sv Luke
Entry to Town Walls
Trg od Kina
Trg od Oružja
Trg Bokeljske Mornarice
Post Office
Trg od Brašna
Trg Sv Tripuna
Jadranski Put
Trg od Salata
Entry to Town Walls
Bay of Kotor
Gurdić Spring
Šuranj
Škaljari
Limili (200m);
Prčanj (4km)
(250m);
Tivat (11km);
Budva (23km)

Kotor

Sights
1 Clock Tower B4
2 Gurdić Gate D6
3 Maritime Museum of Montenegro C4
4 River Gate D2
5 Sea Gate B4
6 St Luke's Church C3
7 St Mary's Collegiate Church D3
8 St Nicholas' Church C3
9 St Tryphon's Cathedral C4
10 Town Walls D3

Activities, Courses & Tours
11 Kayak Montenegro A1

Sleeping
12 Hotel Astoria C4
13 Hotel Monte Cristo D4
14 Hotel Vardar C4
15 Montenegro Hostel C4
16 Old Town Hostel D5
17 Tianis C1
18 Villa Duomo C4

Eating
19 Bastion D3
20 Galion B6
21 Market B4
22 Roda B7
23 Stari Grad C3

Drinking & Nightlife
24 Bandiera D5
25 Citadella B3
26 Havana D4
27 Maximus B3

Shopping
28 Antiques Stanković C3
29 Mon Ami Wine House D3

Information
30 Croatian Consulate B4
31 NLB Montenegrobanka B4
32 Opportunity Bank B4
33 Tourist Information Booth B4

about €15 for a day tour. If you're keen to potter around the Boka on a boat of your own, you'll be disappointed. A licence is required, so most hire companies supply skippers and cater firmly to the top end.

A Day Out On Monty B SAILING
(067-859 309; www.montenegro4sail.com; 4hr/6hr/8hr cruise €295/460/550, additional adults €30/40/50) If you don't have €1000 to blow on a luxury yacht, join British ex-pats Katie and Tim (and their two little doggies) for a day-sail on the 44-ft ketch which doubles as their home (and kennel). The basic price includes up to four adults; children and teenagers sail for free. Smaller groups can split the cost with other travellers on a shared outing.

Avel Yachting SAILING
(032-672 703; www.avelyachting.com; day charter €1200-1500) Charters fancy yachts and launches for day trips or for longer stints.

Kayak Montenegro KAYAKING
(067-382 472; www.kayakmontenegro.com; per hr/4hr/8hr €5/15/25) In the warmer months this Herceg Novi–based crew rents kayaks from the waterfront north of the Old Town.

Festivals & Events

St Tryphon's Day RELIGIOUS
(14 Feb) St Valentine doesn't have the monopoly on 14 February. Kotor's patron saint's feast day is celebrated with Mass, a procession through the streets, folk dances and music.

Traditional Winter Carnival CARNIVAL
(Feb) Carrying on the Venetian Renaissance tradition with two weeks of masked balls, parades and performances.

Camellia Day FLORAL
(mid-Mar) A celebration of the bloom that enlivens many Kotor gardens in mid-March. Includes the Camellia Ball, where a prominent local woman is chosen as the Lady of the Camellia.

Boka Navy Day CULTURE
(26 Jun) Dating back to 1420, on 26 June the traditionally clad sailors are presented with the flag and keys of the city and perform the *kolo* (circle dance).

Kotor Art PERFORMING ARTS
(www.kotorart.org) Kotor's summer arts festival acts as an umbrella for several established events, including the **Children's Theatre Festival** (www.kotorskifestival.com; early Jul), Don Branko's Music Days (featuring international artists performing classical music in Kotor's squares and churches from mid-July to mid-August), Perast's Klapa Festival, and assorted workshops, lectures and touring productions.

WORTH A TRIP

BACK ROAD TO MT LOVĆEN

The journey from Kotor to Mt Lovćen, the ancient core of the country, is one of Montenegro's great drives. Take the road heading towards the Tivat tunnel and turn right just past the graveyard. After 5km, follow the sign to Cetinje on your left opposite the fort. From here there's 17km of good but narrow road snaking up 25 hairpin turns, each one revealing a vista more spectacular than the last. Take your time and keep your wits about you; you'll need to pull over and be prepared to reverse if you meet oncoming traffic. From the top the views stretch over the entire bay to the Adriatic. At the entrance to Lovćen National Park you can continue straight ahead through Njeguši for the shortest route to Cetinje or turn right and continue on the scenic route through the park.

International Fashion Show FASHION
(late Jul) Some seriously big names (including Romeo Gigli in 2008) send their collections down a catwalk set up in front of the cathedral.

Summer Carnival CARNIVAL
(Aug) A condensed version of the main carnival staged at a more tourist-friendly time.

Boka Night CULTURE
(mid-Aug) Decorated boats take to the bay.

Sleeping

Although the Stari Grad is a charming place to stay, you'd better pack earplugs. In summer the bars blast music onto the streets until 1am every night, rubbish collectors clank around at 6am and the chattering starts at the cafes by 8am. Enquire about private accommodation at the tourist information booth.

★Old Town Hostel HOSTEL €
(032-325 317; www.hostel-kotor.me; near Trg od Salata; dm € 12-14, r without bathroom €30, apt €40) If the ghosts of the Bisanti family had any concerns when their 13th-century palazzo was converted into a hostel, they must be overjoyed now. Sympathetic renovations have brought the place to life, and the ancient stone walls now echo with the cheerful chatter of happy travellers, mixing and mingling beneath the Bisanti coat of arms. Comfortable, sociable, reasonable, historical... exceptional.

Montenegro Hostel HOSTEL €
(069-270 510; www.montenegrohostel.com; Trg Bokeljske Mornarice; dm €13-14, s €17, d €50, without bathroom €40;) It couldn't be more centrally located, but that comes at a price – pack earplugs if you're not a heavy sleeper. Otherwise this hostel is a perfectly fine although reasonably basic place to lay your head.

Hotel Monte Cristo HOTEL €€
(032-322 458; www.montecristo.co.me; near Trg Bokeljske Mornarice; r €75-90, apt €115-150; P) It's not going to win any hip design awards but this old stone place offers a cheerful welcome and clean, brightly tiled rooms in a supremely central location. There's a restaurant downstairs, so expect some noise.

Tianis APARTMENTS €€
(032-302 178; www.tianis.net; Tabačina 569; apt €60-120; P) Well located without being in the midst of the melee, this friendly establishment has a clutch of reasonably priced apartments of varying sizes, some of which have magical views across the Škurda River to the Old Town from their terraces.

Hotel Astoria BOUTIQUE HOTEL €€€
(032-302 720; www.kotor.astoriamontenegro.com; Trg od Brašna; s €120-150, d €150-180;) Straddling an awkward line between fantastic and fantastical, the Astoria seems to have been designed by someone with a bulging budget and a *Lord of the Rings* fixation. Corridors are made to look like caves and a teenager's warrior-princess fantasy gazes down on reception, but the rooms are luxuriously furnished and very comfortable. The spacious junior suites have bay views.

Hotel Vardar HOTEL €€€
(032-325 084; www.hotelvardar.com; Trg od Oružja; s €115-169, d €155-230; P) Right on the main square, this lovely old place has had a sumptuous modern makeover with extremely elegant furnishings. We love the fluffy pillows and swirly marble bathrooms but despite the general swankiness, you'll still need the earplugs.

Villa Duomo APARTMENTS €€€
(☎032-323 111; www.villaduomo.com; near Trg Bokeljske Mornarice; apt €120-240; P ❄ 📶) Duomo offers a wonderful blend of modern comforts and traditional ambience. Wooden sleigh beds, old-fashioned phones and writing desks are set against the bare stone walls, alongside plasma TVs, DVDs and, in some rooms, jacuzzis. Breakfast is served on a pretty internal terrace.

Eating

There are dozens of restaurants, bakeries and takeaway joints on Kotor's cobbled lanes. For the sweet-toothed, cherry-filled strudel is a speciality of the region. Self-caterers can stock up at the **market** (⏲7am-2pm) under the town walls, or at the **Roda supermarket** (Jadranski Put; ⏲6am-11pm) on the way to the bus station.

Stari Grad SEAFOOD €€
(☎032-322 025; www.restoranstarigrad.com; Trg od Mlijeka; mains €8-18) Head straight through to the stone-walled courtyard, grab a seat under the vines and prepare to get absolutely stuffed full of fabulous food – the serves are huge. Either point out the fish that takes your fancy or order from the traditional à la carte menu.

Bastion MONTENEGRIN, SEAFOOD €€
(www.bastion123.com; Trg od Drva; mains €8-18; ⏲10am-midnight) At a slight remove from the frenetic heart of the Old Town, Bastion offers a mixture of fresh seafood and traditional meaty grills. If the weather's being well behaved, grab a table outside.

★**Galion** SEAFOOD €€€
(☎032-325 054; Šuranj bb; meals €10-21) With an achingly romantic setting, extremely upmarket Galion gazes directly at the Old Town across the millionaire yachts in the marina. Fresh fish is the focus, served as traditional grills. It usually closes in winter.

Drinking & Nightlife

Kotor is full of cafe-bars that spill onto its squares and fill them with the buzz of conversation. Take your pick.

Havana BAR
(Trg od Zatvora; ⏲8am-1am; 📶) In summer Havana takes over a little square on the dark side of the Old Town, projecting sports or pop videos onto the neighbouring building. When the weather turns, head inside, where Cuban scenes cover the walls and classic cocktails are served from a central bar.

Bandiera BAR
(near Trg od Salata) Tourists don't tend to venture down this darker end of town, where you'll find Che Guevara on the wall and rock music on the stereo.

Citadella BAR
(☎032-311 000; www.cattarohotel.com; near Trg od Oružja) This large terrace bar located on top of the old fortifications is fairly touristy, but you can't beat the views of the bay, town and mountain battlements.

Maximus CLUB
(☎067-216 767; www.discomaximus.com; near Trg od Oružja; admission free-€5; ⏲11pm-5am Thu-Sat, nightly in summer) Montenegro's most pumping club comes into its own in summer, hosting big-name international DJs and local starlets.

Shopping

Mon Ami Wine House WINE
(near Trg od Mlijeka; tastings €4; ⏲9am-3pm & 5pm-midnight) Local boutique wine producers rarely get a look-in on restaurant menus. If you'd like to sample a broader selection of Montenegro's output, this cute little shop offers tasting flights of five wines and three types of *rakija* (fruit brandy). Otherwise, just pick a pretty hand-painted bottle and take your chances.

Antiques Stanković ANTIQUES
(☎069-071 819; www.antiquesstankovic.com; Trg Bokeljske Mornarice) A treasure trove of socialist medals, Roman coins, antique jewellery, traditional garb and other interesting stuff to blow the budget on.

LOCAL KNOWLEDGE

VRMAC RIDGE

'We use the Vrmac ridge as part of our Coastal Challenge but you don't need to be particularly fit to hike it. The route starts at Trojica, the old Austrian fort above Kotor, and heads to Gornja Lastva, an old village where the residents have made a pact not to sell to developers. You can mountain bike along the top as well on what's quite a wide trail.'

Jack Delf, Adventure Race Montenegro

Information

You'll find the **post office** and a choice of banks with ATMs on the main square, Trg od Oružja. The **Accident & Emergency** clinic is in Dobrota.

Limili (082-325 511; Njegoševa 13; per 5kg €7) This dry cleaners offers a reliable next-day bag wash. It's on the road to Muo, past the creepy abandoned Hotel Fjord.

Tourist Information Booth (032-325 950; www.tokotor.me; outside Vrata od Mora; 8am-8pm Apr-Nov, 8am-6pm Dec-Mar) Stocks free maps and brochures, and can help with contacts for private accommodation.

Getting There & Away

The main road to Tivat and Budva turns off the waterfront road at a baffling uncontrolled intersection south of the Stari Grad and heads through a long tunnel.

The **bus station** (032-325 809; 6am-9pm) is to the south of town, just off the road leading to the tunnel. Buses to Herceg Novi (€4, one hour), Budva (€3.50, 40 minutes), Tivat (€2.20, 20 minutes) and Podgorica (€7, two hours) are at least hourly. Further flung destinations include Kolašin (€12, four daily), Dubrovnik (€14, two daily) and Belgrade (€32, seven daily).

A taxi to Tivat Airport should cost around €10.

Prčanj — Прчањ

POP 1130

Heading north along the bay from Kotor to Prčanj, the road narrows to a single lane despite it being two-way, which makes for lots of fun and plenty of honking when a bus meets a truck coming in the opposite direction. After passing through the village of Muo you'll arrive at Prčanj, 5km from Kotor. This formerly prosperous maritime town has lots of old stone buildings, a couple of restaurants, a bakery, a minimarket, a post office and Catholic churches that come in a choice of small, medium and XXL.

Sights

Church of the Birth of the Blessed Virgin Mary — CHURCH

(Crkva Rođenja Blažene Djevice Marije; 7-9pm Mon-Sat, 9-11am Sun) Even the name of this whopping church is outsized. It's said to be the biggest religious building on the Adriatic coast and it certainly dominates this little town in a God-is-watching-you kind of way. It was begun in 1789 but not completed until 1908. At that time, Catholics were in the majority in Prčanj. Now they comprise only 21% of the population.

A grand stairway leads up to a terrace offering commanding views of the bay, enjoyed by the slightly bug-eyed statues of St Peter and St Paul standing sentinel on the church's baroque facade. Inside is an interesting array of sculpture and a skeleton displayed in a glass coffin.

St Nicholas' Church — CHURCH

(Crkva Sv Nikole) Built in the baroque style in 1735, this medium-sized church has a Franciscan monastery attached, although the last monks left in 1908. The church was badly damaged in the 1979 earthquake but wasn't fully restored until 2011. It contains a grand Venetian-built high altar containing an oil painting of St Nicholas flanked by wooden carvings of St Peter and St Paul.

St John the Baptist's Church — CHURCH

(Crkva Sv Ivana Krstitelja) Simple, solid and semi-derelict, this tiny church dates from 1221 or 1397, depending on which resource you believe.

Stoliv — Столив

POP 350

Donji Stoliv (Lower Stoliv) is a pleasant seaside village with a huddle of stone houses surmounted by a grand church, 9.5km from Kotor. It's worth stopping here to take the idyllic but steep half-hour's walk through the olive and chestnut trees to the upper village, **Gornji Stoliv**. Most of the families who lived here for centuries have now left, with only a few houses remaining in use and the rest in varying states of picturesque ruin. A church dedicated to the prophet Elijah (Crkva Sv Ilije) dating from 1553 keeps a lonely vigil. At 250m, the views over the bay to Perast are sublime.

Down in Donji Stoliv several houses offer camping in July and August under their fig and olive trees for about €10 for two people with a car and tent. Facilities are basic (squat toilets with a basket for toilet paper) and water supplies sometimes run out.

Lastva — Ластва

POP 750

From Stoliv, the road rounds the tip of the Vrmac Peninsula and passes the ferry terminal at Lepetane before popping out in the front section of the bay.

Two kilometres further is Lastva, another divided village, but the *gornja* (upper) section of this one has been actively promoted to tourists for its rustic ambience. There's a decent road for starters, leading 3km up the hill. **Gornja Lastva** doesn't offer the same off-the-beaten-track satisfaction as Stoliv, but it's nice to see that this village has been kept alive. Old ladies dressed in black potter about gathering wild herbs, and if you're lucky the parish priest will be around to unlock the 15th-century **St Mary's Church** (Crkva Sv Marije), which reputedly has some accomplished Italian paintings inside. The best time to visit is the first Saturday in August, when a village fair is held.

In **Donja Lastva** there's a summer-only **tourist office** (8am-noon & 5-8pm Mon-Sat, 8am-noon Sun) where you can make enquiries about private accommodation.

Tivat — Тиват

POP 9400

In the throes of a major makeover, courtesy of the multi-million-dollar redevelopment of its old naval base into a superyacht marina, Tivat is becoming noticeably more schmick each year. Only a decade ago its palm-tree-lined waterfront was looking decidedly down-at-heel, and coffee and pizza seemed to be the only forms of sustenance. Now the variety of restaurants rivals anywhere in the country – but then so do the prices.

Tivat has a reputation as one of the sunniest spots on the Boka Kotorska. While it will never rival Kotor for charm, it makes a pleasant stop on a trip around the bay, and a useful base for exploring the sweet villages of the Vrmac and Luštica Peninsulas.

The town is home to the Boka's largest remaining Croat and Catholic community, representing 17% and 21% of its population, respectively.

Sights

Porto Montenegro MARINA, VILLAGE

(www.portomontenegro.com; 7am-1am) Single-handedly responsible for Tivat's transformation, this surreal town-within-a-town occupies 24 hectares which once were the historic Arsenal shipyard and naval base. It's a work in progress, with only 4.5 hectares developed at the time of writing, but it already has five upmarket apartment buildings, a 'lifestyle village' of fancy shops, bars, restaurants and leisure facilities, a museum, and berths for 250 yachts. A Regent Hotel was set to open in May 2014, and eventually 630 luxury yachts will be able to dock here, including 130 superyachts.

The project isn't without controversy: 3500 locals took to the streets to protest the sale of this state asset to foreign investors (an international consortium of the exceedingly rich led by Canadian businessman Peter Munk) and the loss of 480 jobs. Yet many naysayers have been silenced by the improvements that are already evident in the town.

The Porto complex is open to the public and it's a pleasant place to stroll and ogle oppulent yachts – if you're not prone to fits of rage at the injustices of contemporary economics. Kids will love the playground shaped like a pirate ship near the main entrance.

The success of such of a venture relies partially on enticing yacht crews to dock here for the winter, so bars, restaurants and activity providers operate year-round (unlike most of the Montenegrin coast). Prices are generally geared more towards crew-members than oligarchs and, while expensive for Montenegro, are reasonable by European standards.

Naval Heritage Collection MUSEUM

(Zbirka Pomorskog Nasljeđa; Porto Montenegro; 10am-8pm Mon-Sat, 4-8pm Sun) FREE Porto Montenegro doffs its hat to its past with this display devoted to the history of the Arsenal shipyard and naval base, housed in one of the site's old boat sheds. The star exhibits are too big for the museum: the two Yugoslav navy submarines drydocked outside.

Buća-Luković Museum & Gallery MUSEUM

(Muzej i Galerija Buća-Luković; 032-674 591; Trg od kulture; 8am-2pm & 4-10pm Mon-Sat, 4-10pm Sun) FREE Aristocratic families from Perast, Dobrota and Kotor once built their summer residences at Tivat to take advantage of its sunnier outlook. One of the few survivors is this 500-year-old fortified enclosure with its own Catholic chapel which once belonged to Kotor's Buća family.

Ask the staff to unlock the solid stone defensive tower, which houses a collection of Roman bits and bobs. Next door is a well-presented ethnographical museum with fishing and farming artefacts accompanied by photos of them being put to use. Head upstairs for beautiful jewellery and folk costumes, including little handbags and parasols that the women would wear to

Tivat

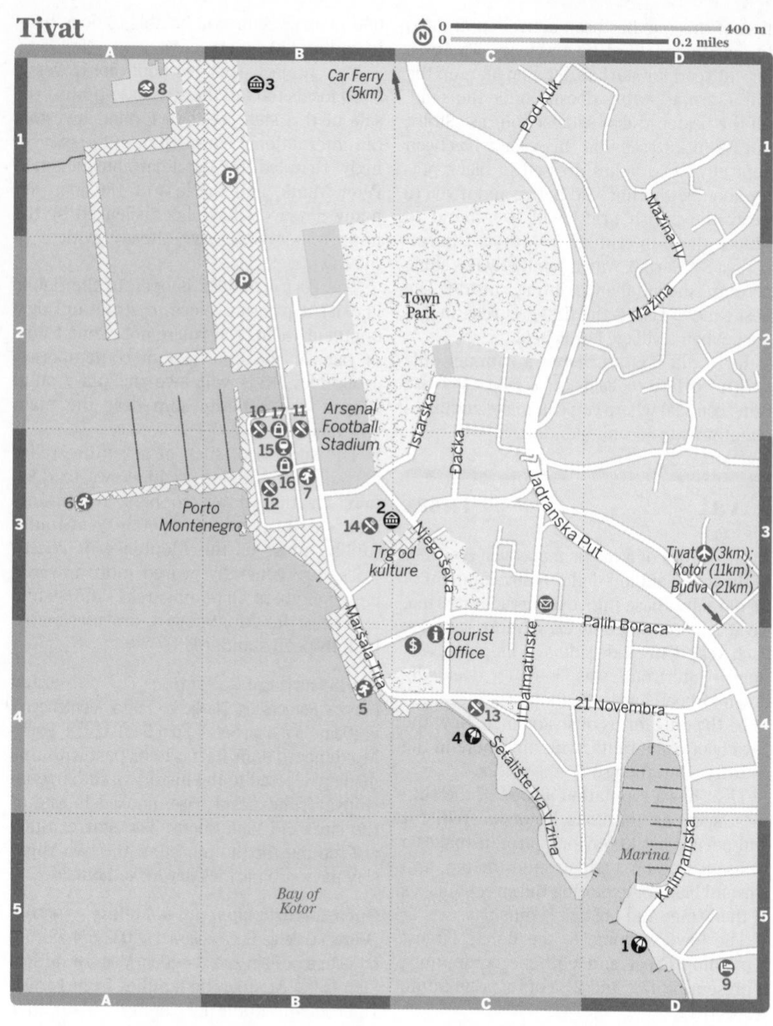

ape Western fashion. The gallery focuses on modern painting and sculpture.

Town Park PARK

(Gradski Park) North of the centre the Town Park is a leafy, peaceful retreat, originally laid out in 1892. At one edge is the headquarters of Tivat's Arsenal football club. We suspect that the club's North London namesake has nothing to fear if its home ground is anything to go by.

Town Beach BEACH

(Gradska Plaža) You're better off heading to the Luštica Peninsula for a proper swim, but Tivat does offer a couple of options if you're desperate for dip. Town Beach is a long concrete platform with a 20m pebbly section right by the main promenade. There's another pebbly beach, **Belani** (Plaža Belane), just past the marina.

Activities

Montenegro Cruising CRUISE

(068-821 300; cruise €20; 10am May-Sep) Offers daily cruises during the tourist season on boats named Vesna (numbered I to V), stopping at Žanjic beach, Herceg Novi, Perast's islands and Kotor; the boat returns

Tivat

Sights
1 Belani Beach ... D5
2 Buća-Luković Museum & Gallery ... B3
3 Naval Heritage Collection ... B1
4 Town Beach ... C4

Activities, Courses & Tours
5 Montenegro Cruising ... B4
6 Montenegro+ ... A3
7 Pura Vida ... B3
8 Purobeach ... A1

Sleeping
9 Hotel Villa Royal ... D5

Eating
10 Al Posto Giusto ... B2
11 Mitsu ... B2
12 One ... B3
13 Prova ... C4
14 Theodorus ... B3

Drinking & Nightlife
15 Clubhouse ... B3

Shopping
16 City Book Store ... B3
17 Pizana Gallery ... B2

to Tivat at 6pm. Budva-based travel agents commonly sell this cruise inclusive of bus transfers, with their clients finishing the cruise at Kotor.

Montenegro+ WATER SPORTS
(069-190 190; www.montenegroplus.me; Jetty 1, Porto Montenegro; 9am-7pm) Offers lessons in wakeboarding and waterskiing (40-minute lesson €80), stand-up paddling (90-minute lesson €35) and sailing a trimaran (12 hours over three days €360); rents kayaks (per day from €30), trimarans (per 1½ hours/day €45/140) and mountain bikes (per day €50); and offers guided kayaking excursions to Perast (€24), the Blue Grotto (€45), Lake Skadar (€65) and the Tara River (€85), and a mountain-biking tour along the Vrmac ridge (€40).

Purobeach SWIMMING
(www.purobeach.com; Porto Montenegro; day-bed incl fruit and first drink €30; 11am-late May-Sep) If you want to witness Mediterranean glamour at close quarters, this water's edge complex offers amateur anthropologists ample opportunities for people-watching. The pool itself is beautifully designed, with tiling reminiscent of a circuit board and an infinity lip connecting it visually with the bay. DJs lay down smooth beats throughout the day and as the sun sets over the bay, patrons slink from their day beds and into the attached restaurants and bars.

Pura Vida DAY SPA
(032-540 356; www.puravida-spa.com; Porto Montenegro; massage from €30; 9am-9pm Mon-Sat, noon-8pm Sun) Of course Porto has a day spa, offering all the plucking, pummelling and pampering treatments you'd expect from a luxury resort.

Festivals & Events

Carnival CARNIVAL
(Feb) Like the other bay towns, Tivat's residents don their Venetian masks in February.

Purgatorije THEATRE
(www.czktivat.co.me; Jul–mid-Sep) The International Festival of Mediterranean Theatre, to use its less punishing title, is a summer-long program of theatre, concerts, film and exhibitions.

November Culture Days PERFORMING ARTS
(Nov) Exhibitions, theatre and concerts to take the chill off the shortening days.

Sleeping

Enquire at the tourist office about private accommodation.

Hotel Villa Royal HOTEL €€
(032-675 310; www.rotortivat.com; Kalimanjska 18; s/d €42/68;) It's not a villa and it's certainly not fit for a king, but this mini-hotel near the old marina has clean bright rooms and friendly staff, making it our pick of Tivat's extremely limited accommodation options... at least until the Regent opens at Porto Montenegro in 2014.

Eating & Drinking

Theodorus CAFE, BAR €
(Trg kulture; mains €3-14;) When you get sick of hanging out with people wearing boat shoes, head to this popular local joint. The menu stretches to cooked breakfasts, tasty sandwiches, pizza, pasta, steaks and salad, or you can just head in for a coffee or a beer. On Friday nights it's Tivat's most popular live-music venue.

Al Posto Giusto ITALIAN €€
(☎031-331 071; www.harmonyoftaste.com; Porto Montenegro; mains €6-19) Out of all of Porto's restaurants, this is the one most geared towards local tastes and hence the one with the buzziest atmosphere. Specials and cartoons are scrawled straight onto the black walls, and there's an open kitchen where you can watch the pizza chefs feeding the wood-fired oven.

Prova MEDITERRANEAN €€
(www.prova.co.me; Šetalište Iva Vizina 1; mains €8-18; ⏰8am-1am) Shaped like a boat with chandeliers that look like mutant alien jellyfish, this upmarket eatery is the very epitome of the new, increasingly chic Tivat. The pasta is excellent.

★**One** ITALIAN €€€
(☎067-486 045; Porto Montenegro; mains €10-20; ⏰8am-1am) Murals and sail-like flourishes on the ceiling invoke the yachtie lifestyle in this smart but informal brasserie, while the menu sails clear across the Adriatic for an authentic take on Italian cuisine. Relax over a cooked breakfast (€6) then stock up on wine at the attached One Gourmet store.

Mitsu JAPANESE €€€
(☎032-540 230; Porto Montenegro; mains €12-16; ⏰11am-11pm) Painted in red and black and hung with large lantern-style light fixtures, this hip eatery is the perfect remedy if you're starting to suffer from an overdose of pasta and grilled seafood. Sushi and sashimi is prepared in an open kitchen on the side of the dining room, and the menu stretches to the odd Chinese and Vietnamese classic.

Clubhouse BAR
(www.facebook.com/TheClubhousePortoMontenegro; Porto Montenegro; ⏰noon-1am) Doing its very best to keep the yacht crews entertained, this lively little Aussie-run bar hosts live music and kooky themed nights, and screens international football and rugby matches. There's a good selection of imported beer, and visiting Antipodeans can drown their homesickness in 'flat white' coffee, Australian shiraz and New Zealand sauvignon blanc.

Shopping

Pizana Gallery ART
(www.pizana.me; Porto Montenegro; ⏰5-11pm) Browse to your heart's content at this gallery, representing many of Montenegro's leading contemporary artists.

City Book Store BOOKS
(www.novaknjiga.com; Porto Montenegro; ⏰9am-11pm) This small store has an English-language section and sells up-to-the-minute print-out copies of major British, French and Russian newspapers.

Information

Tourist Office (☎032-671 324; www.tivat.travel; Palih Boraca 8; ⏰8am-8pm Mon-Fri, 8am-noon & 6-8pm Sat, 8am-noon Sun Jun-Aug, 8am-3pm Mon-Sat Sep-May) Accommodation contacts and information about local sights and walks.

Getting There & Around

AIR

Tivat Airport is 3km south of town and 8km through the tunnel from Kotor. Taxis charge around €5 to €7 for Tivat, €10 for Kotor and €25 for Budva.

Hire-car companies with counters at the airport include Avis, Europcar, In Montenegro, Meridian Rentacar and Sixt.

BICYCLE

Bike Tivat (www.biketivat.com; subscription per day/week €5/30) has four automated docking stations scattered around Tivat and two in Donja Lastva . You'll need to purchase a subscription at the tourist office and then use an electronic card to unlock the bikes. Bikes are free for the first half-hour and then charged at 50c for up to an hour; subscriptions include up to four hours of use.

Mountain bikes can be rented through Montenegro+ (p53).

BUS

Buses to Kotor (€2.20, 20 minutes) stop outside a silver kiosk on Palih Boraca. The main bus station is inconveniently located halfway between Tivat and the airport. From there buses head to Herceg Novi (€3, 10 daily), Kotor (€2, seven daily), Budva (€3, at least hourly), Bar (€6, seven daily), Podgorica (€7, at least hourly) and Belgrade (€28, daily).

CAR

Tivat sits on the western side of the Vrmac Peninsula, which juts out into the Bay of Kotor and divides it in two. The quickest route to Kotor is to take the main road southeast in the direction of Budva, turn left at the major intersection past the airport and take the tunnel. The alternative is the narrow coastal road. For Herceg Novi, take the ferry from Lepetane, 5km northwest of town.

Around Tivat

The overly poetically named **Ostrvo Cvijeća** (Island of Flowers) is accessed by an unlikely looking road that heads behind the airport and through a rundown area where a former tourist complex shelters people displaced by the region's most recent wars. At the very end of the potholed road is the **St Michael the Archangel's Monastery** (Manastir Sv Arhanđela Mihaila). This is the area's most historically significant site. The remains of Roman mosaics have been discovered here, along with the ruins of a 9th-century church and Benedictine monastery. From the early 13th century St Michael's was the seat of the Orthodox bishop of Zeta until it was destroyed by the Venetians in 1452. The sweet little 19th-century **Holy Trinity Church** (Crkva Sv Trojice) stands nearby, shaded by trees and protected by stone walls.

Two more islands stretch out in a line from here but you'll need a boat to access them (a taxi boat from Tivat or Herceg Novi will do the trick). The larger, heavily forested **Sveti Marko** (St Mark's Island) used to be a Club Med and you can still see the huts poking up through the trees. It's a prime spot with a couple of nice beaches so it's bound to be developed sometime.

Beyond this the diminutive **Gospa od Milosti** (Our-Lady-of-Mercy Island) was once the residence of Kotor's Catholic bishops and is now a convent. A wooden statue of the Madonna kept in the church is said to have miraculous powers.

Luštica Peninsula Луштица

Reaching out to form the southern headland of the Bay of Kotor, the gorgeous Luštica Peninsula hides secluded beaches and a dusting of idyllic villages scattered amongst the olive groves of its remote southern edge. If you want to enjoy this magical area while it's still relatively untouched you'd better get in quick. At the time of research a large section of the southern coast was being developed into a golf resort.

The first section of the peninsula facing Tivat is already quite developed. At **Krtoli** the pebbly beaches look over the green swathe of St Mark's Island and the picturesque Our-Lady-of-Mercy Island, which are immediately offshore. If you're looking for a spot to chill out and relax by the water, you could do a lot worse. This area is cheaper and less frantic than most of the coast and some excellent midsized apartment hotels have sprung up. Further west, **Bjelila** is a cute little fishing village comprising a cluster of old stone houses dipping their feet in the water.

Continuing along the peninsula the houses stop, the road gets narrower and the scenery gets greener and prettier. Climbing up the ridge on the way to Rose, a panorama of the bay opens up before you. If you're in the mood for a leisurely drive with a high probability of getting at least temporarily lost, continue on the narrow back roads from Rose that meander through the bucolic olive groves of the southern half of the peninsula. If you see signs for Radovići you're still heading in the right direction.

Along the southern coastline is a string of clean beaches that are popular with day trippers travelling from Herceg Novi by taxi boat.

Sights

Rose VILLAGE

At the peninsula's very tip you'll find this sleepy fishing village (pronounced with two syllables: ro-seh), a blissful stand of stone houses gazing at Herceg Novi across the sparkling waters of the bay. Outside summer, village life winds down to near inertia but from May to September a handful of waterside eateries open their doors to day trippers. If you fancy staying over, ask a local about private accommodation.

Rose's easily reached by taxi boat from Herceg Novi (around €10). Kayak Montenegro stops here on its guided paddle tours or you can hire a kayak and go it alone; it takes about 30 minutes each way.

Dobreč BEACH

Blue-flagged Dobreč is reported to have some of the cleanest waters in Montenegro and is only accessible by sea – usually by taxi boat from Herceg Novi. Kayak Montenegro (p37) tours head here after visiting Rose. Make a day of it, as there's a good restaurant and a little water park for the kids.

Žanjic & Mirišta BEACHES

Sitting in a sheltered cove below the olive groves, Žanjic's 300m-long white pebbly beach attracts up to 1000 people in the height of summer. Neighbouring Mirišta is considerably smaller.

Both are accessible by car but are more commonly reached by boat from Herceg Novi. The daily Boka tours operated by Montenegro Cruising (p52) stop in Žanjic for 90 minutes. Kayak Montenegro's day trips to Mamula Island stop in Mirišta.

Blue Grotto CAVE
(Plava Špilja) A popular cruise stop, the Blue Grotto gets its name from the mesmerising effect of the light reflecting through the clear water. Boats head into the 9m-high cave and usually allow you an opportunity for an iridescent swim. Montenegro+ (p53) offers kayak tours here.

Oblatno BEACH
(www.almara.me) It was perhaps inevitable that the virtually untouched paradise of green headlands and blue waters at Trašte Bay would attract the attention of developers. Only a few years ago there was nothing here but a beautiful stretch of rocky shoreline. More recently it's been commercialised as the chic Almara Beach Club, with a restaurant, day beds, DJs and live music – attracting a young, up-for-it crowd of sunseekers and partygoers.

Yet that's nothing on what's planned – a whole new tourist town, complete with a golf course and marina. We suggest you get here quickly before this rare coastal slice of 'wild beauty', to quote Montenegro's tourist slogan, is gone forever.

Pržno BEACH
At the base of the peninsula, just south of the main town Radovići, is beautiful Pržno (not to be confused with the other Pržno near Sveti Stefan). This gorgeous scallop of white sand sits within a green horseshoe of scrub, pines and olive trees and is a definite candidate for the title of Montenegro's best beach.

Most locals know this beach as Plavi Horizont (Blue Horizon) after a large package-tour hotel which was being demolished when we visited. Its replacement, a €250-million five-star resort tentatively known as Beyond Horizon, is being built by a Qatari company and was due to be completed by the end of 2014. The plans show dozens of individual units, each with its own swimming pool, scattered around the beach. We've not sure what this means for the future of the olive grove or for public access to the beach, but it seems that Pržno's days as a relatively unspoiled paradise may be numbered.

Sleeping

★**Villa Kristina** APARTMENTS €€
(☎032-679 739; www.villakristina.me; Bjelila bb; apt €60-80; ❄ 📶) Kristina's four apartments are decked out with rich colours, chandeliers, tiny kitchenettes and flat-screen teles, and each has its own little balcony gazing over the bay. It's all terribly romantic, which explains why the owners are considering changing the name to Villa Romantica (it may not happen, but forewarned is forearmed). Downstairs, there's a little private beach and a restaurant.

Apartments Briv APARTMENTS €€
(☎032-680 116; www.yubriv.com; Obala Đuraševića bb, Krtoli; apt €70-80; P ❄ @) Step down from the sun deck of this modern block and straight into the water. There are 24 attractive apartments of differing sizes and configurations on offer. Try for the ones on the ground floor that have large terraces facing the water. You can rent a jet ski or borrow a kayak to paddle out to the islands.

Hotel Vizantija HOTEL €€
(☎032-680 015; www.vizantija.com; Kaluđerovina bb; ste €60-80, apt €100; ⏲ Apr-Sep; P ❄ 📶) Vizantija's 12 suites and apartments are simply furnished but spick and span and there's access to the water at the bottom of the property. Make sure your hire car's got some grunt before you tackle the steep driveway.

Eating

Konoba Adriatic SEAFOOD, CAFE €€
(☎031-687 020; Rose bb; mains €5-11; ⏲10am-midnight) Kick back under the vines on the Rose waterfront and munch on a sandwich (€3.50) or a more substantial seafood meal.

Vino Santo SEAFOOD €€€
(☎067-851 662; www.vinosanto.me; Obala Đuraševića bb, Krtoli; mains €10-19; ⏲noon-midnight) If different-restaurant-same-menu fatigue is starting to set in, Vino Santo offers the antidote. The traditional seafood favourites are all present and accounted for, but acclaimed chef Dragan Peričić adds a French twist in the delivery. Enjoy the prawns sautéed in cognac and the serene island views as proficient waiters in black bow ties scurry around.

Naturally Gifted

When you're this little it's easy to be overlooked, so Montenegro overcompensates by being rammed full of extraordinary sights. The coastline is so beautiful that not even the mountains can resist dipping their toes in the clear waters.

Contents

Above Lake Skadar National Park (p95).

GARY JOHN NORMAN / GETTY IMAGES ©

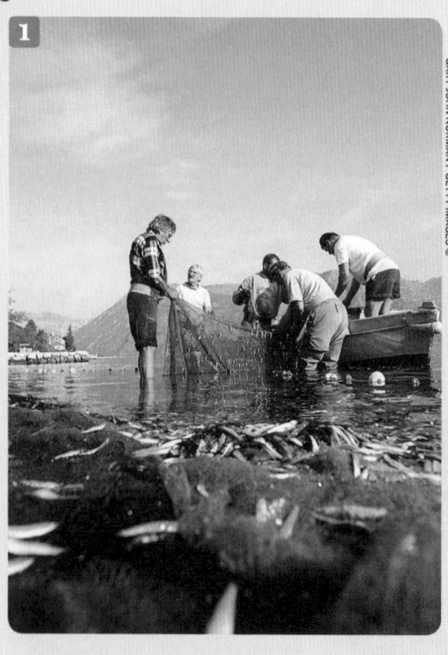

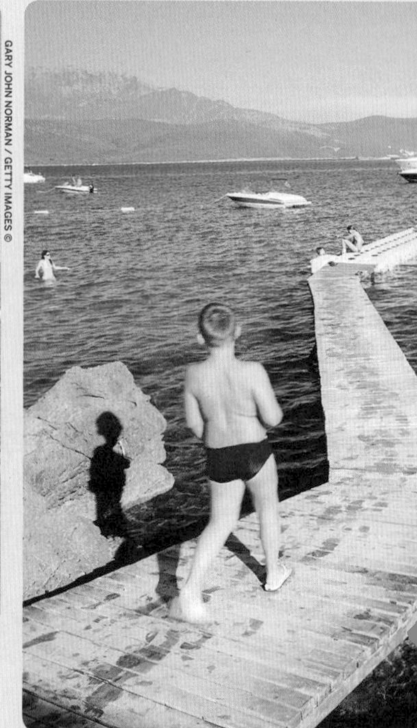

1. Fishermen, Bay of Kotor (p44) 2. Oblatno Beach (p56)
3. Buljarica Beach (p74) 4. Sveti Stefan (p73)

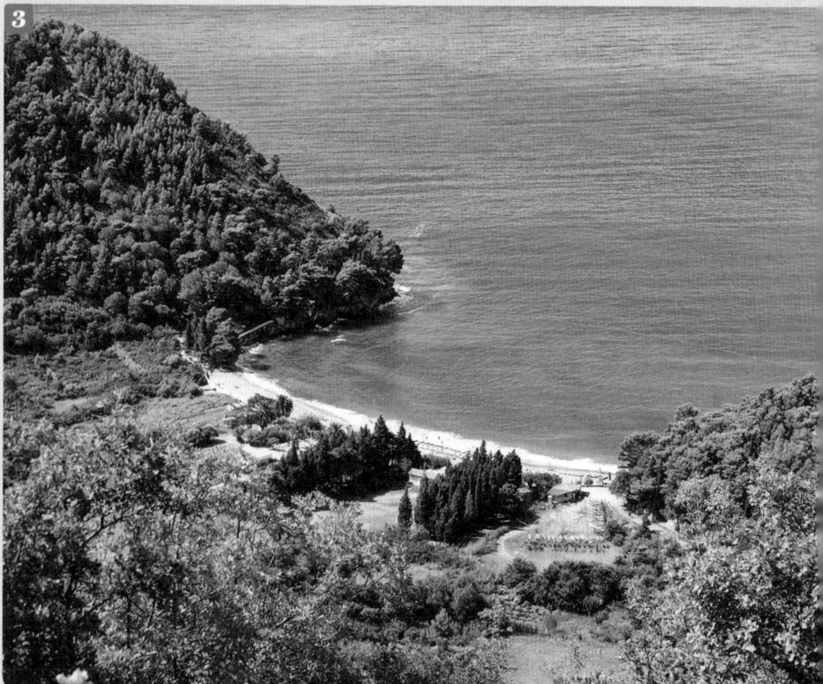

LAURIE NOBLE / GETTY IMAGES ©

Sundrenched Coast

Lord Byron described this coastline as 'the most beautiful encounter between the land and the sea'. Wherever you choose to splash about in the crystalline waters, chances are there will be a mountainous backdrop proving the great Romantic poet right.

Bay of Kotor

The combination of Mediterranean vegetation, historic towns, cute-as-a-button villages and rugged mountains plunging to an opalescent sea makes the Bay of Kotor pretty hard to beat. More fragrant than the ground floor of a department store, the Bay is subtly infused with the scent of wild herbs, perfumed flowers and aromatic trees.

It's little wonder that the inner part of the bay was the first site in Montenegro to be inscribed on the Unesco World Heritage List – recognising both its natural and cultural value.

Walled Towns

For centuries the people of the coast have protected their towns with stone walls, creating a picturesque counterpoint to the natural beauty surrounding them.

At Budva and Ulcinj the ancient fortifications jut out over the azure blue of the Adriatic. Kotor's walls arch high up on the cliffs behind the town. At night they are spectacularly illuminated, forming a halo from their reflections in the still, dark waters of the bay.

Most striking of all is Sveti Stefan, a picture-perfect island village anchored to the coast by the narrowest of causeways. While off-limits to the general public it has survived its transformation into a luxury resort with all of its historic charm intact.

Durmitor National Park (p11

Mountain Majesty

Much of Montenegro's surface looks like it's been dug up by a giant puppy out of freshly laid concrete. Montenegro's mountains push up behind each other, filling most of the land, with only a scattering of sparkling lakes and deeply cut river canyons to give them breathing space.

Durmitor National Park

A lunar landscape of craggy peaks gives way to high plains and twinkling glacial lakes known as 'mountain eyes' – this is the second of Montenegro's World Heritage Sites. The Tara River slices deeply through the Durmitor range, providing one of the world's most dramatic rafting routes and the nation's most popular active attraction. Savin Kuk never quite sheds its cap of snow and in the winter its 3.5km run is adored by enthusiastic skiers and snowboarders.

Biogradska Gora National Park

If you're on the hunt for wood nymphs or satyrs, the 1600 hectares of virgin forest at the heart of the Bjelasica Mountains would be a good place to start.

Mountaintop Monuments

Seemingly sprouting out of the surrounding cliffs, gleaming white Ostrog Monastery is the country's spiritual heart for its Orthodox population and a popular pilgrimage site. At the top of one of Mt Lovćen's highest peaks stands the Njegoš Mausoleum. This tomb for a national hero echoes the grandeur of the black mountain itself, through imposing sculpture, solemn architecture and awe-inspiring views.

Adriatic Coast

Includes ➡

Best Places to Eat

- Blanche (p72)
- Miško (p87)
- Kaldrma (p82)
- Porto (p69)
- Pizza 10 Maradona (p69)

Best Places to Sleep

- Vila Drago (p74)
- Aman Sveti Stefan (p74)
- Vila Levantin (p74)
- Hotel Astoria (p68)
- Haus Freiburg (p85)

Why Go?

The juxtaposition of mountains and sea sends the spirit soaring here. Croatia may hog most of the Adriatic coast but Montenegro's tiny section packs a lot into a very small area. Without the buffer of Croatia's islands, more of Montenegro's shoreline has developed into sandy beaches, culminating in a 12km continuous stretch leading to the Albanian border.

Living on the fault line between civilisations, the people of the coast have fortified their settlements since ancient times. That legacy can be explored in the lively bars and shops of Budva's Old Town, the surreal glamour of Sveti Stefan's village resort, the ramshackle residences within Ulcinj's fortifications and, most evocatively, the lonely and mysterious ruins of Haj-Nehaj, Stari Bar and Svač. Otherwise just spend your days lazing beside azure waters and supping the local vino in outdoor cafes between the oleanders.

When to Go

- Enjoy the beaches and balmy weather in May and June, before the crowds descend.
- July and August see soaring temperatures, crowded beaches and peak prices – but these are the best months to party.
- In September and October you may get some rain, but the air and water temperatures are still warm.

History

From the 4th century BC the ancient Greeks set up colonies along the Illyrian-controlled coast, such as Bouthoe (Budva). Once the Romans had completely smashed Illyria in 168 BC, the region was incorporated into their province of Dalmatia and for over 500 years it benefited from its position near the centre of a great empire. When the decision was made to split the Roman Empire in two, the borderline crossed this section of the coast, leaving most of it within the Greek-influenced eastern (Byzantine) half.

The Serbs reached this part of the coast by the 7th century and put down roots, organising into small clans. These eventually became part of the principality of Duklja (later called Zeta), Montenegro's antecedent. In 1089, only 35 years after the split of Christianity into Catholic (western) and Orthodox (eastern) halves, the rulers of Duklja succeeded in negotiating the creation of a Catholic archdiocese in Bar. Eventually Duklja was brought back into Byzantine control and later incorporated into the Serbian kingdom of Raška. In 1276, Stefan Dragutin overthrew his father to become king of Raška and installed his mother Helen of Anjou as ruler of Zeta, including most of the coast. Helen was a devout Catholic who founded Franciscan monasteries in Bar and Ulcinj.

As Raška became bogged down fighting Byzantium, Bulgaria, Hungary, Venice and the Ottoman Turks, a new force started to gain power in Zeta, the Balšić family. Some historians believe they were originally Orthodox but later converted to Catholicism hoping this would gain them acceptance from the coastal population. In 1368 they had control of Budva, Bar and Ulcinj, but by the end of the century they were forced to oscillate between being a vassal state of the Adriatic's two big players, the Venetians and the Ottomans. By 1443 Venice ruled the coast with the support of powerful families such as the Paštrovići, who were offered a degree of autonomy.

MOVING ON TO ALBANIA?

For tips, recommendations and reviews, head to shop.lonelyplanet.com to purchase a downloadable PDF of the Albania chapter from Lonely Planet's *Eastern Europe* guide.

After enjoying a couple of generations of peace, the people of the coast were once again under siege in 1570, this time from the Ottomans who already ruled most of the interior. Once Ulcinj fell, Bar surrendered without a fight. The Paštrovići resisted but couldn't prevent Budva from being sacked. In 1573 Venice signed a peace treaty confirming Ottoman control of the cities south of Budva, much to the detriment of the Paštrovići who continued to oppose their new overlords. In contrast, Ulcinj became a largely Muslim town, as it remains today.

This situation continued until 1877 when King Nikola's Montenegrin army ended 300 years of Ottoman control in Bar and Ulcinj, in the process finally gaining the seaport that they so desperately craved.

Montenegro disappeared completely after WWI as the whole of this coastal region was subsumed into the Kingdom of Serbs, Croats and Slovenes in 1918 (later Yugoslavia). During WWII both this part of Yugoslavia and neighbouring Albania were occupied by the Italians, who planned to redraw the boundaries to include Ulcinj within Albania and annex Budva directly into Italy, leaving only Bar within their planned puppet Montenegrin state. This was never to eventuate and following the Partisan victory, all of the coastal area was incorporated into Montenegro within the federal Yugoslavia, including Budva for the first time.

Climate

Gorgeously Mediterranean is the best way to describe it. Ulcinj is said to be one of the sunniest spots on the Adriatic, notching up 218 sunny days a year.

Getting There & Away

Budva is connected to the Bay of Kotor by the Jadranski Put (Adriatic highway; also known as 'Jadranska magistrala'). The main route to Cetinje and Podgorica leaves Jadranski Put between Budva and Bečići and climbs steeply into the mountains. Petrovac is connected to Podgorica via a highway leading through Virpazar and the western edge of Lake Skadar. This route can also be reached by a tunnel starting near Sutomore, north of Bar (toll €2.50). A scenic back road links Ulcinj to the southern edge of Montenegro's section of Lake Skadar.

Regular buses connect all the coastal towns with the Bay of Kotor and Podgorica. A railway line links Bar with the centre of the country, including Lake Skadar and Podgorica. There are

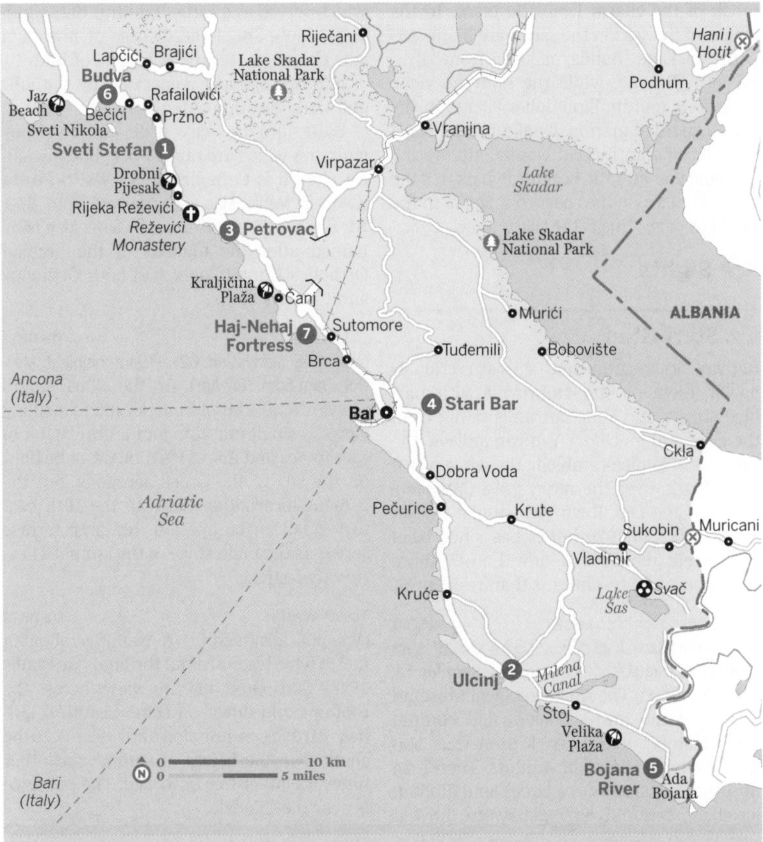

Adriatic Coast Highlights

1. Gazing in wonder at the cutesy beauty of the exclusive walled island of **Sveti Stefan** (p73)
2. Soaking up the summertime beachy buzz of Eastern-tinged **Ulcinj** (p82)
3. Letting the kids off the leash on the **Petrovac** promenade (p74)
4. Delving into the extensive remains of the ruined town of **Stari Bar** (p81)
5. Scoffing a big bowl of fish soup in a stilt-house overhanging the **Bojana River** (p87)
6. Watching the passing parade of beautiful people over the rim of a coffee cup in the cobbled laneways of **Budva's Stari Grad** (Old Town, p64)
7. Hiking to the atmospheric, ruined **Haj-Nehaj fortress** (p80)
8. Snorkelling around the **rocky bays** north of Bar (p78)

ferries from Bar to Italy and bus connections to Albania from Ulcinj.

Getting Around

Jadranski Put is the main road connecting all coastal towns and is well served by buses. In summer, taxi boats are a useful option for short trips between beaches.

Budva Будва

POP 13,400

The poster child of Montenegrin tourism, Budva – with its atmospheric Stari Grad (Old Town) and numerous beaches – certainly has a lot to offer. Yet the child has moved into a difficult adolescence, fuelled by rampant development that has leeched much of the charm from the place. In the height of the season the sands are blanketed with package holidaymakers from Russia and Ukraine, while the nouveau riche park their multimillion-dollar yachts in the town's guarded marina. By night you'll run a gauntlet of scantily clad women attempting to cajole you into the beachside bars. It's the buzziest place on the coast so if you're in the mood to party, this is the place to be.

Sights

Stari Grad

Budva's best feature and star attraction is its Old Town – a mini-Dubrovnik with marbled streets and Venetian walls rising from the clear waters below. You can still see the remains of Venice's emblem, the winged lion of St Mark, over the **main gate** (Map p66). Much of the Old Town was ruined in two earthquakes in 1979 but it has since been completely rebuilt and now houses more shops, bars and restaurants than residences.

Archaeological Museum MUSEUM
(Arheološki muzej; Map p66; ☎033-453 308; Petra I Petrovića 11; adult/child €2/1; ⌚9am-9pm Tue-Fri, 2-9pm Sat & Sun) The Archaeological Museum shows off the town's ancient and complicated history – dating back to at least 500 BC – over four floors of exhibits. There's an impressive collection of Greek and Roman jewellery, ceramics and glassware (how it survived in a town so prone to earthquakes and war is anyone's guess) and an ancient helmet with holes in the back, which suggest that the former owner had at least one very bad day.

Trg Između Crkava SQUARE
Literally the 'square between the churches', this open area below the citadel provides a visual reminder of the once cosy relationship between Orthodox and Catholic Christians in this area.

Beautiful frescoes cover the walls and ceiling of **Holy Trinity Church** (Crkva Sv Trojice; Map p66; ⌚8am-noon & 5pm-midnight summer, 8am-noon & 4-7pm winter), in the centre of the square. Built in 1804 out of stripes of pink and honey-coloured stone, this Orthodox church is the only one of the square's interesting cluster of churches that is regularly open.

The largest of the churches is Catholic **St John's Church** (Crkva Sv Ivana; Map p66), which served as a cathedral until 1828 (Budva is now part of the diocese of Kotor). A side chapel houses the Madonna of Budva – a 12th-century icon venerated by Catholic and Orthodox Budvans alike.

Built into the city walls are two tiny churches which are rarely open. Budva's oldest church is Catholic **St Mary's in Punta** (Crkva Sv Marije; Map p66), dating from 840. **St Sava's Church** (Crkva Sv Save; Map p66), named after the founder of the Serbian Orthodox Church, once had both Orthodox and Catholic altars.

Citadela FORTRESS
(Map p66; admission €2; ⌚9am-midnight May-Oct, 9am-5pm Nov-Apr) At the Stari Grad's seaward end, the old citadel offers striking views, a small museum and a library full of rare tomes and maps. It's thought to be built on the site of the Greek acropolis, but the present incarnation dates to the 19th century Austrian occupation. Its large terrace serves as the main stage of the annual Theatre City festival.

Town Walls FORTRESS
(Map p66; admission €1) A walkway about a metre wide leads around the landward walls of the Stari Grad, offering views across the rooftops and down on some beautiful hidden gardens. Admission only seems to be charged in the height of summer; at other times it's either free or locked. The entrance is near the Citadela.

Modern Gallery GALLERY
(Moderna galerija; Map p66; Cara Dušana 19; ⌚8am-2pm & 6-9pm Mon-Fri, 6-9pm Sat) FREE An attractive gallery displaying temporary exhibitions.

Ričardova Glava BEACH
(Map p66) Immediately south of the Old Town, this little beach has the ancient town-walls as an impressive backdrop. If you wander around the headland, past the much-photographed statue of a naked female dancer, you'll find quieter double-bayed **Mogren Beach**. There's a spot near here where the fearless or foolhardy leap from the cliffs into the waters below.

Plaža Pizana BEACH
(Map p66) By the walls on the northern side of the Old Town, Pizana is 100m of sand and pebbles leading down from an upmarket cafe by the marina.

Budva

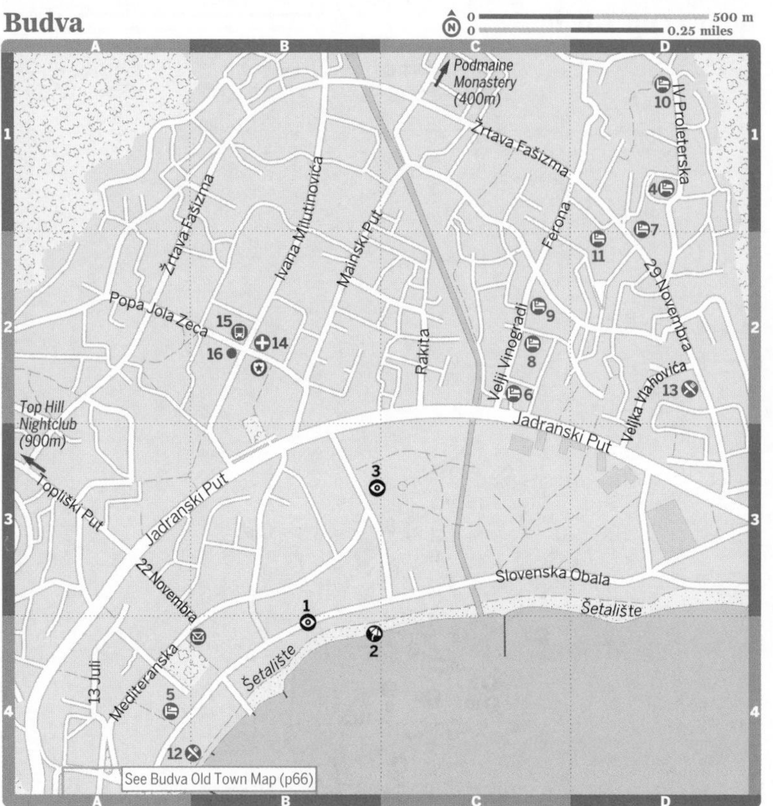

Budva

Sights
- 1 Slovenska Obala ... B4
- 2 Slovenska Plaža ... B4
- 3 Slovenska Plaža tourist village ... B3

Sleeping
- 4 Hippo Hostel ... D1
- 5 Hotel Fontana ... A4
- 6 Hotel Kangaroo ... C2
- 7 Hotel Max Prestige ... D1
- 8 Hotel Oliva ... C2
- 9 Mena ... C2
- 10 Saki Hostel & Apartmani ... D1
- 11 Sun Hostel ... D2

Eating
- 12 Jadran kod Krsta ... B4
- 13 Stari Ribar ... D2

Information
- 14 Accident & Emergency Clinic ... B2

Transport
- 15 Bus Station ... B2
- 16 Meridian Rentacar ... B2

Rest of Budva

Slovenska Plaža BEACH

(Map p65) After the marina the long sweep of Budva's main beach commences, heralded by blaring local pop and endless rows of sun umbrellas and loungers (available for hire at about €3 for each). If you can't get your head around this typically Mediterranean concept, there's no charge for spreading out your towel on the patches of beach set aside for the purpose.

Budva Old Town

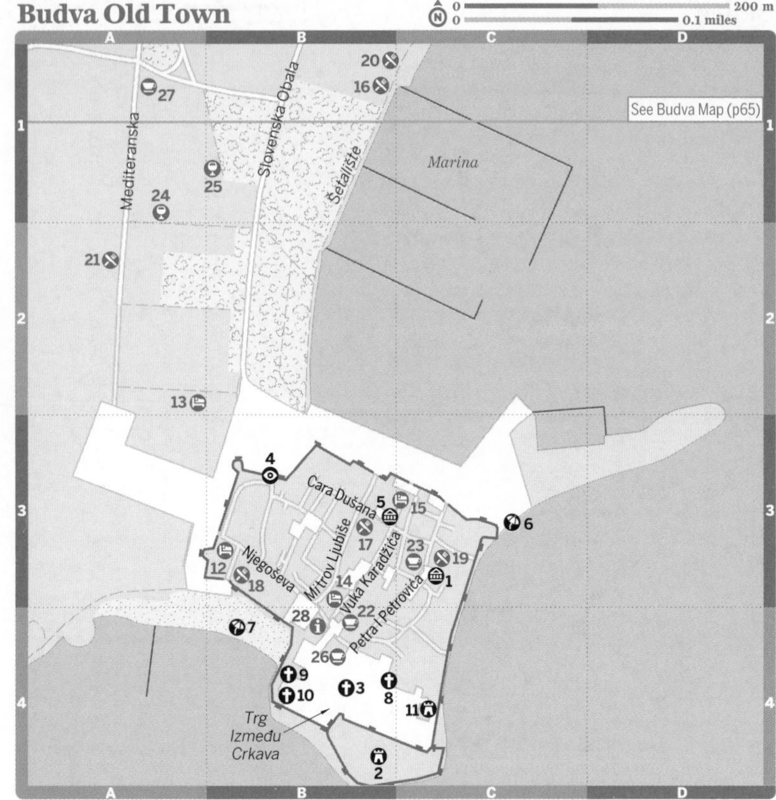

Slovenska Obala STREET

(Map p65) In summer the main beachside promenade is lined with fast-food outlets, beach bars in the guise of pirate ships and famous landmarks, travel agencies hawking tours, market stalls and a fun fair.

Slovenska Plaža tourist village ARCHITECTURE

(Map p65) Anyone with an interest in Yugoslav-era architecture will find this large resort's spacious socialism-meets-Spanish-Mission aesthetic fascinating. Mature trees and modern sculpture are scattered between the terracotta-tiled units connected by white colonnades, and there's a swimming pool and tennis courts galore, which are available for hire by nonguests. The lobby is a wonderful period piece, with white marble floors, brass light fixtures, octagonal handrails, boxy white vinyl couches and potted palms. You really wouldn't be surprised if either Roger Moore's James Bond or Marshal Tito swaggered into view at any time.

Podmaine Monastery MONASTERY

On the surprisingly peaceful northern slopes of town, this monastery features the same stripes of pink and honey-coloured stone as the Stari Grad's Holy Trinity Church. Interesting frescoes inside the church include a Judgement Day scene showing the fate to befall the damned (look for the communist officer with the red star on his military uniform), including being eaten alive by fish and what appears to be a chicken.

From here, a walking track leads up the mountains for 2km to the fortified **Podostrog Monastery**. This was once a residence of Montenegro's *vladikas* (prince-bishops). It was here that Petar II Petrović Njegoš wrote *The Mountain Wreath* and also here that his predecessor Danilo is said to have instigated the savage events that inspired it. The complex's smaller church dates from the 12th century and the larger from the

Budva Old Town

18th. Look above the door for an engraving of the double-headed Montenegrin eagle holding a snake in its claws.

Activities & Tours

Travel agencies on Slovenska Obala peddle every kind of day tour, including the following (with indicative prices): Ostrog (€17); Bay of Kotor cruise (€20); Dubrovnik (€23 to €35); Cetinje and Mt Lovćen (€23); Lake Skadar (€35); Albania (€35); rafting on the Tara River (€60).

You can hire a kayak (€5 per hour) or paddle boat (€6 per hour) from Mogren Beach. A huge range of boats with skippers are available for hire from the marina. A mid-sized launch might charge €400 for a day's fishing, while a flash one could be €1200 or more.

Budva Diving DIVING
(069-060 416; www.budvadiving.com) Based at Pizana; offers intro dives at Mogren Beach (€35) and boat dives at 20 locations for experienced divers (from €30).

Festivals & Events

Before the current global economic meltdown, Budva was actively cultivating a reputation for hosting big events. Even if the €5 million that was reportedly stumped up to entice Madonna to play in 2008 is unlikely to be matched any time soon, it doesn't mean that the city has abandoned its cultural life. A lively calendar of events fills the summer months.

Carnival of Budva CULTURAL
Venetian masked high jinks in April or early May.

International Folklore Festival CULTURAL
(early Jun) Folk costumes and dances from various European countries.

Theatre City PERFORMING ARTS
(www.gradteatar.com) Renowned arts festival happening largely in and around the Old Town for six weeks from mid-June.

Casper Jazz Festival MUSIC
(early Sep) The old town's Casper bar hosts a low-key but excellent jazz festival.

Days of Širun FOOD, CULTURAL
(Oct) A one-day celebration of wine, fish and song on the first Saturday of October.

Sleeping

Expect to pay a hefty premium for digs in the Stari Grad, but apartments in the residential neighbourhoods can be surprisingly reasonable. The tourist office can provide you with information on renting private rooms.

Stari Grad

Montenegro Hostel HOSTEL €
(Map p66; 069-039 751; www.montenegrohostel.com; Vuka Karadžića 12; dm/r €12/50;) Right in the heart of the Old Town, this colourful little hostel provides the perfect base for hitting the bars and beaches. Each floor has its own kitchen and bathroom, and there's a communal space at the top for fraternisation.

A LOAD OF ANCIENT BULL (& SNAKES)

The founding of Budva is celebrated in the sort of mythical soap opera that the ancient Greeks loved so much. Cadmus was the son of Agenor, King of Phoenicia (present-day Lebanon, Syria, Israel and Palestine) and the brother of the beautiful Europa, who the great god Zeus took quite a shine to. Europa must have really liked livestock as Zeus turned himself into a bull in order to seduce her. Hiding amongst her father's flocks, he waited until Europa spotted him, caressed his powerful flanks and jumped on his back. He then raced off with her to Crete, thankfully turning himself back into his godly form before having his way with her (when it comes to Zeus, there was a very fine line between seduction and rape). Europa went on to become the first Queen of Crete and to give her name to an entire continent.

Cadmus was sent to search for his sister, promising not to return without her. He never did find her and ended up founding the Greek city of Thebes, stocking it with brave men that he grew out of the teeth of a sacred water dragon that he had slain (as you do). He then married Harmonia in the sort of A-list shindig that today's gossip magazines would pay a fortune for, with several immortals as guests.

However, killing a sacred water dragon is very bad luck, so Cadmus and Harmonia hitched up their oxen in order to make a fresh start someplace else. Far to the northwest they founded a new city (with no assistance from dragon teeth), naming it Bouthoe (later Budva) after the Greek word for oxen.

The miserable luck didn't lift and Cadmus was heard complaining that if the gods were so fond of scaly critters then he bloody well wished he was one. The gods, never missing an opportunity for a spot of black humour, obliged – promptly turning him into a snake. Harmonia, perhaps with more qualms about cross-species lovin' than her sister-in-law, begged to be allowed to join him and they both slithered off to live happily every after... or something like that.

★Hotel Astoria HOTEL €€€

(Map p66; ☎033-451 110; www.astoriamontenegro.com; Njegoševa 4; s €90-105, d €110-130, ste €130-210; ❄@) Water shimmers down the corridor wall as you enter this chic boutique hotel hidden in the Old Town's fortifications. The rooms are on the small side but they're beautifully furnished; the sea-view suite is spectacular. To top it all off, the wonderful roof terrace is Budva's most magnificent dining space.

Vila Balkan APARTMENTS €€€

(Map p66; ☎033-403 564; www.vilabalkan.me; Vuka Karadžića 2; apt from €105; ❄📶) The five apartments of this historic Stari Grad house have a bit of peeling paint here and there but you'll soon forget about it when you see the sea views and parquet floors. Try for the top floor – it's the same price but a little bigger and has a bathtub.

Rest of Budva

Saki Hostel & Apartmani HOSTEL, APARTMENTS €

(Map p65; ☎067-368 065; www.saki-apartmani.com; IV Proleterska bb; dm €10, apt per person €25; P❄📶) Not quite a hostel and not quite an apartment hotel, this friendly family-run block on the outskirts of town offers elements of both. Individual beds are rented, hostel-style, in a rambling set of rooms. Private apartments have large balconies, but beds have been crammed in where kitchens might otherwise be. Grape and kiwifruit vines shade the pleasant communal terrace.

Sun Hostel HOSTEL €

(Map p65; ☎069-769 212; www.sunhostels.com; Ferona bb; dm/d €10/30; ❄📶) Less a hostel and more cheap shared rooms in an apartment block (sleeping 55 people in 24 rooms), this is cleaner and newer than most of Budva's hostels but perhaps a little less sociable.

Hippo Hostel HOSTEL €

(Map p65; ☎069-256 117; www.hippohostel.com; IV Proleterska 37; dm €11-12, r €28; ⏲Apr-Oct; @📶) Montenegro's longest-standing hostel is a small, tucked-away place with colourful bathrooms and a front garden popular for chilling and socialising in. It can get frantic in the height of summer, but by September it's much more relaxed.

Hotel Oliva HOTEL €€
(Map p65; ☎033-459 429; olivai@t-com.me; Velji Vinogradi bb; s/d €30/58; P ❄ 📶) Don't expect anything flashy, just a warm welcome, clean and comfortable rooms with balconies, and a nice garden studded with the olive trees that give this small hotel its name. The wireless internet doesn't extend much past the restaurant.

Mena HOTEL €€
(Map p65; ☎033-459 310; www.hotelmena.com; Velji Vinogradi bb; s/d €26/43; P ❄ 📶) Trading its previous peach-coloured shell for a makeover in chocolate and cream, midsized Mena has reasonable rates and nicely furnished rooms with balconies. The hot-water cylinders are tiny, so be sure to beat your beau to the first shower.

Hotel Mogren HOTEL €€
(Map p66; ☎033-451 102; www.hotelmogren.com; Mediteranska bb; s/d €64/83; ❄ 📶) A bit like an elderly aunt you've become fond of, the Mogren has seen better days but traces of a glamorous youth occasionally peek through. The rooms are an ode to all things blue: blue built-in wardrobes, blue padded headboards and blue shower curtains. Ask for a room with a view of the Old Town.

Hotel Kangaroo HOTEL €€
(Map p65; ☎033-458 653; www.kangaroo.co.me; Velji Vinogradi bb; s/d €33/50; ❄ @ 📶) Bounce into a large clean room with a desk and terrace at this minimal-frills midsized hotel that's a hop, step and jump from the beach. The owners once lived in Australia, which explains the name and the large 3D mural of Captain Cook's *Endeavour* in the popular restaurant below.

Hotel Fontana HOTEL €€
(Map p65; ☎033-452 153; fontana.lekic@t-com.me; Slovenska Obala 23; s/d €55/70; ❄ 📶) Close to the beach and all the craziness (and noise) of Slovenska Obala in the summertime, Fontana has a holiday-home feel and a terrace cafe for chatting with fellow guests. Rooms are smallish but fine and most of those on the upper levels have sea views.

Hotel Max Prestige HOTEL €€€
(Map p65; ☎033-458 330; www.hotelmaxprestige.com; Žrtava Fašizma bb; s/d/apt €75/100/118; P ❄ 📶 🏊) If you hadn't guessed from the name, this shiny minihotel has slight delusions of grandeur. The exterior is a hodgepodge of pretentious turrets and pediments topped by a garish neon sign, yet the vibe inside is smart and comfortable and we love the kidney-shaped pool surrounded by meticulously kept gardens.

Eating

If you're looking for supplies, head to the **Roda supermarket** (Map p66; ☎452 523; Mediteranska 1; ⏲6am-midnight) near the Old Town. For cheap fast food and delicious gelato you need only stroll along Slovenska Obala.

Stari Grad

★**Pizza 10 Maradona** PIZZERIA €
(Map p66; Petra I Petrovića 10; pizza slice €2) A reader alerted us to this late-night hole-in-the-wall eatery selling pizza by the slice. We can confirm that after a hard night's 're-searching' the city's nightspots, Maradona's crispy based pizza does indeed seem to come straight from the hand of God.

Knez Konoba SEAFOOD €€
(Map p66; ☎069-475 025; Mitrov Ljubiše bb; mains €8-17; ⏲midday-11pm) Hidden within the Old Town's tiny lanes, this atmospheric eatery has only three outdoor tables and a handful inside. The traditional dishes are beautifully presented and often accompanied by free shots of *rakija* (fruit brandy).

Konoba Stari Grad SEAFOOD €€
(Map p66; ☎033-454 443; www.konobastarigrad.me; Njegoševa 14; mains €8-20; ⏲11am-11pm) With an attractive stone-walled interior and a sunny terrace sandwiched between the Stari Grad's walls and beach, this *konoba* (family-run establishment) isn't short on atmosphere – a fact reflected in the prices, which have shot up considerably since the last edition of this book. Still, the seafood's very good and the setting really is lovely.

Rest of Budva

Stari Ribar SEAFOOD, MONTENEGRIN €
(Map p65; ☎033-459 543; 29 Novembra 19; mains €3-12; ⏲7am-11pm) You'll be relieved to learn that the name means Old Fisherman, not Old Fish. This humble eatery in the residential part of town serves grilled fish (fresh, naturally) and meat dishes at local prices. The squid here is definitely worth trying.

★**Porto** SEAFOOD €€
(Map p66; ☎033-451 598; www.restoranporto.com; City Marina, Šetalište bb; mains €8-20;

10am-1am) From the waterfront promenade a little bridge arches over a fish pond and into this romantic restaurant where jocular bow-tie-wearing waiters flit about with plates laden with fresh seafood. The food's excellent and the wine list offers plenty of choice from around the region.

Dona kod Nikole SEAFOOD €€
(Map p66; 033-451 531; www.donakodnikole.weebly.com; City Marina, Šetalište bb; mains €6-20; 8am-midnight) You won't have far to wander back to your luxury yacht from this traditional seafood restaurant bedecked with maritime paraphernalia. It's not as smart or as popular as some others on this strip, but the food's good and live musicians often perform on weekend nights.

Jadran kod Krsta MONTENEGRIN, SEAFOOD €€
(Map p65; 033-451 028; Šetalište bb; mains €6-15; 8am-1am;) With candlelit tables directly on the beach (romantic certainly, but prepare to negotiate some difficult angles as your seat sinks into the pebbles), this long-standing restaurant offers all the usual seafood suspects along with classic Montenegrin dishes from the interior.

Drinking & Nightlife

Stari Grad

★Casper CAFE, BAR
(Map p66; www.facebook.com/casper.budva; Petra I Petrovića bb; 10am-2am Jun-Sep, 5pm-2am Oct-May;) Chill out under the pine tree in this picturesque Old Town cafe-bar. DJs kick off from July, spinning everything from reggae to house. Casper hosts its own jazz festival in September.

Caffe Greco CAFE, BAR
(Map p66; Njegoševa bb; 9am-2am) On summer nights the little square that Greco shares with its neighbour/rival Cafe Jef is packed from wall to wall with revellers. It's easily the busiest spot in the Old Town.

MB Ice Club CAFE, BAR
(Map p66; Njegoševa 44; 8am-1am;) Enjoy coffee, cake or cocktails while soaking in the ambience of the Old Town's main square.

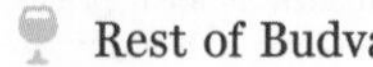

Rest of Budva

Top Hill CLUB
(www.tophill.me; Topliški Put; events €10-25; 11pm-5am Jul & Aug) The top cat of Montenegro's summer party scene attracts up to 5000 revellers to its open-air club atop Topliš Hill, offering them top-notch sound and lighting, sea views, big-name touring DJs and performances by local pop stars.

Perla CAFE, BAR
(Map p66; www.perlabudva.com; Mediteranska bb; 7am-1am;) Billing itself as a 'pop lounge and restaurant', Perla is the schmickest place in Budva to see and be seen – both of which are assisted by its glitzy glass facade. A full menu is available throughout the day (the cooked breakfasts are reasonably priced and excellent), but we prefer to slink in for cocktails.

Hacienda BAR, CLUB
(Map p66; www.haciendabarbudva.com; Mediteranska bb; 8am-2am Jun-Sep) With its tropical foliage, swinging lounges and brightly coloured cushions, Hacienda is a relaxing spot for a daytime cocktail. On summer nights it's a different beast altogether, with DJs creating a nightclub vibe and brawny barmen showing off their glass-juggling skills.

Discoteque Trocadero CLUB
(Map p66; 069-069 086; www.trocaderobudva.com; Mediteranska 4; admission €5, women free; 11pm-5am Jun-Sep) It's not nightclubbing as we know it (where's the dancefloor?) but Trocadero is the best of Budva's indoor clubs. From the mezzanine you can gaze down at punters propping up the little circular tables that are scattered throughout the large oval space. Music ranges from techno to turbo folk, with regular live performances by local starlets.

Information

There are clusters of banks on and around Ulica Mediteranska.

Accident & Emergency Clinic (Map p65; 033-427 200; www.dialysiscenter.me; Popa Jola Zeca bb)

Tourist Office (Map p66; 033-452 750; www.budva.travel; Njegoševa 28; 9am-9pm Mon-Sat, 5-9pm Sun)

Getting There & Around

BUS

The **bus station** (Map p65; 033-456 000; Popa Jola Zeca bb) has frequent services to Herceg Novi (€6, 1¾ hours), Kotor (€3.50, 40 minutes), Bar (€4.50) and Podgorica (€6), and around six buses a day to Kolašin (€10). International destinations include Belgrade (from €26, 15 daily) and Sarajevo (€22, four daily).

You can flag down the Olimpia Express (€1.50) from the bus stops on Jadranski Put to head to Bečići (five minutes) or Sveti Stefan (20 minutes). They depart every 30 minutes in summer and hourly in winter.

CAR

There are plenty of well-marked parking areas but expect to pay about €5 per day or around €1 per hour. Tow trucks earn steady business from the Mediteranska shopping strip.

Meridian Rentacar (Map p65; ☎033-454 105; www.meridian-rentacar.com; Popa Jola Zeca bb) Opposite the bus station; one-day hire from €45.

TAXI

Taxis are in ready supply in Budva, but many of those that hang around the nightspots in the early hours are prone to overcharging. You're better off calling a reputable company. Otherwise check that the cab has a meter and check what rate they charge; €4 per kilometre is not the going rate.

Taxi Slava (☎19715; www.taxibudva.com; flagfall €1, then 80c per km)

Terrae-Taxi (☎19717; www.budvataxi.com) Advertises set fares to the following airports: Tivat (€15), Podgorica (€40) and Čilipi, Dubrovnik (€90).

Around Budva

Jaz Beach — Плажа Јаз

The blue waters and broad sands of Jaz Beach look spectacular when viewed from high up on the Tivat road. While it's not built up like Budva and Bečići, the beach is still lined with loungers, sun umbrellas and noisy beach bars. Head down the Budva end of the beach for a little more seclusion.

Parking will set you back €2.50 and camping is possible (per adult/child/tent/car/caravan €3/1/2.50/1/3), but the facilities are extremely basic and the field can get muddy.

Sveti Nikola — Свети Никола

Known locally as 'Hawaii', Sveti Nikola is Montenegro's largest island, stretching to nearly 2km. Fallow deer wander about on this uninhabited green spot, which is only a nautical mile away from Budva or Bečići Beach. Its rocky beaches make it a popular destination in summer when taxi boats regularly ferry sunseekers to and fro; expect to pay about €15 to €20 return from Budva's marina or Bečići. You'll have more chance escaping the tourist hordes, discarded rubbish and blaring pop music if you hire a kayak and look for a secluded cove on the far side of the island.

Local lore has it that the graves scattered around tiny, whitewashed **St Nicholas' Church** (Crkva Sv Nikole) are those of crusaders who died of an unknown epidemic while they camped nearby. The church itself dates to at least the 16th century but it's rarely open.

Bečići & Rafailovići
Бечићи и Рафаиловићи

Welcome to the Benidorm of Montenegro! Like the Spanish tourist town, Bečići has been completely swallowed by large resort complexes, complete with swimming pools, nightclubs and casinos. If the primary objective of your trip is to flit between the pool, pokies and sand, cocktail in hand, this is the place to do it. Just don't expect any actual engagement with Montenegrin culture.

Bečići and its neighbour Rafailovići share a 1950m-long sandy beach immediately east of Budva. In 1935 it won a Parisian prize and was named the most beautiful beach in Europe, although it's unlikely to win that prize

PARAGLIDING

Montenegro's dramatic craggy peaks make it an obvious candidate for a paragliding hot spot. The most popular launch site is at Brajići, 760m above Bečići on the Budva–Cetinje road. The big attraction here is the view over Budva, Sveti Nikola Island and picture-perfect Sveti Stefan.

Montenegro Adventure Centre (☎067-580 664; www.montenegrofly.com), run by a British-qualified senior paragliding instructor, offers tandem flights for €65, landing on Bečići Beach. Its base is at nearby Lapčići where it offers accommodation and can also organise rafting, hiking, mountain-biking and diving trips. If you're already an experienced paraglider, they'll take you up Mt Lovćen where you can make an unforgettable 1740m descent into the Bay of Kotor itself.

today. It does, however, have a Blue Flag rating for cleanliness and water quality.

Rafailovići is equally built up but retains the vaguest remnants of a village feel. Older-style apartment hotels hug the cliffs and restaurants line the shore. It's a popular spot for families but at high tide there's hardly any beach.

During summer there's usually someone hiring jet skis, pedal boats, banana boats and kayaks from the beach, and taxi boats ply the shore for the trip to Sveti Nikola Island. If you fancy a spot of parasailing you'll need to keep your eyes open to watch where the boats dock. A short ride costs around €25. If the kids are getting restless, there's a large waterpark attached to the **Hotel Mediteran** (www.hotelmediteran.info; Jadranski Put).

Sleeping & Eating

Stella di Mare HOTEL €€
(033-471 567; www.hotel-stelladimare.me; Narodnog fronta bb; s/d €53/71; P ❄ Wi-Fi) It doesn't have a fancy swimming pool or a slice of beach to call its own, but this little hotel has friendly staff, tidy rooms with balconies, and much more reasonable rates than the resorts it rubs shoulders with.

Hotel Splendid RESORT €€€
(033-773 777; www.montenegrostars.com; Jadranski put, Bečići; s €288-358, d €384-454; P ❄ Wi-Fi pool) The rooms are luxurious, but the real star of this mammoth resort is the pool complex. Three outdoor pools (there's another one inside) swirl around palm trees and manicured slices of lawn leading down to the large chunk of beach that the hotel consumes. There's also a lavish health and beauty spa and various spots to eat and drink.

Sentido Tara RESORT €€€
(033-404 196; www.hoteltara.me; Bečići bb; s/d €83/108; P ❄ Wi-Fi pool) Big, modern and bland but close to the beach, the Tara is popular with older Western European travellers. The vibe's low-key and relaxed, and there's a nice stretch of lawn by the pool.

Tri Ribara SEAFOOD €€
(033-471 050; www.triribara.com; Bečićka Plaža 35, Rafailovići; mains €8-18; noon-11pm) Sit only metres from the water and have delicious grilled squid and other seafood silver-served to you by deadly serious waiters. The name means 'three fishermen' and inside the stone walls are covered with nautical miscellanea such as anchors, turtle shells and ancient barnacle-encrusted amphorae.

Pržno Пржно

This charming little spot offers a cramped family-friendly red-sand beach and a surprisingly good selection of restaurants. An enigmatic ruin rests on a craggy island offshore, and just enough old stone houses remain to counterbalance the large-scale resort at the northern end of the beach. The walk from here through the woods to Sveti Stefan is exceedingly beautiful.

Activities

Pro Dive Hydrotech DIVING
(PDH; 069-013 985; www.montenegrodive.com; Obala bb) Based at the Maestral resort, this well-established outfit offers diving trips to various wrecks, caves and reefs. Introductory sessions cost €70, diving courses €330 and it also rents out kayaks (€10 per hour).

Sleeping

Hotel Residence Miločer HOTEL €€
(033-427 100; www.residencemontenegro.com; Jadranski Put; s €69-99, d €79-119; P ❄ Wi-Fi pool) Maybe it's because it's linked to a hospitality school that this new hotel ticks all the right boxes. The decor's fresh and modern, there's secure parking, the breakfast buffets are excellent, and the staff aren't afraid to smile. It's worth paying the additional €10 for a spacious junior suite. The only disappointment is the tiny rooftop pool.

Apartmani Kažanegra APARTMENTS €€
(033-468 738; www.kazanegra.com; Obala 12; apt €80-150; P ❄ Wi-Fi) This stone villa is as close as you can get to the beach without ending up with sandy toes. It houses a range of tidy one- and two-bedroom apartments with private terraces overlooking the sea.

Eating

★ **Blanche** EUROPEAN €€
(062-504 272; www.blanche-restaurant.com; Obala 11; mains €8-24; 10am-midnight) Higher than usual prices and upmarket decor don't necessarily signal quality but in Blanche's case, we weren't left disappointed. Sharing the menu with the usual Dalmatian seafood classics are succulent steaks served with French-style sauces and a wide selection of Italian dishes, with enough twists to keep things interesting.

Konoba More SEAFOOD €€
(☎033-468 255; Obala 18; mains €8-18; ⏰11am-11.30pm) A stereotypically dreamy Mediterranean restaurant with a terrace that juts out over the beach, serving traditional and Italian-tinged fish dishes.

Konoba Langust SEAFOOD €€€
(☎033-468 369; www.langust-przno.com; Obala 34; mains €9-15) This highly rated fish restaurant has been serving traditional seafood meals from its stretch of the Pržno promenade for over 20 years. You can certainly find these dishes cheaper elsewhere but you're unlikely to find them better.

Information

There's an ATM in the lobby of the large Maestral resort at the northern end of town. The **post office** (☎468 202) is at the southern end by the main bus stop and taxi stand.

Getting There & Away

The Olimpia Express bus from Budva to Sveti Stefan stops here (€1.50).

Sveti Stefan Свети Стефан

POP 370

Gazing down on impossibly picturesque Sveti Stefan, 5km south of Budva, provides the biggest 'wow' moment on the entire coast. And gazing upon it is all most people will get to do, as this tiny island – connected to the shore by a causeway and crammed full of terracotta-roofed stone dwellings dating to the 15th century – was nationalised in the 1950s and the whole thing is now the luxurious Aman resort, off limits to all but paying guests.

Sveti Stefan is also the name of the new township that's sprung up onshore. From its steep slopes you get to look down at that iconic view all day – which some might suggest is even better than staying in the surreal enclave below. On the downside, parking is difficult, there are lots of steps and there's little in the way of shops.

Sights

Sveti Stefan Beach BEACH
The main point of coming to Sveti Stefan is to spend as much time horizontal as possible, with occasional breaks to saunter from your recliner to the sea for a cooling dip. The water here gets deep quickly, as if the surrounding mountains could hardly be bothered adjusting their slope. The uncrowded beach on the Budva side of the causeway belongs to the resort. If you don't fancy shelling out €30 for the day-use fee (ie you're not completely insane), the deckchairs on the other side of the causeway get cheaper the further along the beach you go, and there's plenty of rocky but free space near the end.

Miločer & Queen's Beaches BEACHES
At the northern end of Sveti Stefan Beach a path leads over a headland draped in pine and olive trees to the turquoise waters and pink sands of Miločer Beach, which is also known as King's Beach (Kraljeva Plaža). Set back from the tranquil bay and fronted by a loggia draped in sweet-scented wisteria is the Villa Miločer. This grand two-storey stone building was built in 1934 as the summer residence of the Karađorđević royal family, the Serbian monarchs who headed the first Yugoslavia. The whole area is now part of the Aman resort and while you're welcome to walk through, access to the beach will cost you a hefty €75.

Around the next headland, Queen's Beach (Kraljičina Plaža) was a favourite of Queen Marija Karađorđević and it's easy to see why. Cypresses and olive trees provide the backdrop to a pretty 120m curve of reddish sand. You won't get much of a view though, as this beach is set aside exclusively for resort guests. The public path skirts behind a large spa complex which was being constructed at the time of research, and then up through the trees to Pržno.

Praskvica Monastery MONASTERY
Just off the highway in the hills slightly north of Sveti Stefan, this humble monastery, named after the peach-scented water of a brook that flows nearby, rests amongst an ancient olive grove. It was an important political centre for the Paštrovići, a local tribe of Serbian origin whose distinctive cultural traditions have survived along this section of the coast despite numerous foreign occupations.

The monastery was established in 1413 by Balša III of Zeta. The main church, dedicated to St Nicholas (Sv Nikola), has its origins from that time, although it was substantially destroyed by the French in 1812 as punishment for the monks' support of Montenegro's attempt to overtake the Bay of Kotor. Traces of the original frescoes remain on the left wall, but the rest of the church dates to 1847. The current gilt-framed iconostasis

(1863) features paintings by Nicholas Aspiotis of Corfu.

Further up the hill beside a cemetery are an old schoolhouse and the smaller Holy Trinity Church (Crkva Sv Trojice).

The monastery is well signposted from the main road and an easy walk from either Sveti Stefan or Pržno.

Sleeping & Eating

Accommodation fills up quickly in July and August.

★Vila Levantin APARTMENTS €
(☎033-468 206; www.villalevantin.com; Vukice Mitrović 3; r €30-50, apt €50-130; P ❄ 📶 ≋) Modern and nicely finished, with red stone walls, blue-tiled bathrooms and an attractive plunge pool on the terrace, Levantin has a variety of rooms and apartments at extremely reasonable prices. There's a travel agency attached which can sort you out with tours or rooms in private houses.

Crvena Glavica Auto Kamp CAMPGROUND €
(☎069-468070; adult/child/tent/car €2.50/1/3/2; ⏲Jun-Sep) You don't need to be a movie star or oligarch to enjoy Sveti Stefan's million-dollar views. Pitch your tent under the olive trees and stroll past the roving chickens down to the rocky but peaceful shoreline. The outdoor showers and squat toilets are basic though.

★Vila Drago GUESTHOUSE €€
(☎030-468 477; www.viladrago.com; Slobode 32; r €45-60, apt €120-130, mains €5-17; ❄ 📶) The only problem with this place is that you may never want to leave your terrace as the views are so sublime. The supercomfy pillows and fully stocked bathrooms are a nice touch, especially at this price. Watch the sunset over the island from the grapevine-covered terrace restaurant and enjoy specialities from the local Paštrovići clan, such as roast suckling pig.

★Aman Sveti Stefan RESORT €€€
(☎033-420 000; www.amanresorts.com; ste €750-3000; P ❄ 📶 ≋) Truly unique, this island resort offers 50 luxurious suites that showcase the stone walls and wooden beams of the ancient houses. Amazingly there's still a village feel, with cobbled lanes, churches, lots of indigenous foliage and an open-air cafe on the main piazza. But it's a village where you can order a cocktail by a small cliff's-edge swimming pool or slink away for an indulgent massage – and it's not open to the general public. Back on the shore, **Villa Miločer** has a further eight suites by the beach. Nonguests can avail themselves of three eateries: the **Olive Tree** at Sveti Stefan Beach, the **Beach Cafe** at Miločer, and **Queen's Chair**, perched on a wooded hill facing Budva.

Villa Montenegro BOUTIQUE HOTEL €€€
(☎033-468 802; www.villa-montenegro.com; Vukice Mitrović 2; r €245-495, ste €860-1150; P ❄ 📶 ≋) Hidden amongst the rental apartments in the new part of Sveti Stefan, this discreet boutique hotel offers luxurious rooms, including two indulgent suites. The view over the island from the infinity edge pool is exquisite.

Information

The nearest post office and ATM are a 20-minute walk away in Pržno.

Getting There & Away

Olimpia Express buses head to and from Budva (€1.50, 20 minutes) every 30 minutes in summer and hourly in winter, stopping on Ulica Slobode near the Vila Drago.

Petrovac Петровац

POP 1400

The Romans had the right idea, building their summer villas on this lovely bay. If only the new crop of developers had a scrap of their classic good taste. Still, once you get down to the pretty beachside promenade where lush Mediterranean plants perfume the air and a 16th-century Venetian fortress guards a tiny stone harbour, the aberrations up the hill are barely visible. This is one of the best places on the coast for families: the accommodation is reasonably priced, the water is clear and kids roam the esplanade at night with impunity.

In July and August you'll be lucky to find an inch of space on the fine reddish pebbles of the **town beach**, but wander south and there's cypress- and oleander-lined **Lučice Beach**, with a kids' waterslide on its far end. Continue over the leafy headland for another 30 minutes and the 2.4km-long sweep of **Buljarica Beach** comes into view, most of which is blissfully undeveloped – at least for now.

Sights

Roman mosaics RUIN

(Kasnoantički mozaik) Apart from the beaches, Petrovac's most interesting attraction is also its least heralded. In 1902 the foundations of a Roman building complete with mosaics, probably dating from the 4th century, were discovered in an olive grove and here they remain in a precarious state of preservation. A glass shed covers a section of mosaic roughly 10m by 15m; it's invariably locked but you can peer through the windows. Around the shed, extensive brick foundations can be seen.

The site is a little tricky to find: take the path leading through private land opposite **St Thomas' Church** (Crkva Sv Tome) – which is itself around 500 years old and was, at the time of research, being restored. Make your way through the olive grove to the dig site where you will need to watch your footing.

Kastio FORTRESS

This small Venetian fortress by the harbour offers gorgeous views of the beach and the dramatic diagonal stratification of the limestone cliffs melting into the turquoise water below. An interesting socialist realist bas-relief remembering the 'socialist revolution' is partly obscured in the foliage.

Red Commune Memorial House GALLERY, MUSEUM

(Crvena Komuna; 033-404 877; www.crvenakomuna.webs.com; 8am-2pm & 7-10pm) FREE Petrovac became the first communist-run municipality in the Adriatic following an electoral victory in 1919. That auspicious event is celebrated in the Red Commune Memorial House on the waterfront, which contains a modern art gallery and revolutionary museum. The latter consists mainly of photos and documents without any English captions; it doesn't get a lot of visitors these days but the bemused staff will unlock it for you upon request.

Katič & Sveta Nedjelja islands ISLANDS

Directly in front of the town beach is what looks like one sheer rocky outcrop capped with a church and a stand of trees but is actually two islets – Katič and Sveta Nedjelja (Holy Sunday). Holy Sunday Church is said to have been built in gratitude by a Greek sailor who was shipwrecked there. The current church replaces one destroyed in the 1979 earthquake.

Elijah's Church CHURCH

(Crkva Sv Ilije; Nika Anđusa bb) Dedicated to the Old Testament prophet Elijah, this Orthodox church is similar in age to nearby St Thomas', dating from the 14th or 15th century. Unlike St Thomas', it's often open, revealing some beautiful old icons.

Festivals & Events

Petrovac Night MUSIC, FOOD

(Aug) Free fish, wine and beer, majorette parades, performances by Eurovision contestants… who could ask for anything more? It's held on the last Friday and Saturday in August. Yes, that's two nights – but who's counting.

Petrovac Jazz Festival MUSIC

(www.petrovacjazzfestival.net) Three nights of finger-snapping faves in late August/early September.

Sleeping

For private accommodation, try **Mornar Travel Agency** (033-461 410; www.mornartravel.com). It can arrange rooms starting from €23/15 per person in high/low season.

Camping Maslina CAMPGROUND €

(033-461 215; akmaslina@t-com.me; Buljarica bb; per adult/child/tent/car/caravan €3/1.50/3/3/5; P) Just off the road to Buljarica Beach, this well-kept campground has a tidy ablutions block with proper sitdown toilets and solar-powered hot water. As Montenegrin campsites go, this is one of the best.

Hotel Danica HOTEL €€

(033-462 304; www.hoteldanica.net; s/d €55/60; P) With a quiet location under the pine-covered hill immediately west of the town beach, this four-storey hotel is small enough to maintain a relaxed family ambience, but big enough to provide some appealing extras, such as the attractive little pool on the terrace.

Hotel Đurić HOTEL €€

(033-462 005; www.hoteldjuric.com; Brežine bb; s/d €72/96; May-Sep;) There's a vaguely Spanish Mission feel to this smart boutique hotel. All rooms have kitchen facilities and there's a restaurant at the back under a canopy of kiwifruit and grapevines.

Hotel W Grand HOTEL €€

(033-461 703; www.wgrandpetrovac.com; r €80; P) Spacious rooms painted in warm colours are the hallmark of this midsized

LOCAL KNOWLEDGE

DANICA ĆERANIĆ

We asked the Deputy Director of Montenegro's National Tourism Organisation for her top tips.

Favourite Beach?

Ada Bojana – that, for me, is a paradise. I recommend spending one or two nights there, just to relax. Also, I love some of the hidden beaches on the Luštica Peninsula.

Something a Bit Different

Try some of the routes with gastronomic offerings, like the wine routes around Skadar Lake, where you can stop and interact with local producers. Or the places around Kolašin where you can see the traditional way of making cheese. The Old Royal Montenegrin Trails brochure features traditional wine-, cheese- and honey-makers that welcome visitors – although if you don't know the language it may be easier to take a tour.

Favourite Restaurants?

Ćatovića Mlini (p41) in Kotor Bay – I love their fish specialties and the old atmosphere. It's really unique. Also, for atmosphere, try Ćićkova Čarda (p87) by the Bojana River.

Winter Pursuits

Žabljak is very good for skiing and snowboarding, but the infrastructure is better in Kolašin. From 2013, snowkiting will be offered in Žabljak. They say the conditions are better than in Austria because of the wind and the lack of electrical wires.

hotel, although they're starting to look a little scuffed around the edges. Eat up the views from the rooftop terrace while tucking into the breakfast buffet.

Eating

The esplanade is lined with fast-food joints, ice-cream stands, restaurants and cafe-bars.

Voli SUPERMARKET €

(Nika Anđusa bb; 6am-11pm) One street back from the esplanade, Voli is a decent-sized supermarket with an excellent deli and fresh-fruit section, and an ATM outside.

Konoba Bonaca MONTENEGRIN, SEAFOOD €€

(069-084 735; mains €8-15) Set back slightly from the main beach drag, this traditional restaurant focuses mainly on seafood but the local cheeses and olives are also excellent. Grab a table under the grapevines on the terrace and try the *rolnice Bonaca* – rolled and skewered eggplant, tomato, zucchini, mozzarella and prosciutto.

Konoba Mediterraneo MONTENEGRIN, SEAFOOD €€

(mains €8-16) There are no surprises on the menu (a line-up of the usual seafood and meat suspects), but Mediterraneo has a lovely setting under a canopy of citrus trees directly opposite the beach.

Drinking & Nightlife

Terasa & Castelo BAR, CLUB

(terrace/club free/€2) Sip a cocktail and enjoy romantic views over the parapets of the Venetian fortress. DJs spark up both on the terrace and downstairs in the club Castelo on summer nights.

Cuba CAFE, BAR

Live musicians and DJs kick off in the summer at this beachside cafe where the staff all wear Che Guevara T-shirts.

Ponta BAR

(8am-1am) Built into the rocks at the south end of the beach, this is a great location for a sunset cocktail. Later on, covers bands play English-language rock and pop oldies.

Information

Little Petrovac has next to no street signs, but all the main hotels are well signposted from the road into town. You'll find ATMs and a post office off the walkway leading up from the Red Commune House.

Accident & Emergency Clinic (Zdravstvena stanica; 461 055) At the top of town; follow the road from the bus station.

Getting There & Around

Petrovac's **bus station** (068-503 399) is near the top of town. There are regular services to Budva and Bar (each €2.50, 30 minutes), as well as Herceg Novi (€6, five daily), Kotor (€4.50, nine daily) and Ulcinj (€5, eight daily). International destinations include Dubrovnik (€18, daily) and Belgrade (€29, five daily).

Don Street Taxi Service (069-437 966; www.taxi-transfer.me) has metered cabs and advertises the following set fares: Tivat €35, Budva €15, Bar €15, Ulcinj €35 and Podgorica €40.

Around Petrovac

Drobni Pijesak Дробни Пијесак

Hidden in a secluded cove between Sveti Stefan and Rijeka Reževići, Drobni Pijesak is a 240m stretch of 'ground sand' (which is the literal translation of the name) surrounded by green hills and turquoise waters. Every year on 28 June the elders of the 12 Paštrović clans hold the Bankada here, a community court that has its origins in the 16th century. Nowadays its main focus is the restoration and preservation of the tribe's traditions, environmental and cultural conservation and economic development. The day ends with a folk and arts festival.

Rijeka Reževići Риjека Режевићи

Traditional Paštrović-style architecture differs from the rest of Montenegro, favouring rows of terrace houses with stone walls, small windows, single pitched roofs and 'hog's back' curved terracotta tiles. This charming village offers some lovely examples and although gentrification is evident, the focus has been on restoration rather than demolition.

A footpath starting at the car park below the village church leads through the woods to a quiet boulder-strewn beach that offers secluded swimming and good snorkelling. The beachside fish restaurant **Balun** (069-285 652; mains €10-18) is comparatively pricey but it's highly rated by the locals. You can always just order a coffee and a €5 sandwich and gaze over the oleanders to the clear waters below.

Reževići Monastery Манастир Режевићи

Hospitality has always been important at this atmospheric stone complex, just off the highway north of Petrovac. Until the 19th century, the Paštrovići would leave a bottle of wine here for passers-by, one of whom in 1226 was King Stefan the First-Crowned of the Serbian Nemanjić dynasty. It was he who founded the smaller church of the complex, the **Church of the Dormition** (Crkva Uspenja Bogorodice). Once your eyes adjust to the dark interior you'll be able to make out fine frescoes covering the walls. The frescoes in the larger **Church of the Holy Trinity** (Crkva Sv Trojice; 1770) were repainted in the 1970s (the church was badly burnt during WWII) and hence are much more vivid. The iconostasis was painted by Petrovac local Marko Gregović.

Both churches are holding up well considering that they've survived attacks by Ottoman, French and Italian armies. There's usually an elderly black-robed nun holding the fort in the small gift shop selling religious icons and homemade olive oil and honey. Local tradition tells of a Greek or Roman temple and cemetery that once stood on this site.

Just down the hill from the monastery is **Perazića Do**, a small sandy beach bookended by rocky headlands, overshadowed by a hideously large, seemingly abandoned hotel development. Near the highway a stone building (1856) was once a school and now houses a **museum, gallery and library** devoted to the Paštrović tribe, although you'll be lucky to find it open.

Gradište Monastery Манастир Градиште

Perched on a hill overlooking Buljarica Beach, Gradište Monastery is a tranquil collection of stone buildings facing onto a central courtyard. The monastery was first mentioned in documents from 1305 although it's believed to date from 1116. Like many Montenegrin monasteries it's had a rough time over the years at the hands of invading armies and it's been rebuilt several times.

The three churches on the site are renowned for their frescoes. The interior of **St Nicholas' Church** (Crkva Sv Nikole) is completely covered in beautiful paintings of biblical scenes and Serbian royalty dating from 1620. The iconostasis was carved and painted by Vasilije Rafailović of the famous family of artists from Risan. Its neighbour, **St Sava's Church** (Crkva Sv Save), was built in 1864 and has an iconostasis by Nicholas Aspiotis, whose work is also on display at Praskvica Monastery (p73). Look out for a peculiar image of a saint with the head of a donkey on the bottom row of the icon immediately to the right of the iconostasis door. One school of thought suggests that it was St Christopher who received this great blessing after he prayed to be rid of his darned good looks. On a slight elevation is the **Church of the Dormition** (Crkva Uspenja Bogorodice).

Taking the main road south of Petrovac, turn left after the tunnel and take the steep road up to the monastery (park at the bottom, if you're not sure your car is up to it).

Čanj Чањ

Located roughly halfway between Petrovac and Bar, Čanj has a long beach, clear waters and a scrappy strip of beach bars to keep the local teenagers and regional holidaymakers entertained.

Just around the headland, **Kraljičina Plaža** (Queen's Beach) is an appealing curve of pinkish sand that can only be reached by boat. Taxi boats from Čanj operate in the peak season; some offer set departures from Bar for as little as €3.

Bar Бар

POP 13,500

Dominated by Montenegro's main port and a large industrial area, Bar is unlikely to be on anyone's list of holiday highlights but nonetheless is a handy transport hub welcoming trains from Belgrade and ferries from Italy. More interesting are the ruins of Stari Bar (Old Bar) found in the mountains behind.

Unlike the northern part of the coast, which remained largely under the rule of Venice and then Austria, the areas from Bar south spent 300 years under Turkish control. From here on you'll start to notice more mosques and Ottoman-looking buildings, although not in modern Bar itself, which was only founded in 1908.

Sights

Beaches BEACHES
With a large industrial port and marina on its doorstep, Bar's **City Beach** is not the most appealing option for swimming. Heading north, **Šušanj Beach** is popular with Serbian holidaymakers. Beat the crowds in the succession of rocky coves that follow; they are perfect for snorkelling and sheltered swimming. If you're concerned about the Speedos chafing, you can go the full monty at a stony bay just before the rustic ruins of the 11th-century Benedictine monastery of the **Mother of God of Ratac** (Bogorodica Ratac). Destroyed by the Turks in 1571, the remains of its chapel now have a congregation consisting of wild figs and the occasional old lady in black.

King Nikola's Palace MUSEUM
(Dvorac Kralja Nikole; ☎030-314 079; Šetalište Kralje Nikole; adult/child €1/50c; ⏲8am-2pm & 5-11pm) Presenting an elegant facade to the water, King Nikola's Palace was built in 1885 and now houses a collection of antiquities, folk costumes and royal furniture. Its shady gardens contain plants cultivated from seeds and cuttings collected from around the world by Montenegro's sailors.

St Nicholas' Church CHURCH
(Crkva Sv Nikole; Popovići bb) Bar first became the seat of a Catholic diocese in the 9th century and in 1089 it was elevated to an archdiocese, with the archbishop given the title 'Primate of Serbia'. The elegant archbishop's palace sits next to this baroque-style church in the west of town on the route to Stari Bar. These days the archdiocese comprises part of Kosovo and all of Montenegro except for the Kotor diocese, which remains attached to the Croatian arm of the church.

Festivals & Events

Chronicle of Bar PERFORMING ARTS
Plays, exhibitions, literary events and concerts in July and August.

Summer with Stars MUSIC
A series of concerts by regional pop stars in July and August.

Old Olive Tree Gatherings LITERATURE
(⏲Nov) Art and literary festival for children.

Sleeping

It's surprisingly difficult to find decent accommodation in Bar so unless you've got

Bar

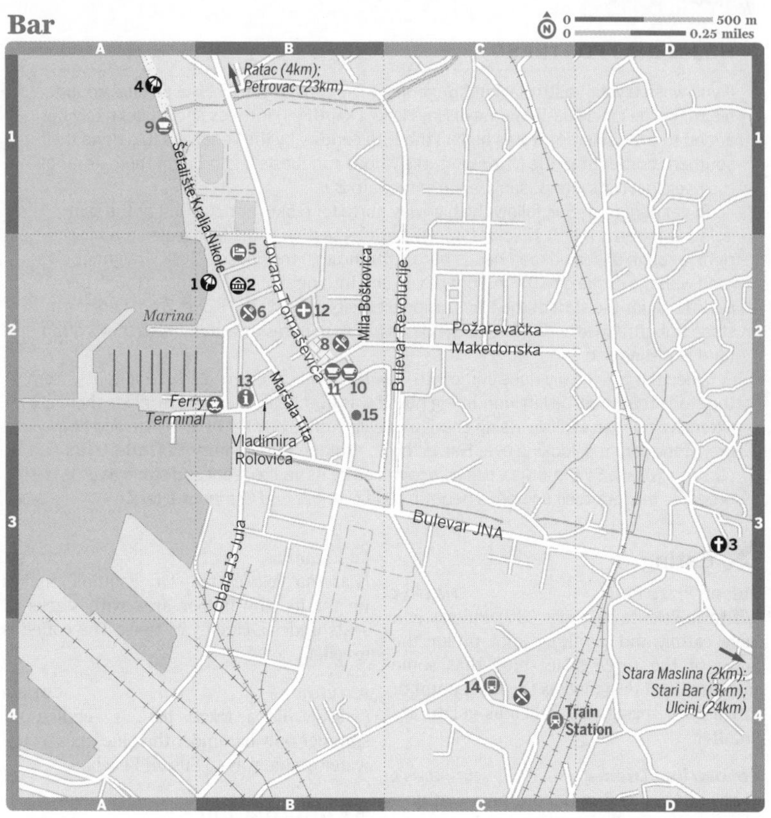

Bar

Sights

1 City Beach ... B2
2 King Nikola's Palace ... B2
3 St Nicholas' Church ... D3
4 Šušanj Beach ... A1

Sleeping

5 Hotel Princess ... B2

Eating

6 Ciao ... B2
7 Konoba Kod Džema ... C4
8 Pulena Pizza Pub ... B2

Drinking & Nightlife

9 Azzuro ... A1
10 Carpe Diem ... B2
11 La Esquina ... B2

Information

12 Accident & Emergency Clinic ... B2
13 Tourist Information Centre ... B2

Transport

14 Bus Station ... C4
15 Meridian Rentacar ... B2

an early or late transport connection, you're better off heading elsewhere. Enquire at the tourist office about private rooms.

Hotel Princess HOTEL €€€
(☎030-300 100; www.hotelprincess.me; Jovana Tomaševića 59; s €83-98, d €126-156, ste €205-275; P ❄ @ ☜ ≋) The standards aren't what you'd expect for the price but this resort-style hotel is the best option in Bar by far. Get your money's worth by lazing for hours at the private beach, swimming pool and spa centre.

WORTH A TRIP

HAJ-NEHAJ FORTRESS

If you wasted your youth playing *Dungeons & Dragons* or you just like poking around old ruins, the lonely battlements of Haj-Nehaj (Хај-Нехај) fortress should definitely be added to your itinerary. It was built in the 15th century by the Venetians to defend their southern border from the Ottoman Turks whose conquests had brought them as far as the river that runs into Šušanj Beach in modern Bar.

To get here from Bar, follow the highway north for 6.5km and turn left at the sign pointing towards the Sv Nikola Hotel. At the intersection of the first sealed road to the right, a rough unsealed road heads hard right through the houses. Walk straight up this road with the castle directly in front of you and turn right at the end into a rough car park. Look for the start of the track amongst the bushes on the slope. From here it's a steep but attractive walk through the pines for 30 minutes on a stony path that's often hard to distinguish.

When the gate finally does come into view the fortifications rise so precipitously from the stone that you'll be left wondering how it was ever built. Once you're inside there are extensive ruins to explore, rising charismatically from a blanket of wild sage and flowers. At the very top, looking over Bar, is the shell of the 13th-century **St Demetrius' Church** (Crkva Sv Dimitrija), easily recognised by its vaulted roof and stone altar. It predates the fort itself and once had separate Catholic and Orthodox altars.

Eating

Pulena Pizza Pub PIZZERIA €
(Vladimira Rolovića bb; mains €3-7) Pulena is a busy eating and drinking spot under the outer of the three spaceships that some zany architect designed as the focal point of town. Pizza, pasta and delicious gelato are on offer.

Konoba Kod Džema MONTENEGRIN €
(mains €4-10; ⏲8am-11pm) This atmospheric stone-walled restaurant is an air-conditioned haven midway between the train and bus stations. Nibble on delicious *pršut* (smoke-dried ham) and bread straight off the griddle while you're waiting for your connection.

Ciao CAFE €
(Šetalište Kralja Nikole bb; mains €4-15) A pleasant place for an omelette, pizza or pasta on the waterfront.

Drinking & Nightlife

The one thing Bar isn't short of is bars.

Carpe Diem CAFE, BAR
(Vladimira Rolovića bb) Part of a swanky strip of bars on a pedestrian-only lane just off the main street, Carpe Diem has comfy outdoor furniture, big screens for the football and large pictures of jazz and blues men on the walls.

La Esquina CAFE, BAR
(Vladimira Rolovića bb) La Esquina makes up for its tiny indoor area with stacks of seats under a canopy of trees. The coffee is excellent.

Azzuro CAFE, BAR
(Šetalište Kralja Nikole bb) A chilled-out summer-only bar under the pine trees by the water on the way to Šušanj Beach.

Information

There are several banks with ATMs around Ulica Maršala Tita and Ulica Vladimira Rolovića.

Accident & Emergency Clinic (☎124; Jovana Tomaševića 42)

Tourist Information Centre (☎030-311 633; www.visitbar.org; Obala 13 Jula bb; ⏲8am-8pm Mon-Sat, 8am-2pm Sun Jul-Sep, 8am-4pm Mon-Fri Oct-Jun) Stocks city maps and useful brochures listing sights and private accommodation.

Getting There & Around

BOAT

Ferries to Bari and Ancona in Italy leave from the ferry terminal *(putnički terminal)* near the centre of town. You can book your **Montenegro Lines** (☎030-311 164; www.montenegrolines.net) ferry tickets here and there's a post office branch and ATM.

In summer you can hail a taxi boat from the marina or beach for a short trip up the coast (from about €3).

BUS

The **bus station** (☎ 030-346 141; Beogradska bb) is adjacent to the train station, 1km southeast of the centre. Frequent buses head to Kotor (€6.50), Budva (€4.50), Ulcinj (€3) and Podgorica (€4.50), and five head to Kolašin daily (€8).

Local buses stop in the centre on Ulica Jovana Tomaševića and head to Stari Bar and north along the coast as far as Čanj.

CAR

From Bar the fastest route to Podgorica is via a toll road (€2.50 each way) that leaves the highway past Sutomore, northwest of Bar.

Meridian Rentacar (☎ 030-314 000; www.meridian-rentacar.com; Jovana Tomaševića 30; 1-day hire from €45) has a branch in the centre of town.

TRAIN

The **train station** (☎ 030-301 615; www.zpcg.me; Beogradska bb) has services to Virpazar (€1.20, 23 minutes, seven daily), Podgorica (€2.40, one hour, nine daily), Kolašin (€5.40, 2½ hours, four daily), Mojkovac (€6.20, 2¾ hours, three daily), Bijelo Polje (€7.20, 3¼ hours, three daily) and Belgrade (€21, 11 hours, two daily).

WORTH A TRIP

THE OLD OLIVE TREE

There are over 100,000 olive trees in the Bar area, many of which have seen more than a millennium. At Mirovica near Stari Bar is a living witness that has stood and mutely waved symbols of peace while the armies of consecutive empires have swept through the land. With 2000 birthdays under its belt, *stara maslina* (old olive tree) is possibly the oldest tree in Continental Europe and one of the oldest of its species in the world.

A ring of white stone protects its personal space from tree-huggers and there's a nominal charge to visit (adult/child €1/50c), but it can be admired nearly as well from the road. Look for the signpost on the Bar–Ulcinj road; at the end of this road, look for the stone wall slightly to the right.

Stari Bar Стари Бар

POP 1870

Impressive Stari Bar, Bar's original settlement, stands on a bluff 4km northeast off the Ulcinj road. A steep cobbled hill takes you past a cluster of old houses and shops to the fortified entrance where a short dark passage pops you out into a large expanse of vine-clad ruins and abandoned streets overgrown with grass and wild flowers.

Findings of pottery and metal suggest that the Illyrians founded the city around 800 BC. In the 10th century the Byzantine town was known as Antivarium as it's opposite the Italian city of Bari. It passed in and out of Slavic and Byzantine rule until the Venetians took it in 1443 (note the lion of St Mark in the entryway) and held it until it was taken by the Ottomans in 1571. Nearly all the 240 buildings now lie in ruins, a result of Montenegrin shelling when they captured the town in 1878.

Sights

★Stari Bar RUINS

(Old Bar; adult/child €2/1; 8am-10pm) A small **museum** just inside the entrance explains the site and its history. From here you can follow the green arrows around the major points of interest. In the western part of the town are the remains of **St Nicholas' Church** (Crkva Sv Nikole) offering glimpses of Serbo-Byzantine frescoes.

The northern corner has an 11th-century fortress with views showcasing Stari Bar's isolated setting amid mountains and olive groves. Nearby are the foundations of **St George's Cathedral** (Katedrala Sv Đorđa), dedicated to Bar's patron saint. Originally a Romanesque church, the Turks converted it into a mosque in the 17th century but the unlucky edifice was yet again in ruins after an accidental explosion of gunpowder.

If you're wondering why **St John's Church** (Crkva Sv Jovana) is in such good nick, it's because it's been completely reconstructed by one of the families associated with the original church. One of the few other buildings to have an intact roof is **St Verenada's Church** (Crkva Sv Verenade), which contains a display of photography from the greater Bar area.

Ottoman constructions include a solid and charming Turkish bathhouse from the 17th or 18th century, the clock tower (1752) and the 17th-century aqueduct that carried water from a spring 3km away; it was reconstructed after the 1979 earthquake.

Omerbašića Mosque MOSQUE

(Omerbašića džamija) Just outside Stari Bar's main gate, this simple construction (dating from 1662) has a square stone base and an

PIRATES OF THE MEDITERRANEAN

Listen up, me hearties, to a swashbuckling tale of murder, theft and slavery. Even before the Venetians took over in 1405, Ulcinj had a reputation as a pirate's lair. That didn't change when the Ottomans wrested control (nominally at least) in 1571. Quite the opposite, in fact. By the end of the 16th century as many as 400 pirates, mainly from Malta, Tunisia and Algeria, made Ulcinj their main port of call – wreaking havoc on passing vessels and then returning to party up large on Mala Plaža.

Pirate captains became celebrities across the eastern Mediterranean, with stories of the Karamindžoja brothers, Lika Ceni, Ali Hodža and the like fuelling the imaginations of avid listeners. Spanish writer Cervantes was one victim; he's said to have spent five years in the vaults by the main square before being ransomed. Legend has it that he appropriated the town's name for his character Dulcinea in *Don Quixote*. Others were less lucky, like the pilgrims bound for Mecca robbed then drowned by Lika Ceni – an act that outraged the sultan and landed the pirate a hefty price on his head.

Along with their usual business of pirating, Ulcinj's crews had a lucrative sideline in slavery. Ulcinj became the centre of a thriving slave trade, with people (mainly from North Africa and some as young as two or three) paraded for sale on the town's main square. Ulcinj is perhaps the only place in the Western Balkans to have had a significant black minority.

elegant minaret enclosed by a stone wall. The domed structure near the entrance is the tomb of Dervish Hasan. Many of the Roma people who make a significant proportion of Stari Bar's remaining population practise Islam.

Eating

Konoba Spilja MONTENEGRIN €

(☎030-340 353; www.konobaspilja.me; mains €3-15; ⊙8am-midnight) So rustic you wouldn't be surprised if a goat wandered through, this is a terrific spot for a traditional meal of seafood or lamb in wine after exploring Stari Bar.

★**Kaldrma** MONTENEGRIN €€

(☎030-341 744; kaldrmarestoran@t-com.me; mains €6-11; ⊙lunch & dinner; ☎) Located on the steep road leading to Stari Bar's main gate (the name means cobblestone), this wonderful little eatery manages to be simultaneously very traditional and slightly hippy-dippy. The focus is on the cuisine of Stari Bar itself, including tender lamb dishes and plenty of seasonal vegetarian options. Accommodation is offered in a sweet little room upstairs with mattresses laid on woven rugs (€25).

Shopping

Wine, Olive Oil, Honey Shop WINE, FOOD

Sells wine from small Montenegrin producers, *rakija* in all its varied forms, and other local produce.

Opal II Filigren JEWELLERY

An excellent place to buy silver filigree jewellery – they've been perfecting their craft over 100 years.

Getting There & Away

Buses marked Stari Bar depart from Ulica Jovana Tomaševića in the centre of new Bar every hour (€1).

Ulcinj Улцињ

POP 10,700

If you want a feel of Albania without actually crossing the border, buzzy Ulcinj's the place to go. The population is 61% Albanian (68% Muslim) and in summertime it swells with Kosovar holidaymakers for the simple reason that it's a hell of a lot nicer than any of the Albanian seaside towns. The elegant minarets of numerous mosques give Ulcinj (Ulqin in Albanian) a distinctly Eastern feel, as does the lively music echoing out of the kebab stands around Mala Plaža (Small Beach).

Sights & Activities

Beaches BEACHES

Mala Plaža may be a fine grin of a cove but it's a little hard to see the beach under all that suntanned flesh in July and August. You are better off strolling southeast where a succession of rocky bays offers clear water and a little more room to breathe.

Each beach has a commercial license, with attendent seasonal beach bars and eateries. If you value your eardrums, avoid those with names like Ibiza and Aquarius and head somewhere like **Sapore di Mare** where you can either plant yourself on a concrete terrace or find a patch of grass under the pines. **Lady Beach 'Dada'** (admission €1.50), true to its unusual name, has a women-only policy, while a section of the beach in front of the **Hotel Albatros** is clothing-optional.

Stari Grad NEIGHBOURHOOD

The ancient Stari Grad overlooking Mala Plaža is still largely residential and somewhat dilapidated – a legacy of the 1979 earthquake. This is part of its charm – this Old Town really does feel old, a fact reinforced by its uneven cobblestones and the paucity of street lighting at night. One suspects that vampires lurk in forgotten basements...

A steep slope leads to the **Upper Gate**, where just inside the walls there's a small **museum** (admission €1; ⏲9am-8pm Tue-Sun) containing Roman and Ottoman artefacts. On the site is a 1510 church that was converted to a mosque in 1693; you can still see the ruined minaret. Just outside the museum is a **fountain** (actually, it's now more of a tap) with an Arabic inscription, a crescent moon and flowers carved into the stone.

Mosques MOSQUES

One of Ulcinj's most distinctive features is its many mosques. Most are fairly simple structures and they're generally more interesting from the outside than inside. An exception is the **Sailor's Mosque** (Džamija Pomoraca; Detarët e Ulqinit bb), which has interesting interior frescoes. This imposing stone structure, right on the waterfront, was completed in 2012, replacing a mosque which predated the Ottomans, which was destroyed in 1931.

Kryepazarit Mosque (Džamija Vrhpazara; Gjergj Kastrioti Skënderbeu bb) was built in 1749 at the intersection of the main streets but was substantially rebuilt following the 1979 earthquake; its name means 'Top of the Market'. Within the same block but set back slightly from the road is the 1728 **Mezjah Mosque** (Džamija Namaždjah; Hazif Ali Ulqinaku 71).

Lamit Mosque (Džamija Ljamit; Kadi Hysen Mujali bb) dates from 1689 but was substantially rebuilt after the 1979 earthquake. The ceiling has interesting green-painted geometric wood panelling. Dating from 1719, **Pasha's Mosque** (Pašina džamija; Buda Tomovića bb) is an elegant complex with a *hammam* (Turkish bathhouse) attached.

St Nicholas' Cathedral CHURCH

(Saborna crkva Sv Nikole; Buda Tomovića bb) Set amongst a picturesque grove of gnarled olive trees below the Upper Gate is this Orthodox cathedral. It's a relative newbie, having been built in 1890 shortly after the Ottomans were booted out, although it's believed to stand on the site of a 15th-century monastery.

Liberty Monument MONUMENT

(Ivan Millutinoviqit bb) On the cliff above Mala Plaža, this imposing monument is a lovely piece of socialist art that's now neglected and covered in graffiti. Its two V-shaped white segments resemble a pair of fighter

VISITING MOSQUES

Unlike in some parts of the Islamic world, respectful non-Muslims are usually welcome to visit mosques in Montenegro, although some mosques don't allow women or have separate areas set aside for them (if you're unsure, ask for permission before entering). Mosques are primarily a place for prayer and most are kept purposefully plain so as not to distract the faithful – so there's usually not a lot to see inside anyway. The interiors of some are decorated with geometric patterns or Arabic calligraphy but the representation of people or animals is strictly forbidden. What they all have in common is a prayer niche aligned at the centre of the wall facing Mecca.

If you're keen to visit, a few protocols should be followed. Clothing should be loose and should cover the body: shorts, singlets, short skirts and tight jeans are a no-no and women will often cover their heads. Shoes must be removed and mobile phones switched off.

Devout Muslims are required to ritually cleanse themselves before entering for prayer, so there's usually a fountain or tap near the entrance. Non-Muslims aren't expected to do so. Don't distract anyone praying by wandering around or talking loudly inside the mosque – in fact, don't enter at all if group prayers or other community activities are taking place.

Ulcinj

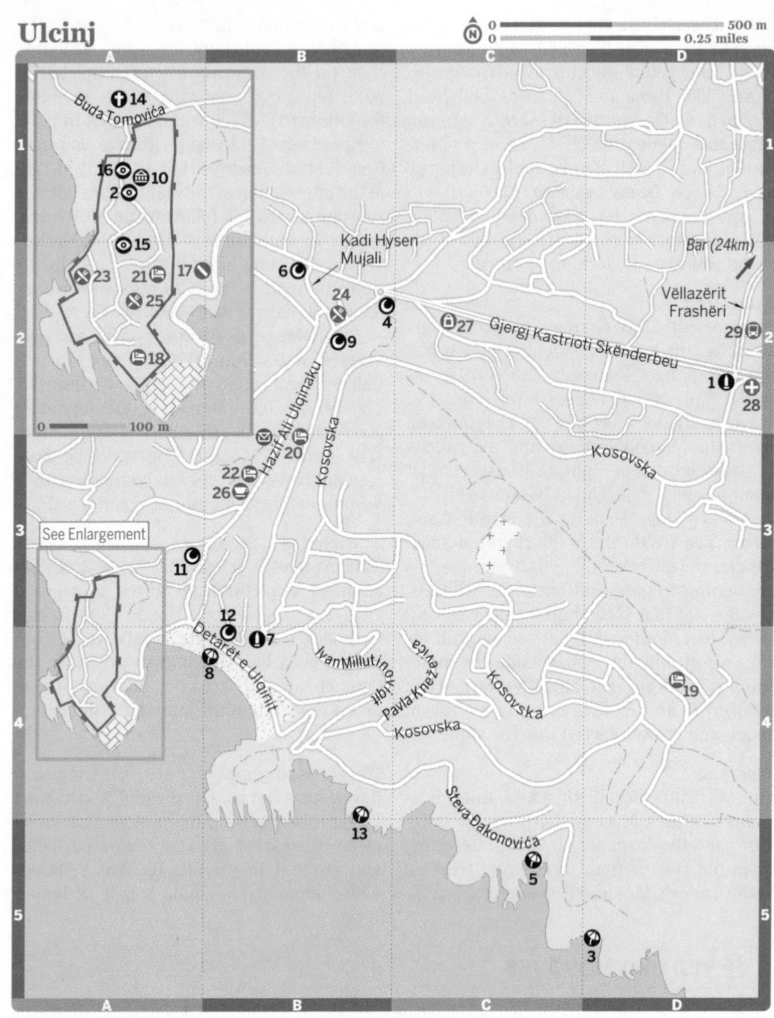

planes that have crash-landed on their noses. Closer inspection reveals them as stylised wings sprouting from the figures facing each other at the centre.

Mother Theresa statue MONUMENT
(Majka Tereza bb) In relatively good nick is this statue of Mother Theresa, the most famous Albanian of recent years (although she was actually born in Macedonia), which stands in front of the clinic on the boulevard named after her.

On the corner adjacent to the statue, there's an interesting **commemorative plaque**: 'In gratitude to the people of Ulcinj for the humanity, solidarity and hospitality they have shown in sheltering and taking care of the persecuted from Kosova during the period March '98 to June '99 – Grateful Kosovars'.

D'Olcinium Diving Club DIVING
(☎067-319 100; www.uldiving.com; Detarët e Ulqinit bb) Local dive sites include various wrecks (this is pirate territory, after all) and the remains of a submerged town. If you've got up-to-date qualifications you can rent gear (€20), take a guided shore dive (€15) or head

Ulcinj

Sights

1 Commemorative Plaque ... D2
2 Fountain ... A1
3 Hotel Albatros Beach ... D5
4 Kryepazarit Mosque ... B2
5 Lady Beach 'Dada' ... C5
6 Lamit Mosque ... B2
7 Liberty Monument ... B4
8 Mala Plaža ... B4
9 Mezjah Mosque ... B2
Mother Theresa statue ... (see 28)
10 Museum ... A1
11 Pasha's Mosque ... A3
12 Sailor's Mosque ... B4
13 Sapore di Mare ... B4
14 St Nicholas' Cathedral ... A1
15 Stari Grad ... A2
16 Upper Gate ... A1

Activities, Courses & Tours

17 D'Olcinium Diving Club ... A2

Sleeping

18 Dvori Balšića ... A2
19 Haus Freiburg ... D4
20 Hotel Dolcino ... B3
21 Palata Venecija ... A2
22 Real Estate Travel Agency ... B3

Eating

23 Antigona ... A2
24 Restaurant Pizzeria Bazar ... B2
25 Restaurant Teuta ... A2

Drinking & Nightlife

26 Rock ... B3

Shopping

27 Market ... C2

Information

28 Accident & Emergency Clinic ... D2

Transport

29 Bus Station ... D2

out on a boat for a day's diving (€50). Night dives also offered (from shore/boat €20/25).

Sleeping

At **Real Estate Travel Agency** (030-421 609; www.realestate-travel.com; Hazif Ali Ulqinaku bb; per person from €15), obliging English-speaking staff can help you find private rooms, apartments or hotel rooms. It also rents bikes (€10) and cars, runs tours and sells maps of Ulcinj.

★Haus Freiburg HOTEL €€
(030-403 008; www.hotelhausfreiburg.me; Kosovska bb; s/d/apt €50/65/85; P) High on the slopes above the town, this family-run hotel has well kitted out apartments and rooms, and a particularly attractive roof terrace with sea views, a swimming pool and small restaurant. Expect to expend 20 minutes walking down to Mala Plaža and a considerable amount of sweat walking back up.

Hotel Dolcino HOTEL €€
(030-422 288; www.hoteldolcino.com; Hazif Ali Ulqinaku bb; s/d €40/50;) You can't quibble over the exceptionally reasonable prices of this modern business-orientated mini-hotel in the centre of town. The quieter rooms at the back have spacious terraces, although the small front balconies are great for watching the passing parade. The hotel's Italian restaurant is reasonably priced, despite being one of the smartest eateries in Ulcinj.

Dvori Balšića HOTEL €€€
(030-421 609; www.hotel-dvoribalsica-montenegro.com; Stari Grad bb; s/d €65/100;) This stone palazzo and its equally grand sister, the **Palata Venecija**, are reached by the cobbled lanes and stairs of the Old Town – not great if you're lugging luggage but very atmospheric nonetheless. The sizeable rooms all have kitchenettes, romantic sea views, and stucco and dark wooden interiors.

Eating

Restaurant Pizzeria Bazar PIZZERIA, SEAFOOD €
(Hazif Ali Ulqinaku bb; mains €4-10; 10am-1pm) An upstairs restaurant that's a great idling place when the streets below are heaving with tourists. People-watch in comfort as you enjoy a plate of *lignje na žaru* (grilled squid), one of the restaurant's specialities.

Antigona SEAFOOD €€
(www.antigonaulcinj.webs.com; Stari Grad bb; mains €7-26) Antigona's clifftop terrace offers perhaps the most romantic aspect of any eatery in Ulcinj, and handsome waiters in bowties only add to the impression. The seafood is excellent too – but be sure to check the price and weight of the fish in advance if you wish to avoid any nasty surprises come bill time. It also rents rooms (from €10 per person).

A SURFEIT OF STREET NAMES

You're unlikely to a find a single street sign in many Montenegrin towns but in Ulcinj you'll sometimes find three different ones per street: a Montenegrin name and an Albanian version of the Yugoslav-era name as well as a new Albanian name. Thus the main boulevard leading east–west at the top of town is either Maršala Tita or Gjergj Kastrioti Skënderbeu, and the main street heading down to the beach is either Ulica 26 Novembra or Rruga Hazif Ali Ulqinaku. In this text we've used the name that was most prominently displayed at the time of research (usually the new Albanian names), but be aware that there is a push to return to the old names.

Restaurant Teuta SEAFOOD, MONTENEGRIN €€
(Stari Grad bb; mains €6-17) The food's good but it's all about the views at this traditional restaurant overlooking Mala Plaža from the battlements of the Old Town.

Drinking & Nightlife

The Mala Plaža promenade buzzes on summer nights. All the bars get packed, fast food is served hand over fist, and nightclubs spark into life.

Rock CAFE, BAR
(Hazif Ali Ulqinaku bb; 7am-3am;) A worthy attempt at an Irish pub with dark wood and electric candles adding to the atmosphere.

Shopping

Market MARKET
(Gjergj Kastrioti Skënderbeu bb) In the covered 'green' market, women in white headscarves sell fresh fruit and vegetables, in competition with the large supermarket next door. On the other side of the supermarket is an attractive little outdoor market selling mainly clothes and shoes. More interesting is the little shop on its edge selling traditional woollen rugs.

Information

There are numerous banks with ATMs along Gjergj Kastrioti Skënderbeu and several internet cafes on Hazif Ali Ulqinaku.

Accident & Emergency Clinic (030-412 433; Majka Tereza bb) There's a pharmacy attached.

Getting There & Away

The **bus station** (030-413 225; Vëllazërit Frashëri bb) is on the northeastern edge of town. Services head to Herceg Novi (€10, daily), Kotor (€9, daily), Budva (€7, eight daily), Podgorica (€6, 12 daily) and Rožaje (€14, daily). International destinations include Shkodra (€6, two daily), Priština (€18, six daily), Sarajevo (€26, daily) and Belgrade (€33, four daily).

A minibus to Velika Plaža or Ada Bojana from Gjergj Kastrioti Skënderbeu will cost about €2.50.

Velika Plaža & Ada Bojana
Велика Плажа и Ада Бојана

The appropriately named Velika Plaža (Big Beach) starts 4km southeast of Ulcinj and stretches for 12 sandy kilometres. Sections of it sprout deckchairs but there's still plenty of space for solitude. To be frank, this large flat expanse isn't quite as picturesque as it sounds and the water is painfully shallow – great for kids but you'll need to walk out a fair way for a decent swim.

On the way to Velika Plaža is the murky **Milena canal** where the local fishermen use nets suspended from long willow rods attached to wooden stilt houses. The effect is remarkably redolent of Southeast Asia. There are more of these contraptions on the banks of the **Bojana River** at the other end of Velika Plaža.

A bridge leads over the river to Ada Bojana, as peculiar a place as you're likely to find in Montenegro. It was formed around a shipwreck between two existing islands in the river mouth, which eventually gathered enough sediment to cover around 520 hectares and create 3km of sandy beach. During its Yugoslav heyday it became one of Europe's premier nudist resorts, with the island completely given over to the footloose and fancy-threads-free. You'd have to be totally committed to the lifestyle to want to stay in the neglected accommodation that's currently offered, but luckily you can pay a day rate to access the island (by car €5, on foot €2). If you'd prefer to keep your gear on, stick close to the rivermouth.

OFF THE BEATEN TRACK

LAKE ŠAS ШАСКО ЈЕЗЕРО

If you've got your own wheels and fancy getting well off the beaten track, this pretty area near the Albanian border makes for a pleasant and peaceful drive. Take the road leading northwest from Ulcinj. After 17km you'll reach the large village of Vladimir where a marked turn-off to the right leads to the lake.

After 2km you'll see to your right the ruins of the once great Zetan city of **Svač** (Šas). Park here and cut across to the top left corner of the rough football field, where you'll find the beginnings of a rocky path. Make sure you're wearing proper shoes as the track is quite rough and there are a lot of thorns.

There's not a lot remaining of Svač apart from some sections of wall and the shells of a couple of buildings, one of which was obviously a church. The town was razed by the Mongols in 1242 and then again by the Ottomans in the 16th century, after which it was abandoned to the dragonflies, bees and butterflies. It's now a rustically beautiful spot, completely unbothered by tourists, offering broad views over the plains towards the Rumija Mountains.

Jump back in the car and continue to follow the signs to the lake, which is 2.5km further. **Lake Šas** (Šasko jezero) covers 364 hectares and is lined with a muddy border of reeds and water lilies, making it an important habitat for the 240 species of bird that are found here. In winter it attracts both dedicated birdwatchers and Italian hunters.

Character-filled **Restaurant Shasi** (☎067-645 045; mains €7-13) is a rambling stone complex built into a cliff by the lake. It's a lovely, quiet spot where the staff spring into action when you arrive and fish soup is served with delicious corn damper. Shasi's specialities are eel, mullet and carp, caught from the pier at the bottom of its yard. It even has its own waterfall.

Activities

This area is making a name for itself as a prime spot for kitesurfing. **Kitesfera** (www.kitesfera.com) and **D'Olcinium Kitesurf Club** (☎069-330 492; www.kitesurfclub.me) are well established.

Eating

Several memorable fish restaurants jut out over the Bojana River near the Ada Bojana bridge. The local speciality is *riblja čorba* (fish soup). Each of these restaurants is worth making the 14km drive from Ulcinj in itself.

Restoran Kod Marka SEAFOOD, MONTENEGRIN €€
(☎030-401 720; Bojana River; mains €8-12) The *riblja čorba* dished up here is sublime, and it's served in a metal pot that will fill your bowl twice over. Some meat dishes are offered as well.

Ćićkova Čarda SEAFOOD, ITALIAN €€
(Bojana River; mains €7-11) Seemingly constructed Robinson Crusoe–style from flotsam and jetsam, this very atmospheric restaurant on the Ada Bojana side of the river serves lots of traditional seafood dishes as well as the usual selection of pasta, risotto, steaks and grills. It's a wonderful spot from which to watch the sunset.

★**Miško** SEAFOOD €€€
(Bojana River; mains €9-17) The most upmarket of the Bojana River restaurants is focussed completely on seafood, including octopus, shrimp, shellfish, a big selection of fresh fish, and, of course, delicious *riblja čorba*. Its motto, with apologies to Julius Caesar: '*Veni, Vidi, Sjedi, Jedi*', or translated from the mix of Latin and Montenegrin 'I came. See! Sit! Eat!'.

Central Montenegro

Includes ➡

Best Places to Eat

- Stari Most (p95)
- Lupo di Mare (p103)
- Kole (p94)
- Konoba Badanj (p96)
- Ibon (p105)

Best Places to Stay

- Villa Miela (p96)
- Hotel Podgorica (p101)
- Aria (p101)
- City Hotel (p102)
- Hotel Marshal (p105)

Why Go?

You can't really say you've been to Montenegro if you haven't visited the region that has always been its physical, spiritual and political heartland. A distinct Montenegrin (as opposed to Serbian) identity formed here from the crucible of resistance to Ottoman hegemony represented by Lovćen, the black mountain.

To reach central Montenegro from the coast you'll first have to skirt two wonderful national parks that provide every excuse for a back-to-nature diversion. Behind the parks are the two capitals: the ancient current one (Podgorica, founded by the Romans) and the newer former one (Cetinje, the royal city). Together they offer the chance to get better acquainted with Montenegrin art and history in their richly endowed galleries and museums.

Continue into the hinterland and you'll reach Ostrog Monastery. In a country with so many religious sites, none comes close to Ostrog in sheer impressiveness.

When to Go

- May is late spring and the perfect time to visit the capital before the sizzling summer begins. August has great weather for exploring Lake Skadar, while Danilovgrad hosts the River Zeta Festival.
- September is not as scorching in the central plains but still warm enough in the national parks.

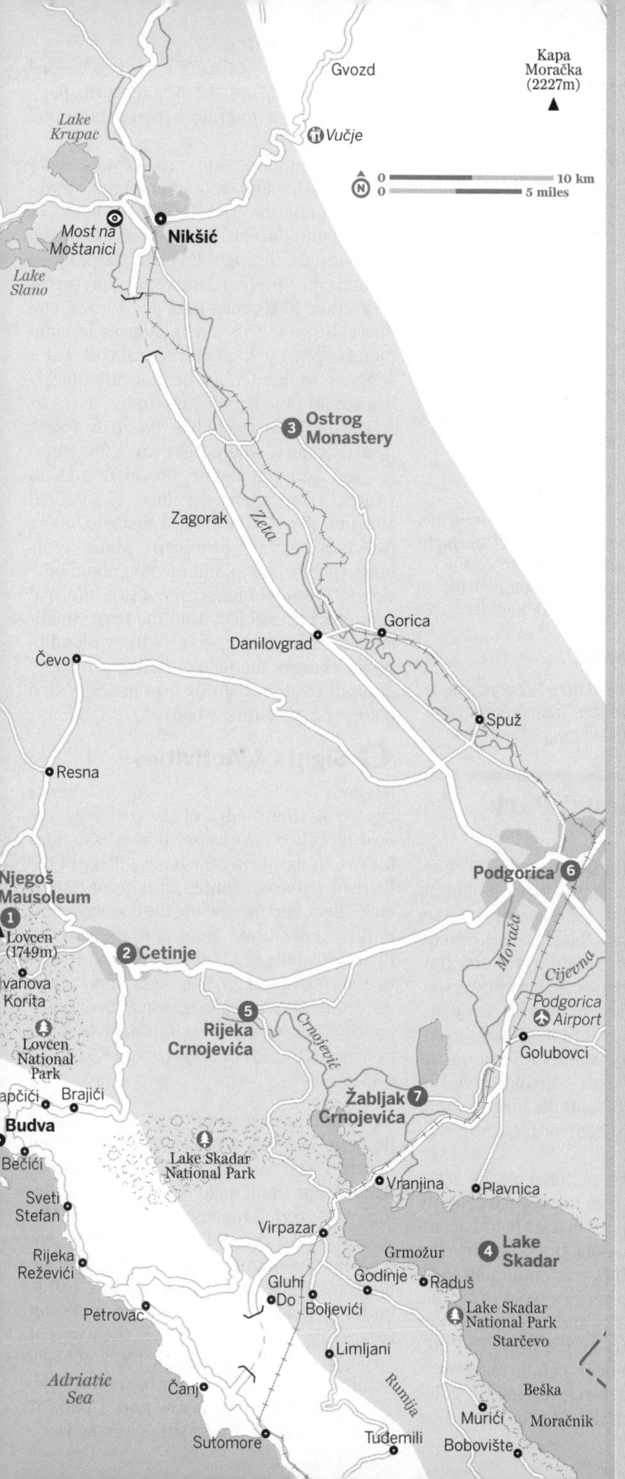

Central Montenegro Highlights

1. Marvelling at the majesty of both the mountains and the monument at the **Njegoš Mausoleum** (p90)
2. Diving into history, art and culture at the **National Museum of Montenegro** (p91) and on Cetinje's streets
3. Gazing in wonder at the improbable cliff-face construction of **Ostrog Monastery** (p104)
4. Cruising the sparkling waters to the island monasteries and bird sanctuaries of **Lake Skadar** (p96)
5. Feasting on the sublime seafood and serene setting of **Rijeka Crnojevića** (p95)
6. Soaking up the nocturnal buzz of Podgorica's **Nova Varoš** (p103) party precinct
7. Braving the snakes and spiders within the usually deserted medieval ruins of **Žabljak Crnojevića** (p99)

> **MOVING ON?**
>
> For tips, recommendations and reviews, head to shop.lonelyplanet.com to purchase a downloadable PDF of the Bosnia & Hercegovina chapter from Lonely Planet's *Eastern Europe* guide.

Climate

Extremes are more noticeable in this region than on the coast. Podgorica is scorching in summer and can reach above 40°C. In the mountains the climate is considerably cooler. Temperatures can drop below freezing any time from October to March.

Getting There & Away

Podgorica has an international airport and is the country's main bus and train hub. The main highway from the coast starts near Sutomore and takes a tunnel (toll charge €2.50) through the mountains to Virpazar and on to Podgorica.

Getting Around

Regular bus services head from Podgorica to Cetinje, Nikšić and Virpazar. Trains connect Podgorica to Virpazar, Danilovgrad and Nikšić.

Lovćen National Park
Ловћен

Directly behind Kotor is **Mt Lovćen** (1749m, pronounced '*lov*·chen'), the black mountain that gave Crna Gora (Montenegro) its name (*crna/negro* means 'black', *gora/monte* means 'mountain' in Montenegrin and Italian respectively). This locale occupies a special place in the hearts of all Montenegrins. For most of its history it represented the entire nation – a rocky island of Slavic resistance in an Ottoman sea. The old capital of Cetinje nestles in its foothills and many of its residents head up here for picnics during summer.

Two-thirds of the national park's 6220 hectares are covered in woods, particularly the black beech that gives it its moody complexion. Even the rockier tracts sprout wild herbs such as St John's wort, mint and sage. The park is home to various types of reptile, 85 species of butterfly and large mammals such as brown bears and wolves. The 200 avian species found here include regal birds of prey such as the peregrine falcon, golden eagle and imperial eagle (but you'll be looking for a long time for the two-headed variety featured on the Montenegrin flag). Several species migrate between here and Lake Skadar.

The mountains are criss-crossed with hiking paths and mountain-biking trails, which can be accessed from Kotor, Budva or Cetinje, and the Coastal Mountain Traversal runs straight through. If you're planning on hiking, come prepared as the temperature is on average 10ºC cooler than on the coast and Lovćen's prone to sudden changes in summer. Despite the high average rainfall, water supplies are limited as the moisture quickly leeches into the karstic limestone.

The park's main hub is **Ivanova Korita** near its centre, where there are a few eateries and accommodation providers and, in winter, a beginners' ski slope. Here you'll also find the **National Park Visitor Centre** (www.nparkovi.me; 9am-5pm), which rents bikes (per hour €2) and offers accommodation in four-bed bungalows (€40). Informal camping is possible within the park (small/large tent €3/5, campervan €10), with additional charges for using established campgrounds (€10) or lighting fires in designated places (€5, including wood).

Sights & Activities

Njeguši VILLAGE

On the northern edge of the park, this endearing collection of stone houses is famous for two things: being the home village of the Petrović dynasty, Montenegro's most important rulers, and for making the country's best *pršut* (smoke-dried ham) and *sir* (cheese). Roadside stalls sell both, along with honey, *rakija* (fruit brandy), hand-woven mats and souvenirs. Otherwise, sit down at the atmospheric **Konoba kod Radonjića** (mains €6-11) to sample the specialities (*pršut* €4.50, *sir* €3.50).

★**Njegoš Mausoleum** MONUMENT

(Njegošev Mauzolej; admission €3; 8am-6pm) Lovćen's star attraction, this magnificent mausoleum (built 1970 to 1974) sits at the top of its second-highest peak, Jezerski Vrh (1657m). Take the 461 steps up to the entry where two granite giantesses guard the tomb of Montenegro's greatest hero. Inside under a golden mosaic canopy a 28-ton Petar II Petrović Njegoš rests in the wings of an eagle, carved from a single block of black granite by Croatian sculptor Ivan Meštrović. The actual tomb lies below and a path at the rear leads to a dramatic circular viewing platform providing the same spectacular views that caused George Bernard Shaw to exclaim 'Am I in paradise or on the moon?'.

A photographer stationed near the entrance has a stash of folk costumes and a computer set up to print out quirky instant souvenirs (photos small/large €3/5).

Avanturistički Park ADVENTURE SPORTS
(☎069-543 156; Ivanova Korita; adult/child €18/12; ⏰10am-6pm May–mid-Nov) This 2-hectare adventure park has zip lines and ropes courses of varying degrees of difficulty set amongst the trees near the National Park Office.

Getting There & Away

If you're driving, the park can be approached from either Kotor or Cetinje (entry fee €2). Tour buses are the only buses that head into the park.

CETINJE CYCLING CIRCUIT

From Cetinje a 53km, day-long circular mountain-biking route follows asphalt roads through Lovćen National Park. You'll ascend 890m in your first 20km to the entrance of the Njegoš Mausoleum, where you can stop for the views and a bite to eat. It's mainly downhill from here, heading in the direction of Kotor before looping through Njeguši and back to Cetinje.

Cetinje Цетиње

POP 14,000

Rising from a green vale surrounded by rough grey mountains, Cetinje (pronounced '*tse*·ti·nye') is an odd mix of former capital and overgrown village where single-storey cottages and stately mansions share the same street. Several of those mansions – dating from times when European ambassadors rubbed shoulders with Montenegrin princesses – have become museums or schools for art and music.

The city was founded in 1482 by Ivan Crnojević, the ruler of the Zeta state, after abandoning his previous capital near Lake Skadar, Žabljak Crnojevića, to the Ottomans. A large statue of him stands in the main square, Dvorski Trg.

Cetinje seems to expect its visitors to flit in and out on tour buses – as indeed most of them do. Accommodation is limited and there are only a few proper restaurants. Come the weekend competing sound systems blast the cobwebs from the main street. If war broke out on a Saturday night you probably wouldn't hear it.

Sights

★National Museum of Montenegro MUSEUM
(www.mnmuseum.org; Narodni muzej Crne Gore; all museums adult/child €10/5; ⏰9am-4pm) The National Museum is actually a collection of four museums and two galleries housed in a clump of important buildings. A joint ticket will get you into all of them or you can buy individual tickets.

Two are housed in the former parliament (1910), Cetinje's most imposing building. The fascinating **History Museum** (Istorijski muzej; ☎041-230 310; Novice Cerovića 7; adult/child €3/1.50) is very well laid out, following a timeline from the Stone Age to 1955. There are few English signs but the enthusiastic staff will walk you around and give you an overview before leaving you to your own devices. Bullet holes are a theme of some of the museum's most interesting relics: there are three in the back of the tunic that Prince Danilo was wearing when assassinated; Prince Nikola's standard from the battle of Vučji Do has *396*; while, in the communist section, there's a big gaping one in the skull of a fallen comrade.

Upstairs you'll find the equally excellent **Montenegrin Art Gallery** (Crnogorska galerija umjetnosti; adult/child €4/2). There's a small collection of icons, the most important being the precious 9th-century *Our Lady of Philermos,* traditionally believed to be painted by St Luke himself. It's spectacularly presented in its own blue-lit 'chapel', but the Madonna's darkened face is only just visible behind its spectacular golden casing mounted with diamonds, rubies and sapphires. Elsewhere in the gallery all of Montenegro's great artists are represented, with the most famous (Milunović, Lubarda, Đurić etc) having their own separate spaces. Expect a museum staff member to be hovering as you wander around.

In 2012 an offshoot of the national gallery opened in a striking building on Cetinje's main street. Dedicated to one of Montenegro's most important artists, who died in 2010, the edgy **Miodrag Dado Đurić Gallery** (Galerija ; Balšića Pazar; ⏰10am-2pm &

Cetinje

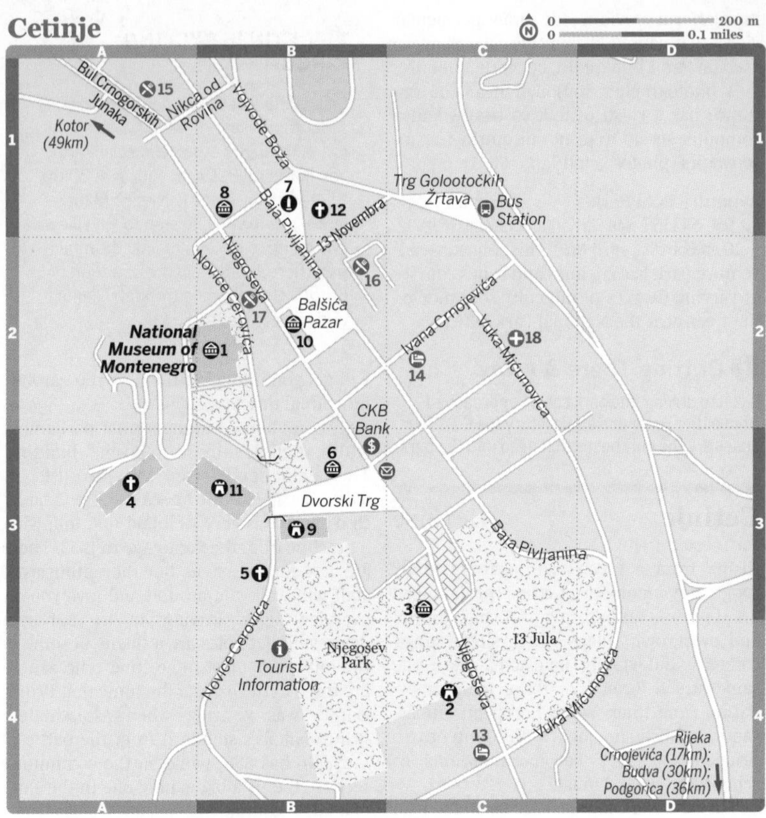

Cetinje

Top Sights

1 National Museum of Montenegro......... B2

Sights

2 Blue Palace.. C4
3 British Embassy.................................. C3
4 Cetinje Monastery A3
5 Court Church.. B3
6 Ethnographic Museum.......................... B3
7 Fairy of Lovćen..................................... B1
8 French Embassy B1
History Museum .... (see 1)
9 King Nikola Museum B3
10 Miodrag Dado Đurić Gallery B2
Montenegrin Art Gallery .... (see 1)
11 Njegoš Museum..................................... B3
Relief Map...................................... (see 11)
12 Vlach Church... B1

Sleeping

13 Hotel Grand.. C4
14 Pansion 22.. C2

Eating

15 Kole A1
16 Market... B2
17 Vinoteka.. B2

Information

18 Accident & Emergency Clinic C2

6-9pm Tue-Sun) is devoted to 20th-century and contemporary Montenegrin art. The same ticket covers both galleries.

Entry to the **King Nikola Museum** (Muzej kralja Nikole; Dvorski Trg; adult/child €5/2.50) is by guided tour, which the staff will only give to a group, even if you've prepaid a ticket. Still, this 1871 palace of Nikola I, last sovereign of Montenegro, is worth the frustration. Although looted during WWII, enough plush furnishings, stern portraits and taxidermied animals remain to capture the spirit of the court.

Opposite the History Museum, the castle-like **Njegoš Museum** (Njegošev muzej; Dvorski Trg; adult/child €3/1.50) was the residence of Montenegro's favourite son, prince-bishop and poet Petar II Petrović Njegoš. The palace was built and financed by the Russians in 1838 and housed the nation's first billiard table, hence the museum's alternative name, Biljarda. The bottom floor is devoted to military costumes, photos of soldiers with outlandish moustaches and exquisitely decorated weapons – these people clearly loved their guns. Upstairs are Njegoš' personal effects, including his bishop's cross and garments, documents, fabulous furniture and, of course, the billiard table.

When you leave the Njegoš Museum turn right and follow the walls to the glass pavilion housing a fascinating large-scale **Relief Map** (admission €1) of Montenegro created by the Austrians in 1917. If it's closed you can peer through the windows.

Occupying the former Serbian Embassy, the **Ethnographic Museum** (Etnografski Muzej; Dvorski Trg; adult/child €2/1) is the least interesting of the seven but if you've bought a joint ticket you may as well check it out. The collection of costumes and tools is well presented and has English notations.

Cetinje Monastery CHRISTIAN MONASTERY

(Cetinjski Manastir; ⏲8am-6pm) It's a case of four times lucky for the Cetinje Monastery, having been repeatedly destroyed during Ottoman attacks and rebuilt. This sturdy incarnation dates from 1786, with its only exterior ornamentation being the capitals of columns recycled from the original building, founded in 1484.

The chapel to the right of the courtyard holds the monastery's proudest possessions: a shard of the True Cross (the *pièce de rèsistance* of many of Europe's churches) and the mummified right hand of St John the Baptist. The hand's had a fascinating history, having escaped wars and revolutions and passed through the hands of Byzantine emperors, Ottoman sultans, the Knights Hospitallers, Russian tsars and Serbian kings. It's now housed in a bejewelled golden casket by the chapel's window, draped in heavy fabric and with an icon of the Baptist at its, ahem, foot. The casket's only occasionally opened for veneration, so if you miss out you can console yourself with the knowledge that it's not a very pleasant sight.

The monastery **treasury** (admission €2) is only open to groups but if you are persuasive enough and prepared to wait around, you may be able to get in (mornings are best). It holds a wealth of fascinating objects that form a blur as you're shunted around the rooms by one of the monks. These include jewel-encrusted vestments, ancient handwritten texts, icons (including a lovely Syrian *Madonna and Child*) and a copy of the 1494 *Oktoih* (Book of the Eight Voices), the first book printed in Serbian. The crown of 14th-century Serbian king Stefan Uroš III Dečanski (who was deposed by his son, murdered and became a Serbian saint) is covered in pearls, large precious stones and priceless Byzantine-style enamels.

If your legs, shoulders or cleavage are on display you'll either be denied entry or given an unflattering smock to wear.

Court Church CHURCH

(Dvorska crkva; Novice Cerovića bb) Built in 1886 on the ruins of the original Cetinje Monastery, this cute little church has a lovely gilded iconostasis but its main claim to fame is as the burial place of Cetinje's founder, Ivan Crnojević, and Montenegro's last sovereigns. If Nikola I and Milena were unpopular after fleeing the country for Italy during WWI, they received a hero's welcome when their bodies were returned and interred in these white-marble tombs in 1989 during a three-hour Orthodox service. While still a part of communist Yugoslavia, a quarter of Montenegro's population were reported to have attended and the royal couple's great-grandson Crown Prince Nicholas (a Parisian architect) was mobbed by royalist fans.

Ulica Njegoševa STREET

Cetinje's main street is pretty Njegoševa, a partly pedestrianised thoroughfare lined with interesting buildings, cafes and shops. At the southern end are two shady parks and the elegant **Blue Palace** (Plavi Dvorac), built in 1895 for Crown Prince Danilo but recently commandeered by the Montenegrin President – hence the manicured gardens. Its neighbour is the equally graceful former **British Embassy**, built in 1912 but Georgian in its sensibilities; it's now a music academy. Just north of the pedestrian-only section is a striking art nouveau building covered in glazed tiles which was once the **French Embassy**.

OFF WITH THEIR HEADS

Decapitated heads were once a common sight in Europe; up until 1802 those of executed criminals were still being displayed on London's Temple Bar. However, the Montenegrins' fondness for chopping off and displaying bits of their enemies was legendary and continued into the 20th century.

The hill above Cetinje Monastery was the repository of many such gruesome trophies, mainly taken from the shoulders of Ottoman Turks. Soldiers would proudly display their own collections as testimony to their prowess in battle. To be fair, the Ottomans shared the same taste in battle souvenirs, so the Montenegrins would often remove the heads of fallen comrades rather than allow the enemy to do it. A Russian officer who stumbled while fighting alongside Montenegrin allies in the early 19th century was startled by a friendly but deadly serious offer to prematurely remove his head lest he be captured.

After the capture of Herceg Novi from the French, it was reported that the Montenegrins used the French general's head as a football. When General Marmont remonstrated with Vladika (later Saint) Petar I about the custom, he was told he could hardly complain as the French had recently chopped off the heads of their own king and queen.

Prince Nikola issued an edict against the practice in 1876, and visiting dignitaries were spared such macabre sights in the capital. Montenegrin soldiers made do with only removing ears and noses instead, a tradition that continued right up to WWI.

Vlach Church CHURCH

(Vlaška crkva; Baja Pivljanina bb) Vlach people can be found throughout the Balkans and much of Central and Eastern Europe. They're believed to be the remnants of the Roman population (either ethnically Latin or Romanised Illyrians) who retreated into the less accessible areas as the Slavs poured in from the north. In Montenegro they formed seminomadic shepherding communities, moving their flocks between summer and winter pastures. While in neighbouring states they retain their own Latin-based language and customs to a greater or lesser degree, in Montenegro they appear to have been assimilated into the Slavic population.

One echo of their presence is this church. While its present appearance dates from the 19th century, it was actually founded around 1450 and therefore predates the Montenegrin founding of Cetinje. The original structure was made of thatch daubed in mud. A sumptuous gilded iconostasis (1878) is the centrepiece of current church.

Take a closer look at the fence around the church: it's made from 1544 barrels of guns taken from the Ottomans during the wars at the end of the 19th century. Two 14th-century *stećci* stand in the churchyard, examples of mysterious carved stone monuments that are found throughout northern Montenegro and neighbouring Bosnia.

Fairy of Lovćen MONUMENT

(Baja Pivljanina bb) During WWI many expatriates answered the call to return to fight for Montenegro. This bronze statue was erected in 1939 to commemorate the 350 American Montenegrins who died when their boat was sunk near Albania.

Sleeping

Pansion 22 GUESTHOUSE €€

(☎069-055 473; pansion22@mtel-cg.net; Ivana Crnojevića 22; s/d €22/40; wi-fi) They may not be great at speaking English or answering emails, but the family who run this central guesthouse offer a warm welcome nonetheless. The rooms are simply decorated yet clean and comfortable, with views of the mountains from the top floor.

Hotel Grand HOTEL €€

(☎041-231 651; www.hotel-grand.me; Njegoševa 1; s/d from €45/65; P wi-fi) Step back into an era of brass trim, dark wood, parquet floors and keys dangling behind disinterested reception staff. While it may have passed for grand in its Yugoslav heyday, the Hotel Grand could hardly be accused of that now. That said, it's not a terrible place to stay and the beds are comfortable.

Eating

Kole MONTENEGRIN, EUROPEAN €

(☎041-231 620; www.restaurantkole.me; Bul Crnogorskih Junaka 12; mains €3-12; 7am-11pm)

They serve omelettes and pasta at this snazzy modern eatery, but what are really great are the local specialities. Try the Njeguški *ražanj*, smoky spit-roasted meat stuffed with *pršut* and cheese.

Vinoteka ITALIAN, MONTENEGRIN €
(Njegoševa 103; mains €4-12) The wood-beamed porch and astroturfed terrace facing the garden is such a pleasant place to sit that the reasonably priced pizza, pasta and Montenegrin cuisine feel like a bonus – the decent wine list even more so. The breakfasts are good too.

Market MARKET €
(off 13 Novembra) The best place to stock up on fruit, vegetables, Njeguški cheese and traditional cured meats.

Information

Accident & Emergency Clinic (Hitna pomoć; 041-233 002; Vuka Mićunovića 2)

Tourist Information (078-108 788; www.cetinje.travel; Novice Cerovića bb; 8am-6pm)

Getting There & Away

Cetinje is on the main Budva–Podgorica highway and can also be reached by a glorious back road from Kotor via Lovćen National Park. The **bus station** (Trg Golootočkih Žrtava) is basically derelict but buses still stop outside, including regular services from Herceg Novi (€7, 2½ hours), Budva (€4, 40 minutes) and Podgorica (€4, 30 minutes).

Lake Skadar National Park Скадарско Језеро

The Balkans' largest lake, dolphin-shaped Skadar has its tail and two-thirds of its body in Montenegro and its nose in Albania. Covering between 370 and 550 sq km (depending on the time of year), it's one of the most important reserves for wetland birds in Europe. The endangered Dalmatian pelican nests here along with 256 other species, including a quarter of the global population of pygmy cormorants. You might spot whiskered terns making their nests on the water lilies. At least 48 species of fish lurk beneath its smooth surface, the most common of which are carp, bleak and eel. Mammals within the park's confines include otters, wolves, foxes, weasels, moles and groundhogs.

On the Montenegrin side, an area of 400 sq km has been protected by a national park since 1983. It's a blissfully pretty area encompassing steep mountains, hidden villages, historic churches, clear waters and floating meadows of water lilies.

Rijeka Crnojevića Ријека Црнојевића

POP 180

The northwestern end of Lake Skadar thins into the serpentine loops of the Rijeka Crnojevića (Crnojević River) and terminates near the pretty village of the same name. It's a charming, tucked-away kind of place, accessed by side roads that lead off the Cetinje–Podgorica highway.

When Montenegro was ruled from Cetinje, this is where the royals came to escape the Black Mountain's winter. The relatively modest house of Vladika Petar I Petrović (St Peter of Cetinje) still stands; you'll recognise it by its ground-floor arches and upper rooms jutting out over the road. The village's main feature is the photogenic arched stone bridge constructed by Prince Danilo in 1853.

During the tourist season there are usually small boats lined up on the river, offering cruises for about €25 per hour. Kayak Montenegro (p37) day trips take to the water here and paddle along the river to the lake.

The village is also the starting point of a two-hour, 7.6km circular walking track that passes through the ruins of **Obod**, the site of the region's first printing press, and on to **Obod Cave** (Obodska Pećina) at the source of the river.

You wouldn't expect it, but this sleepy village is home to one of Montenegro's best restaurants. **Stari Most** (041-239 505; mains €8-25) is well located on the marble riverside promenade, looking to the old bridge from which it derives its name. Fish (particularly eel, trout and carp) is the speciality here and the fish soup alone is enough to justify a drive from Podgorica.

Virpazar Вирпазар

POP 280

This tiny town, gathered around a square and a river blanketed with water lilies, serves as the main gateway to Lake Skadar National Park. Looking over Virpazar are two testaments to its bloody past: the ruins of **Besac castle**, the scene of a major battle with the Turks in 1702; and a striking **bronze sculpture** atop a watchtower memorialising the Partisans who lost their lives in WWII. The path leading to Besac is signposted from the road to Murići about 400m after the post office.

A 15km mountain-biking trail skirts around the Crmnica field, which lies between Virpazar and the tunnel to the coast. The route heads through oak forests and the tiny winemaking villages of **Boljevići**, **Limljani** and **Gluhi Do**. Many of the villagers set up stands along the main roads in summer selling homemade wine and *rakija*.

Another charismatic village is **Godinje**, a cluster of stone houses in the hills to the southeast. Once the cellars of all the houses were linked up, and many are now used for making wine. One reliable stop for a tasting is Miodrag Leković's place – he doesn't have any English but he does have a sign, so he means business. Visitors are welcome onto his vine-covered terrace and served generous pours for a couple of euro.

Tours

Green Boats BOAT TOUR
(Zeleni Brodovi; 069-998 737; greenboats.me@gmail.com; per hr from Virpazar/Vranjina €25/40) Lake cruises are offered every two hours by this association of small local operators; enquire at the tourist office for the next departure. Two-hour cruises are the norm, although longer trips can be arranged. We've heard glowing reports about one particular boat, the **Golden Frog** (069-413 307; www.skadarlakecruise.blogspot.co.uk).

Undiscovered Montenegro ADVENTURE TOURS
(069-402 374; www.lake-skadar.com; Apr-Nov) This excellent agency run by a charming British couple specialises in week-long, all-inclusive, lake-based itineraries (per person €530 including accommodation at Villa Miela, p96), but it also offers an accommodation booking service and day tours. Options include guided hikes (from €30 per person), kayaking (from €40 per person), caving (from €60 per person), boat tours (€20 to €40 per person), fishing (€60 per trip), car safaris (from €60 per person), wine tours (from €30 per person), 'wine-dining' (from €40 per person), honey trails (from €25 per person), and expert-led photo-trekking (from €60 per person) and birdwatching (€250 per trip).

Festivals & Events

Festival of Wine & Bleak FOOD
(Festival vina i ukljeve; mid-Dec) That's 'bleak' as in a type of fish, not Russian theatre. It's a chance to stuff yourself while tapping your toes to traditional music.

Sleeping

Draga's HOMESTAY €
(068-760 711; pedja.vuletic@t-com.me; r €25-30;) Above a family home, these four rooms are simply furnished but clean and very reasonably priced. Two share a bathroom but compensate by having their own terrace offering the most sublime sunrise views over the lake. It's the last inhabited house on the left after the memorial; in winter the backyard disappears into the lake.

★**Villa Miela** GUESTHOUSE €€
(020-3287 0015; www.undiscoveredmontenegro.com; r €80; Apr-Nov) Sitting pretty on the slopes near Virpazar, this lovingly renovated stone farmhouse has four rooms sharing a kitchen, BBQ area, orchard and lake views. In July and August it's reserved for Undiscovered Montenegro's seven-day activity holidaymakers (lucky devils), but shorter stays are accepted at other times.

Jovičević Apartments APARTMENTS €€
(069-281 416; sara.jovicevic@yahoo.com; apt €60;) The Jovičević family rents a couple of atmospheric apartments right in the centre of town. The Cave Apartment (sleeping four) is built into a natural rock wall and has its own ornamental well. A hammock is strung up between the oaks outside, and bikes are available to rent (€10 per day). Better still is the light-filled apartment in an old building right by the monument (sleeping three).

Hotel Vir HOTEL €€
(020-711 120; www.hotelprincess.me; s/d €42/64;) Don't be put off by the ghosts of Yugoslavia past in the reception or the staff's complete lack of English. The rooms at this former state hotel have had a spruce up and some have terraces facing over the lake.

Eating & Drinking

★**Konoba Badanj** MONTENEGRIN €€
(mains €6-12; 8am-midnight) A cool stone-walled interior with solid wooden beams, views of the river and interesting art make this an atmospheric eating option. The fish soup comes with big chunks of fish and delicious scone-like homemade bread.

Silistria MONTENEGRIN €€

(mains €6-11; ⌚8am-midnight Mar-Oct) Restaurants don't come much more swashbuckling than this replica of a 19th-century boat gifted to King Nikola by the Turks, permanently docked by Virpazar's main square. Traditional Montenegrin grilled meat and lake fish are served on deck or below.

Virski Pub PUB

With Nikšićko beer on tap, sport on the TV and pool tables out the back, this is a much more pub-like proposition than your average Montenegrin cafe-bar. If you want to mitigate the damage, the bakery next door sells pizza for €1.

Information

National Park Kiosk By the marina; has no info but sells park entry tickets (€4) and fishing permits (summer/winter per day €10/5).

Virpazar Tourist Office (☎020-711 102; www.visitbar.org; ⌚8am-5pm May-Sep, 8am-4pm Mon-Fri Oct-Apr; 📶) This big new office on the main square can assist you with arranging anything on the lake, including boat trips, wine tastings and private accommodation. Upstairs there are displays about the national park, and the office operates as a storefront for the region's small wine producers.

Getting There & Away

Virpazar doesn't have a bus station but buses on the Bar–Podgorica route stop on the highway. The train station is off the main road, 800m south of town. There are seven trains to/from Bar (€1.20, 23 minutes) and Podgorica (€1.40, 30 minutes) every day.

Murići Мурићи

POP 110

The southern edge of the lake is the most dramatic, with the Rumija Mountains rising precipitously from the water. From Virpazar there's a wonderful drive (or 56km mountain-biking route) following the contours of the lake through the mountains and an enchanting (possibly even enchanted) chestnut forest. The road heads towards the Albanian border before crossing the range and turning back towards Ulcinj. About halfway along the lake a steep side road descends to the village of Murići, a cluster of traditional buildings set around a mosque.

This is one of the lake's best swimming spots. The water's clear, if a little weedy, and swarms of little fish follow your feet as you kick up the nutrients beneath.

AGGRESSIVE TOUTS

We've received many complaints about cars being stopped as they enter Virpazar and given the hard sell for a particular hotel and their boat tours. We strongly recommend that you politely ignore such advances, park elsewhere and speak to the nice folks at the visitor centre before committing to anything.

The **Murići Vacation Resort** (☎069-688 288; www.nacionalnipark-izletistemurici.com; cabin per person €25, campsite per person/car/campervan €5/5/10) has simple log cabins sharing a decent ablutions block, nestled within an olive grove on the lakeshore. There's also a shady outdoor restaurant (mains €5 to €9) but if you're nervous about dogs, this might not be for you.

Islands

An archipelago of islands traces the southern edge of the lake and, in true Montenegrin fashion, many of them shelter monasteries.

Moračnik is one such island monastery dating from at least the early 15th century. Its small domed stone church dedicated to the Holy Virgin is watched over by a tower-like accommodation block occupied by a friendly monk.

In the early years of the new millennium, an exceedingly welcoming community of nuns revived **Beška Monastery** after 300 years of abandonment. Fourteenth-century St George's Church has been completely gutted, pending funds for restoration, but the smaller Church of the Annunciation is in active use. It was built in 1440 and contains traces of once extensive frescoes. An orchard of fruit trees has been lovingly rejuvenated by the sisters; don't be surprised if they offer you some of their homegrown pomegranate juice.

Both this monastery and its neighbour on **Starčevo** were once famous for producing religious scripts. Starčevo Monastery was named somewhat unflatteringly after the hermit who founded the monastery in 1377; it translates as Old Man's Monastery. Revived in the last three decades, Starčevo has an old man once again – a hermit monk who would prefer not to be disturbed (entertaining tourists isn't part of the hermit job description).

LOCAL KNOWLEDGE

KRSTINJA PETRANOVIĆ, LAKE SKADAR

When Krstinja isn't working at the National Park Visitor Centre or the Virpazar Tourist Office, she acts as the secretary of the Green Boats Association.

Top Recommendations

I always start by asking [visitors] what their interests are, as there are a lot of activities they can do here. We have a lot of hiking trails, they can rent a kayak, and of course there are the boat trips.

A Typical Two-Hour Cruise

Starting from Virpazar you would first go to the prison island Grmožur and then to a beach near the small fishing village of Pristan – nobody has lived there since the 1979 earthquake. Then you would head to Raduš, another fishing village, which is situated at the deepest part of the lake where there's an underwater spring. We always allow at least 25 minutes for swimming on our trips. After that you could go to the middle of the bird reserve before heading back.

Visiting Local Wineries

If you come to the tourist office we can tell you which of the small wineries is definitely open for visitors – we can even call ahead to check for you and to let the owner know you're coming. Even if the winemaker doesn't speak any English, there's often someone in the family who can. It shouldn't cost more than €5 for tastings.

Grmožur, closest to Virpazar, is topped by a fortress (1843) that was used mainly as a prison and nicknamed 'the Montenegrin Alcatraz'.

On the other side of the causeway, in the swampy northwestern reaches of Lake Skadar, stands **Kom Monastery** (www.manastirkom.org). Its Church of the Dormition (1415) has the best-preserved frescoes of any of the lake's many churches.

Getting There & Away

Moračnik, Beška and Starčevo are best reached from Murići. Boats are easy to find in summer, but you might need to ask around at other times. Expect to pay about €20 per hour.

Grmožur is a regular stop on boat trips from Virpazar and Vranjina (the boats are considerably cheaper from Virpazar).

Kom is most easily reached by boat from Vranjina. In the height of summer it can be approached by a path leading through the marshes from near Žabljak Crnojevića.

Vranjina — Врањина

POP 210

The twin hills on Vranjina island are nicknamed Sofia Loren by the locals for reasons that become apparent when they're viewed from afar. The main **National Park Visitor Centre** (020-879 103; www.nparkovi.me; admission €2; free with National Park entry ticket; 8am-4pm, to 6pm summer) rests in the shade of their cleavage on the opposite side of the causeway leading to Podgorica from Virpazar. This modern facility has excellent displays about all the national parks, not just Lake Skadar, including lots of taxidermied critters and an ethnographic section that features folk costumes and tools. You can buy national park entry tickets (€4) and fishing permits (per day summer/winter €10/5) from a kiosk outside.

Montenegro's largest wine company, **Plantaže** (9am-9pm), sells its range from a shop built into a cave by the car park. In the busy months tour operators set up kiosks nearby.

Kings Travel (069-310 050; www.kingsmn.com; May-Oct) offers a variety of boat tours, from €20 per hour for a barge to €65 per hour for a 'fast boat'; both take up to five passengers. The Green Boats also depart from here, although they charge more from Vranjina than they do from Virpazar.

Just along the causeway are the remains of the 19th-century fortress **Lesendro**. The busy highway and railway tracks prevent land access to the site.

The Vranjina walking trail leads to **St Nicholas' Monastery** (Manastir Sv Nikole), a 13th-century complex that's been destroyed in many wars; the current building dates from the 19th century. The monastery is a regular stop on boat tours.

Plavnica Плавница

Day trippers from Podgorica escape the summer heat at the upmarket **Plavnica Eco Resort** (020-443 700; www.plavnica.info; ste €130-180; P ❄ 📶 🏊), where there's an impressive pool (day use €10) set within an amphitheatre that's sometimes used for live performances. The resort has a suitably glam boat that's used for lake tours, and you can hire catamarans (€70 per hour), canoes (€4), kayaks (€3) and pedal boats (€6).

It may have all the ambience of a reception hall, but the cavernous restaurant (mains €7 to €18) is an excellent place to try the local *krap* (relax, it's the Montenegrin word for carp). Upstairs are four lavishly furnished suites, each sleeping two adults and potentially a small child.

To get here, head towards Podgorica from the National Park Visitor Centre. After 11km turn right at the large white war memorial in Golubovci and head back down in the direction of the lake for 6km. The resort's at the end of the road.

Žabljak Crnojevića Жабљак Црнојевића

For a brief time in the 15th century, between the fall of Skadar (now Shkodra in Albania) and the founding of Cetinje, this was the capital of Zetan ruler Ivan Crnojević. Now the enigmatic ruins stand forlornly on a lonely hillside surrounded by lush green plains with only some rather large snakes and spiders as occupants.

Walking up from the small village that time forgot at its base, the 14m-high, 2m-thick walls look intimidating enough, yet even these couldn't withstand the hammering the Ottoman invaders gave them in 1478 when the town was finally abandoned.

The site's a little hard to find but well worth the effort. Heading towards Podgorica, turn left at the only set of traffic lights in Golubovci. After the railway bridge and the one-way bridge, turn left. Continue for about 4.5km until you see a bridge to your left. Cross the bridge and continue to the car park near the village. Take the stone stairs heading up from the path near the river and follow your nose past the village church and along the overgrown path.

Podgorica Подгорица

POP 151,000

Podgorica (pronounced 'pod·go·ri·tsa') is never going to be Europe's most happening capital but if you can get past the sweltering summer temperatures and concrete apartment blocks, you'll find a pleasant little city with lots of green space and some excellent galleries and bars.

The city sits at the confluence of two rivers. West of the broad Morača is what passes for the business district. The smaller Ribnica River divides the eastern side in two. To the south is Stara Varoš, the heart of the Ottoman town. North of the Ribnica is Nova Varoš, an attractive, mainly low-rise precinct of late-19th to early-20th-century buildings housing a lively mixture of shops and bars. At its heart is Trg Republika, the main square.

Sights

Museums & Galleries of Podgorica MUSEUM
(Muzeji i Galerije Podgorice; 020-242 543; Marka Miljanova 4; 9am-8pm) FREE Despite Cetinje nabbing most of the national endowment, the new capital is well served by this collection of art and artefacts. There's an interesting section on Podgorica's history which includes antiquities exhumed from Doclea, its Roman incarnation, the remains of which are in the northern fringes of the modern city. Look out for Petar Lubarda's large canvas *Titograd* (1956) in the foyer.

Stara Varoš NEIGHBOURHOOD
Podgorica's oldest neighbourhood retains traces of the 400 years in which it was the centre of a bustling Ottoman Turkish town. The blocky **clock tower** (Sahat Kula; Trg Bećir-Bega Osmanagića) overlooking the square was useful for signalling Muslim prayer times. In the maze of streets behind it, two mosques remain. You wouldn't know to look at it, but the **Doganjska Mosque** (Nemaljića bb) has its origins in the 15th century. More impressive is the 18th-century **Osmanagić Mosque** (Spasa Nikolića bb), which Turkish money has helped to restore.

At the confluence of the two rivers is the ruin of the **Ribnica Fortress** (Tvrđava na Ribnici), built by the Ottomans after their conquest in 1474. The best-preserved element is a little arched bridge crossing the Ribnica. The pebbly Morača riverbank now

Podgorica

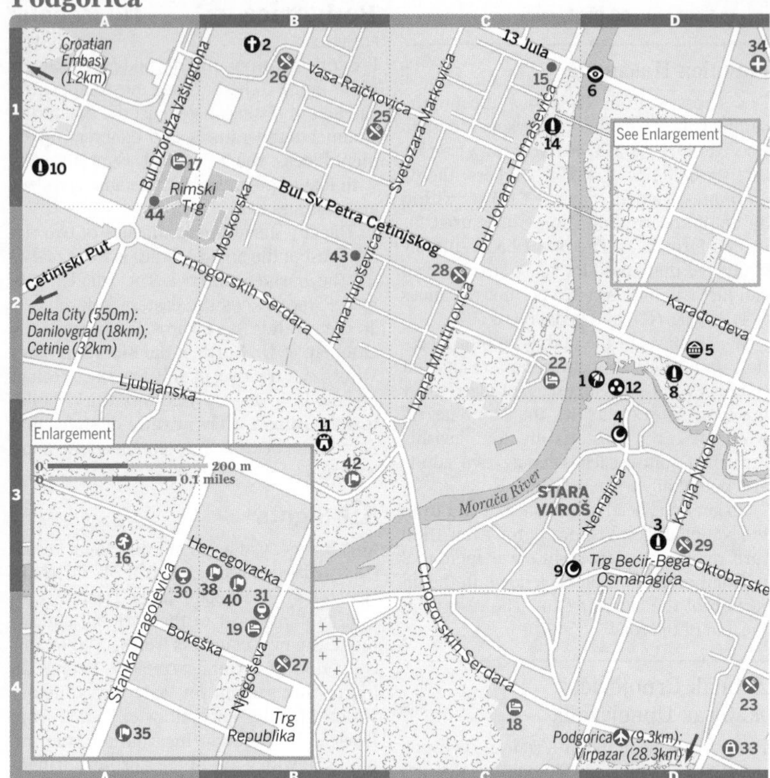

serves as Podgorica's main **beach**, complete with a summertime bar, deckchairs and sun umbrellas.

Petrović Palace PALACE, GALLERY
(Dvorac Petrovića; ☎020-243 513; www.csucg.co.me; Ljubljanska bb; ⏱9am-2pm & 5-10pm Mon-Fri, 10am-2pm Sat) FREE The Contemporary Art Centre operates two galleries in Podgorica. The bottom two floors of this former palace are given over to high-profile exhibitions, while the top floor has an oddball collection of traditional and modern art (Indonesian batik, a metal palm tree from Iraq, revolutionary themed paintings from South America) from its days as Yugoslavia's gallery devoted to art from countries belonging to the Non-Aligned Movement.

The leafy grounds contain interesting sculptures, a tiny church and another exhibition space in the former guardhouse (Perjanički Dom). Temporary exhibitions are also staged in the small **Galerija Centar** (☎020-665 409; Njegoševa 2; ⏱10am-1pm & 2-6pm Mon-Fri, 10am-1pm Sat) FREE.

Cathedral of Christ's Resurrection CHURCH
(Saborni Hram Hristovog Vaskrsenja; www.hramvaskrsenjapg.org; Bul Džordža Vašingtona) The large dome, white stone towers and gold crosses of this immense Serbian Orthodox cathedral are a striking addition to Podgorica's skyline. Work commenced in 1993 and it's still a long way from completion, but you can usually enter and check out the glistening gold frescoes inside.

Public Sculpture MONUMENTS
For a city formerly known as Titograd (literally 'Tito-city'), there is an inordinate number of royal sculpture dotted around its many parks. The most imposing is the huge bronze statue of **Petar I Petrović Njegoš** standing on a black marble plinth on the Ce-

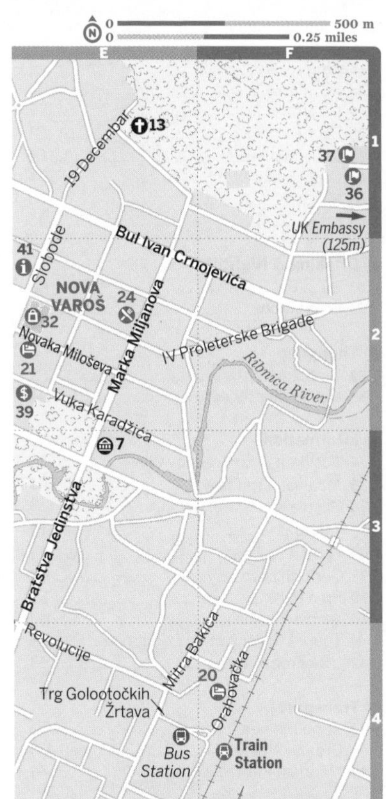

tinje edge of town. A large equestrian statue of **Nikola I** struts grandly opposite the parliament at the head of a lovely park with manicured hedges and mature trees.

You won't find Tito anywhere but there is a spectacularly cheesy statue of Russian singer **Vladimir Visockij** near the **Millennium Bridge**, pictured shirtless with a guitar and a skull at his feet.

St George's Church CHURCH

(Crkva Sv Đorđa; 19 Decembar bb) Sitting behind castle-like walls on the lower slopes of Gorica hill (Podgorica means 'under Gorica'), this little Orthodox church is the city's oldest. Inside, the remains of centuries-old frescoes are more interesting than the relatively modern gilded iconostasis. More fascinating still is the thoroughly creepy overgrown cemetery behind the enclosure.

Activities & Tours

Timberland PLAYGROUND

(Stanka Dragojevića bb; admission €1.50; 9am-11pm Apr-Oct) Let the little ones off the leash in this colourful private playground.

Montenegro Adventures ADVENTURE TOURS

(020-208 000; www.montenegro-adventures.com; Jovana Tomaševića 35) This well-respected and long-standing agency creates tailor-made adventure tours, country-wide. It can organise mountain guides, cycling logistics, kitesurfing, hiking, cultural activities, accommodation, flights... you name it.

Sleeping

Most visitors to Podgorica are here for business, either commerce or government-related. Hotels set their prices accordingly and private accommodation isn't really an option.

Aria HOTEL €€

(020-872 572; www.hotelaria.me; Mahala bb; s €56-76, d €93, apt €132-205;) An oasis of green lawns in the scorched field surrounding the airport, this new hotel offers better value than its city equivalents and is a great option if you've got a badly timed flight. The interiors offset dark wooden furniture with local stone. Airport transfers included.

Hotel Evropa HOTEL €€

(020-623 444; www.hotelevropa.co.me; Orahovačka 16; s €40-55, d €70-90; P@) It's hardly a salubrious location, but Evropa is handy to the train and bus stations and offers good clean rooms with comfortable beds, writing desks and decent showers. Despite its diminutive size there's a sauna and ample parking.

Hotel Kerber HOTEL €€

(020-405 405; www.hotelkerber.co.me; Novaka Miloševa 6; s €56-79, d €99;) It's an odd set-up, with the hotel accessed from the rear of a central city shopping centre draped in fake ivy. However, the rooms are good, clean and surprisingly quiet. Plus the name is pronounced a bit like 'carebear', which is kinda cute. The 'economic' single would be great value if the shower wasn't directly above the toilet.

Hotel Podgorica HOTEL €€€

(020-402 500; www.hotelpodgorica.co.me; Bul Sv Petra Cetinjskog 1; s €125-155, d €170-180, ste €190-200; P@) A wonderful showcase of 1960s Yugoslav architecture, the

Podgorica

Sights

1	Beach	D2
2	Cathedral of Christ's Resurrection	B1
3	Clock tower	D3
4	Doganjska mosque	D3
5	Galerija Centar	D2
6	Millennium Bridge	D1
7	Museums & Galleries of Podgorica	E3
8	Nikola I statue	D2
9	Osmanagić Mosque	C3
10	Petar I Petrović Njegoš statue	A1
11	Petrović Palace	B3
12	Ribnica Fortress	D2
13	St George's Church	E1
14	Vladimir Visockij Statue	C1

Activities, Courses & Tours

15	Montenegro Adventures	C1
16	Timberland	A3

Sleeping

17	Best Western Hotel Podgorica	A1
18	City Hotel	C4
19	Hotel Eminent	B4
20	Hotel Evropa	F4
21	Hotel Kerber	E2
22	Hotel Podgorica	C2

Eating

23	Big Market	D4
24	Laterna	E2
25	Leonardo	B1
26	Little Market	B1
27	Lupo di Mare	B4
28	Mantra	C2
29	Maxi	D3

Drinking & Nightlife

30	Buda Bar	A3
31	Greenwich	B4

Shopping

32	Gradska Knjižara	E2
33	Mall of Montenegro	D4

Information

34	Accident & Emergency Clinic	D1
35	Albanian Embassy	A4
36	Bosnia & Hercegovinian Embassy	F1
37	French Embassy	F1
38	German Embassy	B3
39	Prva Bank	E2
40	Serbian Embassy	B3
41	Tourist Organisation Podgorica	E2
42	USA Embassy	B3

Transport

43	Adria Airlines	B2
	Croatia Airlines	(see 43)
44	Meridian Rentacar	A1

Podgorica has been luxuriously modernised yet retains its period charm – the river-stone cladding blending into stone the shade of Montenegro's mountains. The best rooms have terraces facing the river.

City Hotel HOTEL €€€
(020-441 500; www.cityhotelmn.com; Crnogorskih serdara 5; s €75-95, d €100-120, apt €130-170; P ❄ @) A business-orientated makeover in 2008 has thankfully kept the 1970s exterior angularity of this city-fringe hotel, while the surrealist art of Dado Đurić has prevented a total beige-out inside. There's a small gym, comfy furnishings and helpful English-speaking staff.

Best Western Hotel Podgorica HOTEL €€€
(020-406 500; www.bestwestern-ce.com/montenegro; Bul Sv Petra Cetinjskog 145; s/d from €135/205; P ❄) Even the standard rooms are spacious at this upmarket hotel, focused squarely on the business market. Expect the usual generically smart decor and marble bathrooms. Parking is available for €15 per day.

Hotel Eminent HOTEL €€€
(020-664 646; www.eminent.co.me; Njegoševa 25; s €85-95, d €130-135; ❄) Given its location and excellent facilities, the Eminent seems to be set up for businesspeople keen on an after-work tipple. The front rooms can be noisy but the comfortable mezzanine apartments open on to a covered verandah at the rear.

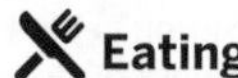

Head to the **little market** (Moskovska bb) or the **big market** (Bratstva Jedinstva bb) for fresh fruit and vegetables, and the large **Maxi** (Kralja Nikole bb; 7am-midnight Mon-Sat, 7.30am-3.30pm Sun) supermarket for other cooking supplies.

Laterna PIZZERIA, MONTENEGRIN €
(020-232 331; Marka Miljanova 41; mains €4-13; 9am-midnight Mon-Sat;) Farm imple-

ments hang from the rough stone walls creating a surprisingly rustic ambience for the centre of the city. A selection of meat and fish grills is offered, but it's hard to go past the crispy-based pizza – it's quite possibly Montenegro's best.

★Lupo di Mare SEAFOOD €€
(Trg Republika 22; mains €8-20; 8am-midnight) As you may have guessed from the name, there's a distinct Italian bent to this excellent seafood restaurant. Nautical knick-knacks hang from the pale stone walls and there's an interesting wine list, heavily slanted towards regional producers.

Leonardo ITALIAN €€
(020-242 902; www.leonardo-restoran.com; Svetozara Markovića bb; mains €5-17; 8am-midnight;) Leonardo's unlikely position at the centre of a residential block makes it a little tricky to find but the effort's well rewarded by accomplished Italian cuisine. The pasta dishes are delicious and reasonably priced, given the upmarket ambience, while the €5 pizzas should leave even those on a budget with a *Mona Lisa* smile.

Mantra INDIAN €€
(Ivana Milutinovića 21; mains €6-11;) In a country where any cuisine from further away than Italy is considered exotic, this opulently decorated Indian restaurant comes as a pleasant surprise – and a welcome relief for vegetarian travellers bored of pizza and pasta, and vegans sick of salad. Ask for 'spicy' if you want any hint of a kick.

Drinking & Nightlife

Podgorica's nightlife is centred on Nova Varoš, particularly in the blocks west of Ulica Slobode. The hippest strip right now is Ulica Bokeška.

Buda Bar BAR
(067-344 944; www.facebook.com/Budabarpg; Stanka Dragojevića 26; 8am-2am) A golden Buddha smiles serenely as you meditate over your morning coffee or search for the eternal truth at the bottom of a cocktail glass. This is one slick watering hole; the tent-like semi-enclosed terrace is the place to be on balmy summer nights, especially when there's a local starlet performing.

Greenwich BAR
(www.facebook.com/greenwichpg; Njegoševa 29; 8am-3am) The name may remain but the decor's shifted from London to Los Angeles (is that Barbra Streisand on the ceiling?), in this popular late-night cafe-bar.

Shopping

The pedestrian-only section of Hercegovačka is Podgorica's best window-shopping strip. Two malls, **Delta City** (www.deltacity.me; Cetinjski Put; 9am-10pm Mon-Sat, 9am-8pm Sun) and **Mall of Montenegro** (www.mallofmontenegro.com; Bul Bratstva i Jedinstva; 9am-10pm Mon-Sat, 9am-8pm Sun), have opened in recent years.

Gradska Knjižara BOOKS
(Trg Republika 40; 8am-10pm) Head upstairs for a small but interesting selection of English-language titles, including translations of Balkan classics.

Information

Accident & Emergency Clinic (Hitna Pomoć; 124; Vaka Djurovića bb)

Tourist Organisation Podgorica (020-667 535; www.podgorica.travel; Slobode 47; 8am-8pm Mon-Fri)

Getting There & Away

BUS

Podgorica's **bus station** (020-620 430; Trg Golootočkih Žrtava 1) has a left-luggage service, a post office, an ATM, a restaurant and regular services to all major towns, including Herceg Novi (€9, three hours), Kotor (€7, 2¼ hours), Budva (€6, 1½ hours), Ulcinj (€6, one hour) and Cetinje (€3.50, 30 minutes).

International destinations include Priština (€17, daily), Sarajevo (€19, six daily), Dubrovnik (€19, daily) and Belgrade (€27, frequent).

CAR

Hire-car agencies with counters at Podgorica Airport include Alamo, Avis, Europcar, Hertz, National and Sixt. Local agency **Meridian** (020-234 944; www.meridian-rentacar.com; Bul Džordža Vašingtona 85) also has a city office; one-day hire starts from €30.

TRAIN

From Podgorica's **train station** (020-441 211; www.zpcg.me; Trg Golootočkih Žrtava 13) there are services to Bar (€2.40, one hour, nine daily), Virpazar (€1.40, 30 minutes, seven daily), Nikšić (€2.80, one hour, five daily), Kolašin (€5, 90 minutes, five daily), Bijelo Polje (€5.20, two hours, six daily) and Belgrade (€20, 10 hours, three daily).

Getting Around

TO/FROM THE AIRPORT

Podgorica airport is 9km south of the city. Taxis from the airport charge a standard €15 fare to the city centre but metered taxis from Podgorica to the airport should cost less than €8.

BUS

It's not difficult to explore Podgorica on foot but if you fancy trying a local bus, they cost 80c for a short journey.

TAXI

Alo Taxi (☎19700)
City Taxi (☎19711; www.citytaxi.com)

Danilovgrad Даниловград

POP 5200

Little Danilovgrad, located 18km northwest of Podgorica, is worth a short stop en route to Ostrog or Nikšić. There's a smattering of cafes on the main street, Ulica Baja Sekulića, which runs between two attractive squares.

The one nearest the Zeta River is dominated by an impressive socialist realist **monument** featuring two likely lads and a staunch woman topped by a red star. Below the monument there's a wonderful **sculpture garden** featuring dozens of interesting works carved out of white marble, ranging from the classic to the space-age.

In late August the three-day **River Zeta Festival** takes place featuring wooden raft and kayak races; diving, fishing and beauty contests; and an organic-food festival.

Ostrog Monastery Манастир Острог

Resting in a cliff face 900m above the Zeta valley, the gleaming white **Ostrog Monastery** (Manastir Ostrog) is the most important site in Montenegro for Orthodox Christians, attracting up to a million visitors annually. Even with its numerous pilgrims, tourists and trashy souvenir stands, it's a strangely affecting place.

The **Lower Monastery** (Donji manastir) is 2km below the main shrine. Stop here to admire the vivid frescoes in the **Holy Trinity Church** (Crkva Sv Trojice; 1824). Behind it is a natural spring where you can fill your bottles with deliciously fresh water and potentially benefit from an internal blessing as you sup it.

From here the faithful, some of them barefoot, plod up the steep road to the top. Halfway up, the beautiful stone walls of the little domed **Church of St Stanko the Martyr** (Crkva Sv Mučenika Stanka) gleam golden in the sunset. Nonpilgrims and the pure of heart may drive directly to the main car park and limit their penitance to just the final 200m.

The **Upper Monastery** (Gornji manastir; the really impressive one) is dubbed 'Sv Vasilije's miracle', because no one seems to understand how it was built. Constructed in 1665 within two large caves, it gives the impression that it has grown out of the very rock. Sv Vasilije (St Basil), a bishop from Hercegovina, brought his monks here after the Ottomans destroyed Tvrdoš Monastery near Trebinje.

Pilgrims queue to enter the atmospheric shrine where the saint's fabric-wrapped bones are kept. To enter you'll need to be wearing a long skirt or trousers (jeans are fine) and cover your shoulders. Most women also cover their heads with a scarf. It's customary to back out of the doorways and you'll witness much kissing of lintels and making of signs of the cross from the devout. At the very top of the monastery is another cave-like chapel with faded frescoes dating from 1667.

A **guesthouse** (☎020-811 133; dm €5) near the Lower Monastery offers tidy single-sex dorm rooms, while in summer sleeping mats are provided for free to pilgrims in front of the Upper Monastery.

Getting There & Away

There's no public transport but numerous tour buses head here from all of the tourist hot spots. Expect to pay about €17 to €20 for a day trip from the coast.

If you're driving we strongly recommend that you take the excellent new road from Danilovgrad to the monastery. The old road leaves the main Podgorica–Nikšić highway 19km past Danilovgrad. It's extremely narrow, twisting and steep and in a very poor state of repair; in short, it's terrifying.

Nikšić Никшић

POP 57,000

Montenegro's second-biggest city isn't high on most tourists' must-see lists and neither should it be. But if you fancy a blow-out in a lively student town, Nikšić (pronounced '*nik*·shich') has an array of establishments that offer a more genuine (not to mention cheaper) Montenegrin experience than the tourist-populated bars of Budva. What else would you expect in the town that produces Nikšićko Pivo, the nation's favourite beer?

Nikšić isn't just a university town; it's also one of Montenegro's main industrial centres, supporting a large steel mill and bauxite mine.

Sights

Nikšić Heritage Museum MUSEUM, PALACE

(Zavičajni muzej Nikšić; Trg Šaka Petrovića; adult/child €1/50c; 9am-1pm & 5-8pm Tue-Sat, 9am-noon Sun) King Nikola must have kept the country's builders busy as there's yet another of his palaces here (adding to those in Cetinje, Podgorica and Bar). Now used as a museum it's badly in need of a renovation rescue to deal with the water stains and general decay.

Start upstairs to the right in the prehistoric section (where there are various flints dating to the 3rd millennium BC) and progress past the bronze armour and iron spearheads to the lovingly decorated guns, jewel-encrusted armour and embroidered clothes in the ethnographic section. WWII is covered by photographs and memorabilia but none of the explanations are in English. You'll find that the graves of many of the fallen Partisan comrades pictured here are in the nearby cemetery. Outside the museum are *stećci*, similar to those outside Cetinje's Vlach Church (p94).

St Basil of Ostrog's Cathedral CHURCH

(Saborna crkva Svetog Vasilija Ostroškog; Trg Šaka Petrovića) Sitting grandly on top of a pine-covered hill, Nikšić's hefty Serbian Orthodox cathedral was built between 1895 and 1900. A central dome floods the interior with light and massive chandeliers hang from the ceiling. The exquisite iconostasis is painted in the realistic style popular in the early 20th century, as opposed to the Byzantine look of the more recent icons. Look for local saints Peter of Cetinje and Basil of Ostrog on either side of the sanctuary doors.

Freedom Square SQUARE

(Trg Slobode) The heart of Nikšić is this large open area at the centre of Ulica Njegoševa, the main street. On summer nights what seems like the entire population – from toddlers to the elderly – parade up and down the square. On one side is a hefty bronze equestrian statue of King Nikola, while the other side has a fountain set around a modern sculpture.

Onogošt Fortress FORTRESS

The original Nikšić was built within sturdy walls on a rocky hill to the west of the current town. This was the site of a 4th-century Roman military base that was taken over by the Goths and fortified. Part of it has been restored and is used as a summer stage, although when we visited it was covered in graffiti and broken glass.

From Ulica Njegoševa take Ulica Narodnih Heroja to the end, where you'll see the fortress ahead of you.

Tours

Anitra Travel Agency ADVENTURE TOURS

(040-200 598; www.tara-grab.com; Njegoševa 12) Owned by the same company as Kamp Grab (p114), this local agency can arrange all kinds of active expeditions, including rafting, canyoning, hiking, fishing, mountain-biking and jeep safaris.

Sleeping & Eating

★ **Hotel Marshal** HOTEL €€€

(040-223 504; www.marshalgroup.me; Partizanski Put bb; s €50-75, d €100; P ❄ 📶) On the northern fringe of the city, 2.5km from the centre, this shiny new hotel is the best place to stay in Nikšić by far. Ask for a rear room; they're quieter and have mountain views. Breakfast is served on the terrace of the 1st-floor restaurant.

★ **Ibon** PIZZERIA, CAFE €

(Trg Šaka Petrovića; mains €2-6.50; 7.30am-11pm) Facing the park near the museum, this flash cafe's terrace is a lovely spot for a morning coffee (a mere snip at 80c) and an omelette or pancake. The pizza's excellent too.

Fontana ICE CREAM €

(Njegoševa bb; snacks €1-3) A popular spot on the main drag for enjoying coffee, cakes and delicious ice cream. The blue-grey and chrome interior makes you feel a little like you're sitting in a classic Cadillac.

Konoba Portun MONTENEGRIN €€

(040-212 336; Njegoševa bb; mains €6-12; 8am-11pm) The city centre's only proper restaurant is accessed by an unlikely corridor leading from the main street. The usual national specialities come in massive serves, accompanied by fries and vegetables.

Drinking

The main strip goes crazy on a Saturday night. There seems to be a higher concentration of bars and cafes on Njegoševa than anywhere else in the country and on the weekends most seem to operate under the assumption that the loudest is the best.

De Bova BAR
(Novice Cerovića bb) One of the few quiet establishments in town is this pub-like place where you can have a beer while photos of Jimmy Page and The Beatles look on.

Information

You'll find banks with ATMs, the post office and pharmacies on the main street, Njegoševa.

General Hospital (Opšta bolnica; ☎040-244 216; Radoja Dakića bb)

Getting There & Away

BUS

The **bus station** (☎040-213 018; Gojka Garčevića bb) is next to the main roundabout and has toilets, restaurants and a left-luggage counter (€1). Domestic destinations include Kotor (€8.50, three hours, seven daily), Budva (€7.50, two hours, 10 daily), Podgorica (€3.50, one hour, frequent), Plužine (€6.50, one hour, six daily) and Žabljak (€9, 2½ hours, six daily). International services include Trebinje (€6.50, three daily), Sarajevo (€15.50, three daily) and Belgrade (€26, every second day).

TAXI

Nik Taxi (☎19733)

TRAIN

Train Station (☎040-214 418; www.zpcg.me; Gojka Garčevića bb) Five trains a day head to/from Podgorica (€2.80, one hour) via Danilovgrad and Ostrog.

Around Nikšić

Travelling west on the road to Trebinje in Hercegovina, a large sign on the left (3.5km after the small roundabout on the edge of town) points to **Most na Moštanici**, an ancient Roman bridge. It's hard to find as there are no other signs once you leave the main road. Coming off the road turn sharp left and then right. Veer left after about 300m and head alongside the village. After a kilometre you'll see the bridge near a sturdy little church. The bridge's five graceful arches span a ditch that's now completely dry: it seems that it has outlasted the river itself!

Heading in the same direction, a few kilometres past the turn-off to the bridge, you'll pass **Lake Slano** (Slansko jezero) on your left. Although it's an artificial structure (there's a dam at one edge), its sparkling blue waters, low-lying islands and green borders make for a beautiful vista. There are a few tiny villages on the shore but there's no straightforward route down to the water; take whatever turn-off you can find and wind your way down. You'll be unlikely to find more than a few people fishing or sunbathing.

More popular is **Lake Krupac** (Krupačko jezero), another dammed lake to the northwest of town, which is sometimes tagged 'Nikšić's sea'. It has a small sandy beach, a couple of beach bars, picnic spots under the poplar trees and pedal boats, jet skis and kayaks for hire. The waters are stocked with California trout.

There are four ski slopes at **Vučje** (☎067-319 719; www.vucje.me; day pass adult/child €10/5), 21km northeast of Nikšić on the road to Šavnik.

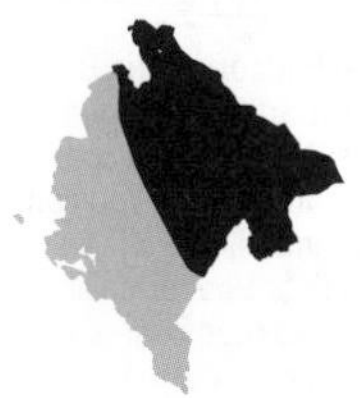

Northern Mountains

Includes ➡

Best Places to Eat

- Konoba kod Rada Vlahovića (p110)
- Vodenica (p111)
- Savardak (p111)
- Aqua (p120)
- Zlatni Papagaj (p117)

Best Places to Stay

- Eko-Oaza Suza Evrope (p116)
- Hotel Soa (p117)
- Bianca Resort & Spa (p110)
- Brile (p110)
- Eko Selo Meadows (p116)

Why Go?

The mountainous north's premier attractions are its three national parks. Durmitor combines soaring peaks with the depths of the Tara Canyon, allowing for excellent skiing in winter and rafting in summer. Biogradska Gora shelters large swathes of ancient forest within the protecting arms of the Bjelasica mountains. If you're after something more extreme, serious mountain-lovers can take on the lofty reaches of Prokletije, the Accursed Mountains.

Locals will try to dissuade you from going anywhere other than Kolašin and Žabljak as these are the only towns that have a significant level of tourist infrastructure. This serves to give an off-the-beaten-track feel to almost any other place you might choose to explore.

You don't need to be an action hero to experience the beauty of this untamed region. Just hire a car for a few days and let the back roads lead you somewhere unexpected.

When to Go

- In January and February spend your days skiing and your nights feasting in front of an open fire.
- July and August have the best hiking weather, with average Durmitor temperatures in the low 20s (Celsius).
- Watch the forest explode in colour in September and October as autumn hits Biogradska Gora.

Climate

It shouldn't surprise anyone that this mountainous region is cooler than the rest of the country. Average high temperatures range from just above freezing in January to the low 20s in August.

Getting There & Away

The main highway between Podgorica and Belgrade cuts through Mojkovac and Bijelo Polje and is well served by buses. A major road connects Nikšić to Durmitor National Park. You can travel to Kolašin, Mojkovac and Bijelo Polje by train from Serbia in the north or Podgorica and Bar in the south. There are also road connections with Bosnia, Serbia and Kosovo.

Northern Mountains Highlights

1. Floating through paradise, rafting between the kilometre-plus walls of the **Tara Canyon** (p114) in Durmitor National Park
2. Being dwarfed by the scale of the views enveloping the **Andrijevica–Kolašin road** (p109)
3. Searching for wood nymphs in the primordial forest of **Biogradska Gora National Park** (p111)
4. Time-warping to the 13th century as you step through the gates of the **Morača Monastery** (p109)
5. People-watching as the evening promenade descends on **Rožaje's main street** (p118)
6. Seeking that peaceful Eastern feeling between the mosques and mountains of **Gusinje** (p121)
7. Taking a white-knuckle ride between the sheer cliffs and green depths of the **Piva Canyon** (p116)

Getting Around

South of Bijelo Polje, the Podgorica–Belgrade highway joins another highway leading through Berane and Rožaje. Buses take both of these routes. The road from Mojkovac to Žabljak is in excellent condition but gets twistier as it leaves the Tara Canyon and climbs into the mountains; this isn't a regular bus route. Plav is the most isolated town but it's reached by a scenic road used by frequent buses to Berane. It's possible to circle the Bjelasica mountains completely in a 136km loop. The most spectacular section is from Kolašin to Andrijevica, but it is prone to landslides in bad weather and avoided by buses.

It's possible to travel between Kolašin, Mojkovac and Bijelo Polje by train.

Morača Canyon
Кањон Морача

Heading north from Podgorica it doesn't take long before the scenery becomes breathtaking. The highway gets progressively more precarious as it follows the Morača River into a nearly perpendicular canyon, 300m to 400m deep. If you're driving, pull over into one of the viewing areas to enjoy it properly as this is an extremely busy and unforgiving stretch of road.

The river continues after the canyon recedes and near its banks, 46km from Podgorica, you'll find the **Morača Monastery** (Manastir Morača). Along with Ostrog, Cetinje and Piva, this is one of the most important Orthodox monasteries in Montenegro, with some of its most accomplished religious art.

As you enter the walled compound into a garden courtyard where the bees from the monks' hives dance between the hydrangeas and roses, it's like stepping back into the 13th century, when the monastery was founded. To the right, the small **St Nicholas' Church** (Crkva Sv Nikole) has faded frescoes on its facade which were once as vivid as those inside. You can still make out the Madonna and Child above the door and an archangel on either side.

The larger **Church of the Dormition** (Crkva Uspenja Bogorodice) has external frescoes by the celebrated master Đorđe Mitrofanović, as well as beautiful doors inlaid with geometric patterns. In the vestibule there's a fascinating vision of Christ sitting in judgment, attended by saints. A slide of flames shoots the damned into hell where two-headed people-eating sea monsters do their worst. Look for the angels spearing little demons in the face to prevent them from tipping the scales of justice.

The church's treasures include Mitrofanović's *The Virgin Enthroned with Child, Prophets and Hymnographers* (1617), which sits within the iconostasis, to the left of the sanctuary door. The other master at work here was Kozma, whose icon of *Saints Sava and Simeon* (1645), on the right-hand wall, includes a border showing the construction of the monastery (the latter saint was the founder's grandfather). Also look to the left of the iconostasis for the icon of St Luke (by an unknown painter) depicting the apostle painting an icon of the Madonna and Child; this is probably a reference to the famous *Our Lady of Philermos* icon which now hangs in Cetinje.

Kolašin Колашин

POP 2800

Kolašin (pronounced 'ko·*la*·shin') is Montenegro's main mountain resort. Although the skiing's not as reliable as in Durmitor, Kolašin's much easier to get to (it's just off the main highway, 71km north of Podgorica) and has ritzier accommodation offerings. Like most ski towns, it looks far prettier under a blanket of snow but even in summer it's a handy base for exploring Biogradska Gora National Park or other parts of the Bjelasica Mountains.

Most things of interest, including banks and a post office, are set around the two central squares (Trg Borca and Trg Vukmana Kruščića) and the short street that connects them (Ulica IV Proleterske).

Sights & Activities

Heritage Museum MUSEUM
(Zavičajni muzej; Trg Borca 1; 8am-3pm) FREE
Trg Borca contains a stirring statue of a young man and woman marching forward, guns and communist flag aloft. They look like they're about to liberate the museum building, which served as a prison during WWII. Inside, the collection consists mainly of photos and there aren't any explanations in English, but the idealistic faces of the town's young comrades, many of whom lost their lives fighting the Nazis, are captivating. There's also an ethnographic section and an art gallery.

> **MOVING ON?**
>
> For tips, recommendations and reviews, head to shop.lonelyplanet.com to purchase downloadable PDFs of the Kosovo or Serbia chapters from Lonely Planet's *Eastern Europe* guide.

Kolašin 1450 Ski Resort SKIING
(020-717 845; www.kolasin1450.com; skiing half-day/day/week pass €12/20/104) Located 10km east of Kolašin, at an elevation of 1450m, this ski centre offers 30km of runs (graded green, blue, red and black) reached by various ski lifts, as well as a cafe and restaurant in attractive wooden chalets. You can hire a full ski or snowboard kit for €13 per day and there are shuttle buses from Bianca Resort & Spa; they're free if you're a hotel guest or if you purchase your ski pass from the hotel. The ski season lasts roughly from December to mid-April.

Hiking HIKING
Three marked hiking paths start from Trg Borca and head into the Bjelasica mountains. From the ski centre there's a 16km, five-hour loop route through the forest to Mt Ključ (1973m). A continuation of the trail knocks off Zekova Glava (2117m) and passes Lake Pešić (Pešićko jezero), skirting beneath Bjelasica's highest peak. On the loop back it visits the spring that is the source of the Biogradska River before heading up Troglava (2072m).

Before setting out on any of these hikes, stop in at the tourist office for advice and maps.

Mountain Biking MOUNTAIN BIKING
A 93km mountain-biking route running through remote countryside from Podgorica to Kolašin is detailed in the *Wilderness Biking* pamphlet (ask for it at the tourist office). There are plenty of places in Kolašin to hire bikes (including from Trg Borca in summer), so you could cycle to Podgorica and catch the train back.

Explorer Tourist Agency ADVENTURE TOURS
(020-864 200; www.montenegroexplorer.co.me; Mojkovačka bb) Located near the bus station, this agency specialises in action-packed holidays. It can arrange hiking, skiing, rafting, mountain biking, canyoning, caving, mountain climbing, jeep safaris, horse riding, paragliding and fishing expeditions. It also hires mountain bikes.

Sleeping

Premium prices are charged during the ski season, with the absolute peak being around New Year. In summer it's possible to stay high in the mountains in a traveller-friendly version of a traditional *katun* (wooden shepherd's hut); enquire at the tourist office or book through one of the adventure travel agencies.

Brile HOTEL, RESTAURANT €€
(020-865 021; www.montenegrohotelsonline.com/eng/hotel/46/brile.html; Buda Tomovića 2; s/d €35/70, mains €5-10;) On the edge of the main square, this attractive family-run hotel has comfy rooms with polished wooden floors. There's a sauna for an après-ski defrost and a restaurant downstairs serving warming comfort food like roasts, grilled meat, pizza and pasta. It also rents out bikes and skis.

Hotel Čile HOTEL €€
(020-865 039; www.zlatnido.com; Braće Miloševič bb; s/d €35/46, apt €60-80;) The name starts with a 'chill', but you'll be perfectly snug in this friendly minihotel near the centre of town. The studio apartments have a little more space than the double rooms and are fitted out with kitchenettes and stereos.

★**Bianca Resort & Spa** RESORT €€€
(020-863 000; www.biancaresort.com; Mirka Vešovića bb; s/d from €79/108;) Take one large angular hotel with quirky hexagonal windows, completely gut it and give it a designer rustic look and you end up with an atmospheric, idiosyncratic and first-rate ski resort. After a hard day's skiing you can soothe out any bumps and bruises in the luxury spa, which includes a large indoor pool, sauna, Turkish bath and gym.

Eating

★**Konoba kod Rada Vlahovića** MONTENEGRIN €€
(Trg Vukmana Kruščića; mains €6-8) Set on the square that was the heart of the old Turkish town, this rustic eatery is a standard-bearer for Montenegrin mountain cuisine, such as *kačamak* (polenta porridge with mashed potato), *cicvara* (creamy polenta), *popara* (bread-based porridge) and tender roast lamb that falls off the bone.

Vodenica MONTENEGRIN €€

(☎020-865 338; Dunje Dokić bb; mains €5-7) Set in a traditional watermill, Vodenica offers a taste of traditional stodgy mountain food designed to warm your belly on cold nights. Ease back and let your arteries clog over a bowl of *cicvara* or *kačamak*.

Savardak MONTENEGRIN €€

(☎069-051 264; savardak@t-com.me; mains €8-9) Located 2.8km from Kolašin on the road to the ski centre, Savardak serves traditional food in what looks like a big haystack with a chimney attached. Eat in the atmospheric interior or sit at outdoor tables by the stream. Four-person apartments (€40) are available in a thatch-roofed wooden chalet next door.

Information

Bjelasica & Komovi Regional Tourism Organisation (☎020-865 110; www.bjelasica-komovi.com; Trg Borca 2; ⏲9am-8pm Mon-Fri, 9am-noon & 4-8pm Sat & Sun) When it's open (it's often not) this impressive wooden information centre, very prominently located near the main square, should be your first port of call for information on hiking and mountain-biking routes. It can help arrange all manner of mountain activities and tours, including visits to local honey and cheese producers. It also rents out mountain bikes (per half-day/day €7/10).

Cultural Centre (Dom Kulture; Trg Borca 2; per hr 50c; ⏲10am-8pm Mon-Fri, noon-8pm Sat) Has an internet room above a souvenir shop.

Kolašin Tourist Office (☎020-864 254; www.kolasin.travel; Mirka Vešovića bb; ⏲8am-8pm Mon-Fri, 9am-3pm Sat) The town's tourist office is very useful for arranging private accommodation (including *katun* stays) and for information on local activities.

Getting There & Away

The **bus station** (☎020-864 033; Mojkovačka bb) is a wooden shed by a scrappy parking lot on the road leading into town, about 200m from the centre. Destinations include Pljevlja (€7, 2½ hours, five daily), Podgorica (€5, 1½ hours, frequent), Bar (€8, 2½ hours, five daily), Budva (€10, three hours, six daily) and Kotor (€12, 3¾ hours, four daily).

Kolašin's **train station** (☎020-441 492; www.zpcg.me) is 1.5km from the centre, with services to Bijelo Polje (€2.20, 30 minutes, four daily), Podgorica (€5, 90 minutes, five daily) and Bar (€5.48, 2½ hours, four daily). Buy your tickets on the train.

Biogradska Gora National Park Биоградска Гора

Nestled within the Bjelasica mountain range, this pretty national park has as its heart 1600 hectares of virgin woodland – one of Europe's last three remaining primeval forests. King Nikola is to thank for its survival; on a visit in 1878 he was so taken by the beauty of **Lake Biograd** (Biogradsko jezero) that the locals gifted him the land and he ordered it to be preserved.

The main entrance to the park is between Kolašin and Mojkovac on the Podgorica–Belgrade highway. After paying a €2 entry fee you can drive the further 4km to the lake. It really is exquisitely pretty and oh-so-green. If you're knowledgeable about such

BJELASICA MASSIF

The Bjelasica massif dominates northeastern Montenegro with 10 grand peaks higher than 2000m. The unfortunately named Crna Glava (Black Head) is the highest at 2139m.

Any preconception you may have of Montenegro's mountains as grey and barren will be shattered as the snows recede and reveal virgin forest (within the protected environs of Biogradska Gora National Park) and meadows teeming with wildflowers. In the higher pastures you'll find *katuns*, round thatched structures that have been used for centuries by seminomadic shepherds when they bring their flocks here in summer. It's a much more forgiving environment than the Orjen, Lovćen or Durmitor ranges and therefore easier to explore.

Trails are accessed from the towns that encircle the mountain: Kolašin, Mojkovac, Bijelo Polje, Berane and Andrijevica. The best times for hiking are at the end of summer and in autumn when the forests are a mash of colours. Be prepared for sudden drops in temperature and storms. Local tourist offices should be able to provide you with maps, information, advice and contacts for guides. Otherwise, talk to one of the agencies specialising in adventure holidays.

things, you'll be able to spot beech, fir, juniper, white ash, maple and elm trees. Occasional tour buses pull in, but a 10-minute stroll should shake the masses and quickly return you to tranquillity.

Most of the busloads head directly to **Restoran Biogradsko Jezero** (mains €5.70-9). It has a wonderful terrace where you can steal glimpses of the lake through the trees as you tuck into a traditional lamb or veal dish.

You can hire rowboats (€8 per hour) and buy fishing permits (€20 per day) from the **park office** (☎020-865 625; www.nparkovi.me; campsite per small tent/large tent/caravan €3/5/10, cabin €20; ⏰7.30am-8.30pm) by the car park. Nearby there's a campsite and a cluster of 12 small windowless log cabins, each with two or three single beds. The ablutions block for the cabins is much nicer than the campsite's basic squat toilets.

From the car park, a 17km loop track heads up **Mt Bendovac** (1774m) for awesome lake views before continuing up **Mt Razverše** (2033m). Apart from a couple of steep climbs, it's a fairly straightforward six-hour hike.

Getting There & Away

The nearest bus stop is an hour's walk from the lake, at Kraljevo Kolo, and the nearest train station is a 90-minute walk, at Štitarička Rijeka.

Mojkovac Мојковац

POP 3600

Despite being on the doorstep of two national parks, Mojkovac (pronounced '*moy*·ko·vahts') doesn't have a lot to offer tourists – at least not yet. Over recent years there's been a concerted effort to clean up the toxic legacy of centuries of silver, lead and zinc mining. Now that the task has been largely completed, the United Nations Development Programme has turned its attention to encouraging adventure tourism and organic farming – watch this space.

The centre of town is triangular Trg Ljubomira Bakoča, encompassing a pretty little park and a large pompous statue of Janko Vukotić, who led Montenegrin forces in a victory against Austria-Hungary in the WWI Battle of Mojkovac. Everything is laid out around the square, including a bank and a post office at its pointy end.

Surrounding it is a slew of decaying apartment blocks which residents have made an effort to decorate with flower boxes. On the approach to town there's a WWII memorial resembling a giant tooth; Mojkovac lost 10% of its population in the war.

A steep path leads from the centre of Mojkovac on a 17km (six-hour) loop through the surrounding mountains; take trail 310 and return on 319 and then 301. Mojkovac's railway station is the starting point of a 309km, six- to seven-day mountain-biking loop (Top Biking Trail 3: Eastern Enchantment) which takes in Biogradska Gora National Park, Gusinje, Plav and Rožaje.

Sleeping

Hotel Dulović HOTEL €€
(☎050-472 615; hoteldulovic@t-com.me; Trg Ljubomira Bakoča bb; s/d €20/40; 📶) Hidden in the corner of the square behind the park, this midsize hotel is a strictly perfunctory affair that's personality-less but clean. There's a restaurant downstairs that provides a decent cooked breakfast.

Hotel Palas HOTEL €€
(☎050-472 508; hotelpalasmojkovac@t-com.me; Podgorica–Belgrade hwy; s/d €24/43; P) Montenegro's pointiest hotel has the form of a set of interconnecting triangles collapsing into each other like a matryoshka doll. The rooms are clean and serviceable in an early-1980s kind of way, but it's certainly no palace.

Eating

Eating options are limited to a couple of shabby restaurants and bakeries selling the ubiquitous *burek* (meat or cheese pastry) near the bus station. The square has two grocery stores and several cafe-bars, some of which serve cake and ice cream.

Getting There & Away

Mojkovac's large **bus station** (☎050-470 133; Podgorica–Belgrade Highway) is a major stop on the Podgorica–Belgrade route. Destinations include Podgorica (€6, two hours,), Kolašin (€4, 35 minutes,), Pljevlja (€6.50, two hours) and Belgrade (€19, 9½ hours).

The **train station** is harder to find: take the road between the Hotel Palas and the cemetery; veer left past the timber yard; and keep going to the southern outskirts of town. Trains head from here to Bar (€6.20, 2¾ hours, three daily), Podgorica (€4.40, two hours, six daily) and Bijelo Polje (€1.20, 15 minutes, five daily).

Durmitor National Park
Национални парк Дурмитор

Magnificent scenery ratchets up to stupendous in this national park, where ice and water have carved a dramatic landscape from the limestone. Forty-eight peaks soar to over 2000m in altitude, with the highest, **Bobotov Kuk**, reaching 2523m. From December to March Durmitor is a major ski resort, while in summer it's a popular place for hiking, rafting and other active pursuits.

The park is home to enough critters to cast a Disney movie, including 163 species of bird, about 50 types of mammals and purportedly the greatest variety of butterflies in Europe. It's very unlikely you'll spot bears and wolves, which is either a good or bad thing depending on your perspective. We were assured that the wolves are only dangerous if they're really starving at the end of a long winter.

Durmitor National Park covers the Durmitor mountain range and a narrow branch heading east along the Tara River towards Mojkovac. **Žabljak**, at the eastern edge of the range, is the park's principal gateway and the only town within its boundaries. It's not very big and neither is it attractive, but it has a supermarket, a post office, a bank, hotels and restaurants, all gathered around the car park masquerading as the main square.

West of the park, the Tara forms the border with Bosnia and joins the Piva River near Šćepan Polje.

Sights

Dobrilovina Monastery MONASTERY

Near the eastern boundary of the national park, 28km from Mojkovac, this monastery has an idyllic setting in lush fields hemmed in by the mountains and Tara River. Don't be fooled by the tranquillity; this complex has been destroyed and rebuilt several times since it was founded (sometime before 1593, when it first appears in the written record).

If you knock at the accommodation wing, a black-robed nun will unlock the church but only if she's satisfied that you're appropriately attired. Dedicated to St George (Sv Đorđe), the frescoes that remain inside the church are faded but very beautiful.

Tara Bridge BRIDGE

The elegant spans of the 150m-high Tara Bridge were completed just as WWII was starting. At the time it was the largest concrete arched vehicular bridge in Europe. Its 365m length is carried on five sweeping arches, the largest of which is 116m wide.

In May 1942, with large numbers of Italian and German troops stationed in Žabljak, the Partisan command gave the order to blow up the bridge. The honour went to one of its engineers, Lazar Jauković, who planted the bomb that destroyed his beautiful creation. Jauković was captured by the Italians and Četniks (Serb royalists) and executed on the remains of his bridge. When it was rebuilt in 1946, Jauković's bravery was acknowledged by a plaque that still stands by the bridge today.

Tara River & Canyon RIVER

Slicing through the mountains at the northern edge of the national park like they were made from the local soft cheese, the Tara River forms a canyon that at its peak is 1300m deep. By way of comparison, Colorado's Grand Canyon is only 200m deeper.

The best views are from the water, which explains why rafting along the river is one of the country's most popular tourist activities. If you'd rather stay dry and admire the canyon from afar, head to the top of **Mt Ćurevac** (1625m) – although even this view is restricted by the canyon walls.

The viewpoint isn't well signposted and it's hard to find. From Žabljak's central square take the main road east and before you leave the town, turn left at a sign reading 'Restoran Momčilov Grad'. Shortly after, turn right and follow this road as it climbs the hill. Where there are forks, chose the road that loops up and follow signs that say 'Tepca'. Eventually there are some small wooden signs pointing to Ćurevac or *vidikovac* (viewpoint). Stop at the grassy parking spot with the national park information boards and clamber up the small track behind.

Black Lake LAKE

(Crno jezero) Eighteen glacial lakes known as *gorske oči* (mountain eyes) dot the Durmitor range. The Black Lake, a pleasant 3km walk from Žabljak, is the largest and the most visited part of the national park. The rounded mass of **Međed** (The Bear; 2287m) rears up behind it, casting an inky shadow into the waters. An easy 3.6km walking track circles the lake.

Activities

★Rafting

A rafting expedition along the Tara is one of the things that enduring Montenegro memories are made of. The river has a few rapids but don't expect an adrenaline-fuelled white-water experience. You'll get the most excitement in April and May, when the last of the melting snow revs up the flow. Various operators run trips between April and October.

The 82km section that is raftable starts from Splavište, south of the Tara Bridge, and ends at Šćepan Polje on the Bosnian border. The classic two-day trip heads through the deepest part of the canyon on the first day, stopping overnight at Radovan Luka. Summit Travel Agency (p116) offers a range of rafting trips out of Žabljak (half-/one-/two-day tour €50/110/200).

Most of the day tours from the coast traverse only the last 18km from Brstanovica – this is outside the national park and hence avoids hefty fees. You'll miss out on the canyon's depths but it's still a beautiful stretch, including most of the rapids. The buses follow a spectacular road along the Piva River, giving you a double dose of canyon action.

If you've got your own wheels you can save a few bucks and avoid a lengthy coach tour by heading directly to Šćepan Polje. It's important to use a reputable operator; in 2010 two people died in one day on a trip with inexperienced guides. At a minimum make sure you're given a helmet and life-jacket – wear them and do them up.

One good operator is **Kamp Grab** (☎040-200 598; www.tara-grab.com; half-day incl lunch €44, 2-day all-inclusive €180), with lodgings blissfully located 8km upstream from Šćepan Polje. To get there, you'll need to cross the Montenegrin side of the border crossing and hang a right (tell the guards you're heading to Grab); the last 3.5km is unsealed. Accommodation is available in six-person bungalows with shared toilets (€33), three-person rooms with en suites (€45), or you can pitch a tent (€3.30 plus €1.10 per person) or borrow one of theirs (€3.50 per person). Grab also offers guided **riverboarding** (or hydrospeed as it's known here), where you direct yourself down the river on what looks like a kick board (€35).

ADVENTURE RACE MONTENEGRO

Started by a bunch of British expats operating outdoor adventure businesses, the Adventure Race (www.adventureracemontenegro.com) should be high on the agenda for anyone who fancies themselves an action man or wonder woman. Held in late September/early October, there are now two separate events.

The **Coastal Challenge** is one day of kayaking, mountain biking, trekking and orienteering amid the exceptional scenery of the Bay of Kotor. For the truly hardcore, the **Expedition Challenge** is a gruelling two-day, almost nonstop, team-based race that also includes rafting and traversing the northern mountains in the night.

For Jack Delf, one of the event's founders, drawing attention to Montenegro's unique environment is a key part of his motivation.

'We consciously stage the Expedition Challenge in areas where bears, lynx and wolves are thought to live,' says Delf. 'Montenegro is the last country in Europe to have the continent's big five mammal species – the bear, the wolf, the chamois, the wild boar and the lynx. They exist separately in other places but not all together in the wild. These animals could be a major draw for Montenegro, but we need to stop them being wiped out first. Currently nobody knows how many there are, what they do or where they go. My goal is to raise €100,000 to get EuroNatur to tag the bear and the lynx.'

The Expedition Challenge has struggled to find sponsorship to cover its costs, let alone raise money, and consequently the event wasn't held in 2012. The Coastal Challenge, on the other hand, returns modest profits which are donated towards local charities. In the meantime, the situation for Montenegro's wildlife remains precarious.

'The last confirmed live bear sighting was five years ago,' says Delf. 'I've heard of two that have been killed since then, including one that was found decapitated. The traditional mentality here is "my father took me hunting and I want to take my son hunting". We need to get the message across that if you do that, your son will be the last to see a bear in this country.'

Tara Tour (☎069-086 106; www.tara-tour.com) offers an excellent half-day trip (€40, including two meals) and has a cute set of wooden chalets in Šćepan Polje with squat toilets and showers in a separate block; accommodation, three meals and a half-day's rafting costs €55.

Hiking

Durmitor is one of the best-marked mountain ranges in Europe. Some suggest it's a little too well labelled, encouraging novices to wander around seriously high-altitude paths which are prone to fog and summer thunderstorms. Ask the staff at the National Park Visitors Centre about tracks that suit your level of experience and fitness.

One rewarding route is the hike to the two **Škrčka Lakes** (Škrčka jezera), in the centre of a tectonic valley, where you can enjoy magnificent scenery and stay overnight in a mountain hut. If you're considering an assault on Bobotov Kuk or a serious winter expedition, it's best to arrange a local guide.

In any case, check the weather forecast before you set out, stick to the tracks, and prepare for rain and sudden drops in temperature. A compass could be a lifesaver. *Durmitor and the Tara Canyon* by Branislav Cerović (€12 from the Visitors Centre) is a great resource for mountaineers and serious hikers.

Skiing

(⌚Jan-Mar) Even in the height of summer **Savin Kuk** (2313m), 5km from Žabljak, wears a pocket of snow. On its slopes you'll find Durmitor's main ski centre. Its 3.5km run starts from a height of 2010m and is best suited to advanced skiers. At the time of writing, the ski lift operator was bankrupt, the business failed to sell at auction and a scramble was on to find someone to take on the lease. Hopefully by the time you're reading this the situation will be resolved.

On the outskirts of Žabljak, near the bus station, **Javorovača Ski Centar** (☎067-800 971) has a gentle 300m slope that's good for kids and beginners, and a year-round restaurant.

One of the big attractions for skiing in the national park is the cost: day passes are around €15, weekly passes €70, and ski lessons cost between €10 and €20. You can rent ski and snowboard gear from **Sport Trade** (☎052-361 010; Vuka Karadžića 18, Žabljak; ⌚8am-1pm & 3-8pm) for around €10 per day.

PARK FEES

The road to Black Lake is blocked off just past the National Park Visitors Centre and an entry fee is charged (per day €2, free for under-seven-year-olds). If you're planning on staying in the area for more than a few days, it's worth purchasing a 10-day ticket (€7). Drivers will need to park outside the gates (€2) and walk the remaining 500m to the lake. Keep hold of your ticket in case you bump into a ranger.

Canyoning

Just south of the national park, near Šavnik, the remarkable 2.7km-long **Nevidio Canyon** on the Komarnica River is at points only metres wide, earning it the name *nevidio* (invisible). It's extremely beautiful but dangerous; July and August are the safest months to explore it, and then only in the company of professional guides. Canyoning expeditions generally take about three to four hours and participants should be able to swim and have a high level of fitness.

Anitra (p105) organises expeditions out of Nikšić (price on application), as does Summit (p116) out of Žabljak (€120 per person including lunch, minimum two people).

Ziplining

Want to take flight? Two zip lines have been set up at **Avanturistički Park** (☎069-543 156; Black Lake; forest/lake/combined €6/7/10; ⌚10am-7pm daily Jul & Aug, 10am-6pm Sat & Sun Jun & Sep,) by the shores of Black Lake, offering criminal amounts of fun. The shorter one zips across the forest from a height of 14m, while the longer one will hurtle you for 350m clear across the lake.

Rock climbing

Two rock walls have been prepared on the side of the mountain at **Pirlitor**, but you'll need your own ropes. The easier eastern wall has six lines graded 3+ to 4+ on the French scale, reaching to about 10m. There are 14 routes on the 30m-high western wall, graded from 5b to 7b+.

To get here from Žabljak, head towards the Tara Bridge, turn left at Vrela and follow the signs. The access road is very rough and is best attempted with a four-wheel drive.

WORTH A TRIP

PIVA CANYON

The highway north from Nikšić meets the Piva River after passing through 40km of verdant farmland. It then tangoes with the river until they both reach the border at Šćepan Polje. The river was blocked in 1975 by the building of a 220m-high hydroelectric dam at Plužine, flooding part of the Piva Canyon to create Lake Piva, which reaches depths of over 180m.

Great care was taken to move the **Piva Monastery** (Manastir Piva) to higher ground, a feat that took 12 years to complete. This Serbian Orthodox monastery holds the distinction of being the only one to be built during the Ottoman occupation. It was constructed between 1573 and 1586 with the permission of the Ottoman Grand Vizier, who was a relative of its founder. The Muslim Vizier was given the unusual honour of featuring in one of the church's many magnificent frescoes with his head still attached to his body. Inside the church, note the internal door leading into the nave, which is beautifully inlaid with stars, trees and geometric patterns.

The road alongside the river is quite a feat of engineering in itself. It clings to the cliffs and passes through 56 small tunnels carved out of the stone in the years following WWII. The narrow but equally spectacular route through the mountains from Žabljak joins this road near Plužine. Heading north from here the route gets even more spectacular, with the steep walls of the canyon reflected in the deep green waters below.

Accommodation is available at the rafting camps (p114) around Šćepan Polje and in various *eko sela* (eco villages), scattered around Plužine and the back road to Žabljak. One excellent option is **Eko Selo Meadows** (☎069-718 078; www.meadows-eco.com; Donja Brezna bb; s/d/tr/q €20/30/42/50, mains €6-10; P), signposted from the highway, 17.5km south of Piva Monastery. Set on a flat plain edged by hills, the complex consists of a large restaurant serving local specialities (such as nettle soup, lamb in milk, *cicvara*, *kačamak* and grilled trout) and a collection of tidy wooden cabins. They're simply furnished, but each has its own bathroom.

Tours

Summit Travel Agency ADVENTURE TOURS
(☎052-360 082; www.summit.co.me; Njegoševa 12, Žabljak) As well as rafting trips, owner Anna Grbović can arrange jeep tours (€100 for up to three people), mountain-bike hire (€1.50/8 per hour/day) and canyoning expeditions (€120 per person).

Sleeping

Summit Travel Agency can arrange private accommodation starting from around €10 per person.

★Eko-Oaza Suza Evrope CABINS, CAMPGROUND €
(☎069-444 590; ekooazatara@gmail.com; Dobrilovina; campsite per tent/person/campervan €5/1/10, cabin €50; ⊙Apr-Oct) Consisting of four comfortable wooden cottages (each sleeping five people) and a fine stretch of lawn, this magical family-run 'eco oasis' offers a genuine experience of Montenegrin hospitality. From here you can walk down to a beach by the river or up to Lake Zaboj (1477m). Home-cooked meals are provided on request, and kayaking, fishing, rafting and jeep safaris can be arranged.

Autokamp Mlinski Potok CAMPGROUND €
(☎069-497 625; campsite per person/car €3/1) With a fabulously hospitable host (there's no escaping the *rakija* shots), this private campsite above the Visitors Centre is a sociable option. It's a fairly basic set-up but there are showers and sit-down toilets. Private rooms are also available.

Autokamp kod Boće CAMPGROUND €
(☎052-361 340; www.kampkodboce.me; Razvršje; campsite per tent €2.50, cabin/apartment €6/20) Two kilometres south of Žabljak, this nicely set out campground has tidy A-frame cabins (each with two single beds), a small camp kitchen and a toilet block with showers. There's not much English spoken, but the owners are very friendly.

Mountain Huts HUTS €
(per person Sušica/Škrčka €15/6.50, campsite per small/large tent €3/5; ⊙15 Jun-15 Sep) The National Park Visitors Centre takes bookings for the fully made-up beds in their hut at Lake Sušica (Sušičko jezero). The other park-administered hut, located between the large and small Škrčka Lakes, is more basic; you'll need to bring everything you need.

You can pitch a tent anywhere within the park for the same fee.

★Hotel Soa HOTEL, RESTAURANT €€
(☎052-360 110; www.hotelsoa.com; Njegoševa bb, Žabljak; s €55-82, d €75-110, ste €130-160; 📶) Let's hope Durmitor's hoteliers are taking note, as this newcomer could teach them a thing of two. Rooms are kitted out with monsoon shower heads, Etro toiletries, robes and slippers. There's a playground, bikes for hire (€2/8 per hour/day) and an appealing terrace restaurant (mains €4 to €18). But best of all, the staff are genuinely friendly and the prices reasonable.

Ski Hotel HOTEL €€
(☎052-361 088; www.skihotelzabljak.com; Narodnih heroja bb, Žabljak; s/d €40/80; P 📶 🏊) While the interiors don't live up to the promise of the Swiss chalet-style building, the rooms are more than adequate. A sauna, a small gym and an indoor pool sweeten the deal.

MB Hotel HOTEL, RESTAURANT €€
(☎052-361 601; www.mbhotel-mn.com; Tripka Đakovića bb, Žabljak; s/d €30/55; P 📶) In a quiet back street halfway between the town centre and the bus station, this little hotel has simple rooms, English-speaking staff and an attractive restaurant serving a mix of local and international dishes (mains €3 to €10).

Eating & Drinking

Žabljak's best eateries are the restaurants attached to Hotel Soa and MB Hotel.

Zlatni Papagaj PIZZERIA, CAFE €
(Vuka Karadžića 5, Žabljak; mains €4-13; 📶) The 'Golden Parrot' has the feel of a pirate lair, with wine-barrel tables, a wooden ceiling hung with chandeliers and a thick fug of cigarette smoke in the air. The menu offers a crowd-pleasing selection of pizza and steaks.

Konoba Luna MONTENEGRIN €
(Njegoševa bb; mains €2-7; ⏲6am-midnight) The Montenegrin equivalent of a greasy spoon, this humble cafe-bar serves good cheap meals in simple surrounds. The menu stretches from *kačamak* and grilled lamb to spaghetti and omelettes.

Čudna Šuma CAFE, BAR
(Vuka Karadžića bb, Žabljak) Living up to its intriguing name (meaning 'Strange Forest'), this cafe-bar somehow manages to be rustic and hip at the same time.

Information

National Park Visitors Centre (☎052-360 228; www.nparkovi.me; ⏲7am-5pm Mon-Fri, 10am-5pm Sat & Sun Jan & Jun-mid-Sep, 7am-3pm Mon-Fri mid-Sep-Dec & Feb-May) On the road to the Black Lake, this centre includes a wonderful micromuseum focusing on the park's flora and fauna. The knowledgable staff answer queries and sell local craft, fishing permits (river/lake €20), maps (€5) and hiking guides (€12).

Žabljak Tourist Office (☎052-361 802; www.montenegro-mountains.com/zabljak-durmitor/me; Trg Durmitorskih ratnika, Žabljak; ⏲7am-10pm mid-Jun-Sep, 8am-8pm Oct–mid-Jun) Operates in a wooden hut in the main square/car park.

Getting There & Away

All of the approaches to Durmitor are spectacular. The most reliable road to Žabljak follows the Tara River west from Mojkovac. In summer this 70km drive takes about 90 minutes. If you're coming from Podgorica the quickest way is through Nikšić and Šavnik. The main highway north from Nikšić follows the dramatic Piva Canyon to Šćepan Polje. There's a wonderful back road through the mountains leaving the highway near Plužine, but it's impassable as soon as the snows fall.

The bus station is at the southern edge of Žabljak, on the Šavnik road. Buses head to Nikšić (€9, six daily), Podgorica (€9.50, three daily) and Pljevlja (€4.50, three daily).

Pljevlja Пљевља

POP 19,200

The road over the vertigo-inducing Tara Bridge, 23km east of Žabljak, heads north to Montenegro's third-largest city. Although it has ancient roots (Roman and before that Illyrian), Pljevlja is a scrappy kind of town, with crumbling footpaths and a liberal dusting of graffiti. While much of the surrounding countryside is extremely pretty, there's also a fair bit of heavy industry including a large coalmine and thermal powerplant.

Despite its prominent mosques Pljevlja is predominantly an Orthodox town (73%) and nearly half of the population identifies their ethnicity as Serbian. But then the Serbian border is less than 10km away.

Sights

Hussein Pasha Mosque MOSQUE
(Husein Pašina Džamija; ☎052-323 509; Vuka Kneževića bb) Built in 1569 and boasting the highest minaret in the Balkans (42m), this is

the most beautiful mosque in Montenegro. Its interiors are unusual as they're painted with elaborate frescoes featuring geometric patterns and floral motifs. If it's locked (as it often is), you'll get a taste from the paintings around the entrance.

Holy Trinity Monastery MONASTERY
(Manastir Sv Trojice) Dating from 1537, this impressive monastery occupies a sublimely peaceful nook tucked into the hills, a kilometre north of the town. Ottoman-style buildings hung with flowerboxes form a backdrop to a solid church with a sumptuously painted interior and gilded iconostasis. Behind the church a small waterfall tumbles into a pond.

Sleeping & Eating

Hotel Oazza HOTEL €
(052-353 049; hoteloazza@gmail.com; RVI bb; s/d €29/37;) If circumstances conspire to detain you in Pljevlja overnight, this hotel on the eastern edge of town offers perfectly adequate little rooms. Approaching Pljevlja from Žabljak, turn right into the road to Prijepolje and look for the sign.

Restoran Milet Bašta MONTENEGRIN €
(Dr Sava Dimitrijevića bb; mains €3-5; 8am-11pm;) Grab a seat in the garden (the interiors haven't moved on since the demise of Yugoslavia) and tuck into a good honest serve of the local cuisine (trout, grilled meat, *cicvara*, *kačamak* etc) at proper local prices.

Information

Tourist Office (052-300 148; www.pljevlja.travel; Kralja Petra 43)

Getting There & Away

Bus Station (cnr Miloša Tošica & III Sandžačke;) Buses head to Žabljak (€4.50, 1¼ hours, three daily), Mojkovac (€6.50, two hours, five daily), Kolašin (€7, 2½ hours, five daily), Podgorica (€10, four hours, eight daily) and Budva (€14, 5½ hours, three daily). International destinations include Belgrade (€18, three daily) and Sarajevo (€9, daily).

Bijelo Polje Бијело Поље

POP 15,400

Montenegro's fourth-largest city, Bijelo Polje (pronounced 'bi·*ye*·lo *po*·lye') was once part of the evocatively named Sandžak of Novi Pazar, the Ottoman-controlled region that separated Montenegro from Serbia until 1912. Today 42.4% of the town's population identify their ethnicity as Bosniak or Muslim, 36.3% as Serb and 16.1% as Montenegrin. It's one of the most diverse cities in Montenegro with mosque minarets and church bell towers sprouting in nearly equal profusion.

The broad Lim River skirts the somewhat shabby town centre, where you'll find lots of cafe-bars, pizzerias, banks and the **post office** (Tomaša Žižića 2).

Sights

Church of St Peter the Apostle CHURCH
(Crkva Sv Apostola Petra; Kneza Miroslava bb) Predating the Ottoman invasion, this 1196 church lost its towers when it was converted into a mosque. Once again a church it's currently in the process of sprouting new towers, which look somewhat grafted on. Inside, the scant remains of frescoes contrast with the bright red of the episcopal throne and a modern iconostasis.

Sleeping & Eating

MB Dvori HOTEL, RESTAURANT €€
(050-488 571; mbdvori@t-com.me; Podgorica–Belgrade Hwy; s/d €35/61, mains €5-11; P) Southwest of town, this highway hotel has an old-fashioned ambience with little gables, wooden shutters and terracotta tiling. The rooms looking over the fields at the back are preferable to those facing the road. The restaurant serves excellent crispy-based pizza.

Getting There & Away

The bus station is on the highway, near the town centre. Services head in both directions on the Podgorica–Belgrade highway.

There's a large train station further along the highway, 2.5km north of town, with services to Bar (€7.20, 3¼ hours, three daily), Podgorica (€7, two hours, six daily), Kolašin (€2.20, 30 minutes, four daily), Mojkovac (€1.20, 15 minutes, five daily) and Belgrade (€17, eight hours, six daily).

Rožaje Рожаје

POP 9500

Rožaje is Montenegro's most easterly town, nestled within the mountainous folds bordering Serbia and Kosovo. Ninety-six percent of its population are Muslim and the song of muezzins can be heard echoing from its minarets at prayer times. It's fascinating to sit by the main square and watch the evening promenade. While this social ritual is common to every town in Montenegro, here you'll spot plenty of men strolling together arm in arm and some (but by no means most) women wearing hijabs (head coverings).

With a backdrop of rocky cliffs and plenty of old wooden houses achieving a look bordering on designer decrepitude, Rožaje could be very pretty indeed. The main thing preventing that happening is the scandalous state of the Ibar River, which seems to be used as the main waste disposal. Plastic bags full of household refuse line its banks as it gurgles through town.

During the late 1990s the town's mosques provided shelter for refugees from neighbouring Kosovo.

Sights

Ganića Kula TOWER
(Trg IX Crnogorske Brigade bb) Residential towers of this sort were once common throughout eastern Montenegro, Kosovo and Albania. Not just a defence against invaders, a *kula* was particularly useful for protecting the menfolk during interfamily blood feuds. There are gun slits on the bottom floor and only small barred windows on the next two. The wooden top floor provides a little more comfort, with bigger windows and a carved balcony. There's a small collection of artefacts inside but the tower is rarely open.

Sultan Murad II Mosque MOSQUE
(Đzamija Sultana Murata II; Mustafa Peđancia bb) Rožaje's main mosque has multiple domes and twin minarets. Tiling in geometric patterns completely covers the interior and includes an image of the Kaaba in Mecca above the prayer niche.

Kurtagić Mosque MOSQUE
(Kurtagića Džamija; Mustafa Peđancia 14) An attractive wooden minaret is a reminder of its venerable age, as are the extremely low doors leading inside, but the stone cladding on the street frontage owes more to the 1967 than 1697, when this mosque was actually built.

Sleeping & Eating

Duga HOTEL, RESTAURANT €
(☎051-278 266; resoran_duga@hotmail.com; s/d €15/30, mains €5-8.50; P 📶) Duga's dark wooden trim and flower boxes give it an old-fashioned homely ambience, a feeling only enhanced by the friendly staff. The ageing rooms are clean but basic – and at these prices, who could complain? There's a popular restaurant on the front terrace that serves pasta and traditional grills. It's located on the highway, 2.5km west of Rožaje.

Hotel Rožaje HOTEL €€
(☎051-240 000; www.hotelrozaje.montenegro.com; Maršala Tita bb; s/d €50/90; ❄ @ 📶 🏊) This distinctive wonky M-shaped hotel is one of the best places to stay in town, but it's been operating on half-steam since it was seized by the state while its owners are on trial for money laundering. The vibe is a bit tense and only limited services are offered, but the rooms are excellent, with opulently draped curtains, thickly embroidered bedspreads and attractive en suites.

Drinking

Tajson Caffe CAFE
(Maršala Tita bb; ⏲7am-midnight) At first we thought this place was called 'The Best Of Caffe' as that's what all the signage says. It actually is the best of Rožaje's cafe-bars and its comfy couches provide ringside seats for the promenade on the main square.

Information

Tourist Office (☎051-270 158; www.torozaje.me; 13 Juli bb; ⏲8am-4pm)

Getting There & Away

From Rožaje the main highway continues into Serbia, 22km to the northeast. On a windy road heading southeast is Montenegro's only border crossing with Kosovo.

The **bus station** (☎051-271 115) is on the highway above the town centre, with services to Herceg Novi (€18, 7¼ hours, four daily), Bar (€13, five hours, daily), Ulcinj (€14, 5¾ hours, daily), Podgorica (€11, four hours, three daily) and Gusinje (€6, two hours, daily). International destinations include Peć (€5, two daily), Priština (€10, daily) and Belgrade (€14, seven daily).

Plav Плав

POP 3800

Although only 33km as the crow flies, there's a border and a whole heap of mountains between Rožaje and Plav, necessitating an 83km drive through Berane and Andrijevica. From Andrijevica the road follows the Lim River through lush fields as the imposing Prokletije Mountains (Montenegro's highest)

LOCAL KNOWLEDGE

MONTENEGRO'S MOST EXTRAORDINARY DRIVES

- Around the Bay of Kotor (p32)
- Kotor to Cetinje via Lovćen National Park (p48)
- Nikšić to Šćepan Polje along the Piva Canyon (p116)
- The mountain road from Plužine to Žabljak (p118; summer only)
- Žabljak to Mojkovac along the Tara River (p117)
- Plav to Andrijevica and over the mountains to Kolašin (p109)
- Kolašin to Podgorica along the Morača Canyon (p109)
- Virpazar to Ulcinj along the southern edge of Lake Skadar (p97)

begin to reveal themselves. As if knowing that such beauty demands a mirror, picturesque **Lake Plav** (Plavsko jezero) has positioned itself to provide it. It's devastatingly pretty, with swarms of tiny fish swimming between the reeds and water lilies lining its edges, and a chorus of birds and frogs singing of their contentment to call it home.

The human occupants seem rather less appreciative, judging by the amount of rubbish washing into it from the township. The lakeside road passes a crop of massive turreted houses that either take their inspiration from fairy tales or nightmares – take your pick.

Like Rožaje, Plav is a predominantly Muslim town (91%), with 80% of the people identifying their ethnicity as Bosniak or Muslim and a further 9% as Albanian. It seems to produce some very unusual characters, such as the overweight shirtless fellow with the prodigious moustache wandering around with red braces attached to his shorts; or the busty blond waitress (equal parts Bet Lynch and Candy Darling) who clears leftover cans, serviettes and food from her tables directly into the Plav River.

Plav is another of those towns that doesn't believe in street names, so you'll have to follow your nose through the twisting laneways of its hilly *čaršija* (old market area).

Sights & Activities

The minarets of multiple mosques are the most prominent feature of the centre. The most imposing is the **Sultana Mosque** (Džamija Sultanija; 1909) near the main roundabout, capped by a set of large and small domes. Nearby is the **Old Mosque** (Stara Džamija; 1471), which is easily spotted by its decorated wooden minaret.

If you continue down from the roundabout to the main street, turn right and head up the hill, you'll reach the **Redžepagić Mosque** (Redžepagića Džamija; 1774). A slender minaret made of geometrically arranged panels of wood extends from a steeply pitched and tiled roof, which in turn is mounted on a solid stone base with a beautifully carved enclosed wooden porch. Intricate floral motifs are carved on the door.

Slightly up the hill is the **Redžepagića Kula** (officially built in 1671, although possibly 16th century), another defensive tower like the one in Rožaje. The bottom two floors have stone walls more than a metre thick, capped by a wooden storey with lovely jutting balconies.

The **pier** extending over the lake is a good spot to swim from, or you can hire paddle boats (€2 per hour) or kayaks (€1 per hour) nearby.

Sleeping & Eating

Good accommodation and eating options are thin on the ground. The best options are outside of the town.

Aqua BUNGALOWS, RESTAURANT €
(☎051-252 432; visitaqua@gmail.com; Brezojevica bb; r €25, mains €3-12) Hugging the lake's western shore near the beginning of the road to Gusinje, this complex has simple freestanding bungalows (sleeping up to four people) and a handful of rooms with three single beds. It's a simple set-up but reasonably comfortable. Upstairs, the restaurant offers lake views to accompany pizza, pasta, salad, fish and meat dishes.

Lake Views CAMPGROUND €
(☎068-591 044; campsite/dm €5/8) Set in a field by the lake on the approach to Plav, this is a lovely spot to pitch a tent. The squat toilets are less lovely, however. There is also a handful of hostel-like rooms below the associated restaurant.

Komnenovo Etno-Selo HOTEL €€
(☎051-255 350; www.kuladamjanova.com; Vojno Selo bb; s/d €39/54) Located on the south shore of the lake (reached by the back road from Plav), this large complex conjures up an 'ethno' ambience with its wood and stone construction. The theme continues with the traditional specialities served in the restaurant (breakfast is included in the room rates). Activities on offer include fishing, horse riding and guided mountain expeditions.

Information

Plav Tourist Office (☎063-231 428; ⏰8am-4pm Mon-Fri, 9am-3pm Sat) They don't speak much English but the staff here are friendly and surprisingly helpful, considering. They stock the *Prokletije Hiking & Biking* map (€4, scale 1:50,000), which outlines on its reverse 10 bike paths and 15 hiking tracks.

Getting There & Away

Regular services from Berane (€3, one hour) pull into the bus station on the main road.

Around Plav

Holy Trinity Monastery Манастир Св Тројице

On the approach to Plav, in the last village before the lake, Brezojevica Monastery is a study in rural tranquillity. Meadows of yellow and purple flowers line the riverbank broken by the occasional abandoned stone building.

Holy Trinity Church (Crkva Sv Trojice) has had a hard life. The present structure was built in the 16th century on 13th-century foundations but was damaged during WWII and left to decay, used only by the local Orthodox community for funerals. It's a testimony to the religious revival of recent years that the monastery is being restored. There's a new stone gate leading from the highway, topped by a shiny golden Orthodox cross. Inside the church are the faded remains of original frescoes, although the only subject that's easy to discern is the *Dormition of the Mother of God* over the door.

Gusinje Гусиње

It's difficult to understand why Plav has such a shabby, frontier-town feel when Gusinje (pronounced '*gu*·si·nye'), 10km further towards nowhere, is such a tidy and laidback place. The setting is idyllic, surrounded by verdant farmland hemmed in by the rugged majesty of the Prokletije Mountains. You could easily lose a day exploring the back roads and villages either by bicycle or car.

While the 1700-strong community is overwhelmingly Muslim, the town's two mosques coexist comfortably with both an Orthodox and a Catholic church. The most impressive architecturally is the **Vizier's Mosque** (Vezirova Džamija; 1626). This stone structure has a wooden porch and minaret that are similar to the mosques in Plav but better preserved. It's interesting to note the four prominent communist graves in the little cemetery.

In the centre of Gusinje you'll find a post office, an ATM, cafes and plenty of options for pizza or *burek*.

Prokletije National Park Национални парк Проклетије

The Prokletije mountains are a large expanse of wilderness forming the border with Albania and Kosovo. In 2009 protection was extended to a 160 sq km expanse on the Montenegrin side when it was declared the country's fifth national park. On the Albanian side there are two national parks: 26 sq km Theth and 80 sq km Valbona Valley. Ambitious plans are afoot for the whole mountain range to be declared a cross-border Balkans Peace Park.

It's ironic really, as both the Slavic and Albanian versions of the mountain range's name mean 'accursed', a reference to the harsh environment of these jagged peaks. They reach their highest point at Jezerski Vrh (2694m) on the Albanian side of the border and also include Montenegro's loftiest peak Kolac (2534m). This magnificently scenic area may well rate as one of Europe's least explored.

From both Gusinje and Plav, yellow signs point to various walking tracks and give both the distance and estimated time required for each. Within a few hours you can reach glacial lakes and mountain springs. One invaluable resource is the *Prokletije Hiking & Biking* map, available from the Plav Tourist Office.

If you're interested in doing some serious mountaineering, it's best to talk to one of the agencies specialising in adventure tourism as you'll need help in arranging guides, accessing mountain huts and dealing with red tape if you wish to cross the Albanian border.

Dubrovnik (Croatia)

POP 30,000

Includes ➡

Best Places to Eat

- Oyster & Sushi Bar Bota Šare (p130)
- Lucin Kantun (p130)
- Sugar & Spice (p129)
- Oliva Gourmet (p132)
- 360° by Jeffrey Vella (p132)

Best Places to Stay

- Karmen Apartments (p129)
- Hotel Bellevue (p129)
- Fresh Sheets (p127)
- Villa Klaić (p129)
- Begović Boarding House (p127)

Why Go?

Why have we included a Croatian city in a book on Montenegro? The first reason is practical: many travellers to Montenegro fly into Dubrovnik airport, which is, after all, only 17km from the border. More importantly, it seems inconceivable that you'd come this close and not visit one of the most beautiful cities in the entire Mediterranean, if not the world. Its proximity to the Bay of Kotor makes at least a day trip practically obligatory.

Dubrovnik is simply unique. It leaves many speechless: its beauty is bewitching, its setting sublime. Regardless of whether you are visiting Dubrovnik for the first time or the hundredth, the sense of awe when you set eyes on the remarkable Old Town, ringed by its mighty defensive walls, never fades. Indeed it's hard to imagine anyone becoming jaded by the city's marble streets, baroque buildings and the endless shimmer of the Adriatic.

When to Go

- St Blaise's Day in February is marked by pageants and processions, while a carnival sees in Lent.
- Sate your cultural appetite during the prestigious Summer Festival in July and August.
- In October sea temperatures are still warm enough for swimming along the coastline.

History

After the Slavs wiped out the Roman city of Epidaurum (site of present-day Cavtat) in the 7th century, survivors fled to the safest place they could find – a rocky islet separated from the mainland by a narrow channel. By the end of the 12th century the city they founded, Ragusa (later called Dubrovnik), had become an important trading centre on the coast. It came under Venetian authority in 1205, finally breaking away from its control in 1358. Through canny diplomacy the Republic of Ragusa maintained good relations with everyone – even the Ottoman Empire, to which it began paying tribute in the 16th century.

Centuries of peace and prosperity allowed art, science and literature to flourish, but most of the Renaissance art and architecture in Dubrovnik was destroyed in the earthquake of 1667, which killed 5000 people and left the city in ruins. The earthquake also marked the beginning of the economic decline of the republic. The final *coup de grâce* was dealt by Napoleon in 1808.

Caught in the cross-hairs of the war that ravaged former Yugoslavia, Dubrovnik was pummelled with some 2000 shells in 1991 and 1992.

Sights

The Old Town

Pile Gate CITY GATE

(Map p130) The natural starting point of any visit to Dubrovnik, this fabulous city gate was built in 1537. Notice the **statue of St Blaise**, the city's patron saint, set in a niche over the Renaissance arch. As you pass through the inner gate (1460) you're struck by the gorgeous view of the main street, **Placa**, or as it's commonly known, Stradun, Dubrovnik's pedestrian promenade.

★City Walls & Forts FORTRESS

(Gradske Zidine; Map p130; adult/concession 70/30KN; 9am-6.30pm Apr-Oct, 10am-3pm Nov-Mar) No visit would be complete without a leisurely walk around the spectacular city walls, built between the 13th and the 16th centuries. They're the finest of their kind in the world, enclosing the entire old town within a stone barrier 2km long and up to 25m high. The main entrance is by the Pile Gate, but you can also enter at the **Ploče Gate**; the walls can only be walked clockwise.

★War Photo Limited GALLERY

(Map p130; 326 166; www.warphotoltd.com; Antuninska 6; admission 30KN; 9am-9pm Jun-Sep, 9am-3pm Tue-Sat & 9am-1pm Sun May & Oct) An immensely powerful experience, this state-of-the-art photographic gallery features exhibitions curated by photojournalist Wade Goddard, who worked in the Balkans in the 1990s. War Photo declares its intention to 'expose the myth of war... by focusing on how war inflicts injustices on innocents and combatants alike'. There's a permanent exhibition on the upper floor devoted to the war in Yugoslavia.

Franciscan Monastery & Museum MONASTERY

(Muzej Franjevačkog Samostana; Map p130; Placa 2; adult/concession 30/15KN; 9am-6pm) Over the doorway of this monastery is a remarkable *pietà* sculpted in 1498. Inside is a mid-14th-century cloister – one of the most beautiful late-Romanesque structures in Dalmatia – and the third-oldest functioning pharmacy in Europe (since 1391). The small monastery museum has a collection of relics, liturgical objects and pharmacy equipment.

Dominican Monastery & Museum MONASTERY

(Muzej Dominikanskog Samostana; Map p130; off Ulica Svetog Dominika 4; adult/concession 20/10KN; 9am-6pm May-Oct, to 5pm Nov-Apr) This imposing structure is an architectural highlight, built in a transitional Gothic-Renaissance style. Constructed around the same time as the city walls in the 14th century, the stark exterior resembles a fortress more than a religious complex. The interior contains a graceful 15th-century cloister, a large church and the monastery's impressive art collection.

Rector's Palace PALACE

(Map p130; Pred Dvorom 3; adult/concession 35/15KN, audioguide 30KN; 9am-6pm May-Oct, to 4pm Nov-Apr) The Gothic-Renaissance Rector's Palace was built in the late 15th century and is adorned with outstanding sculptural ornamentation. It was built for the rector who governed Dubrovnik, and it contains his office, private chambers, public halls and administrative offices. Interestingly, the elected rector was not permitted to leave the building during his one-month term without the permission of the senate. Today the palace has been turned into a museum evoking the glorious history of the republic.

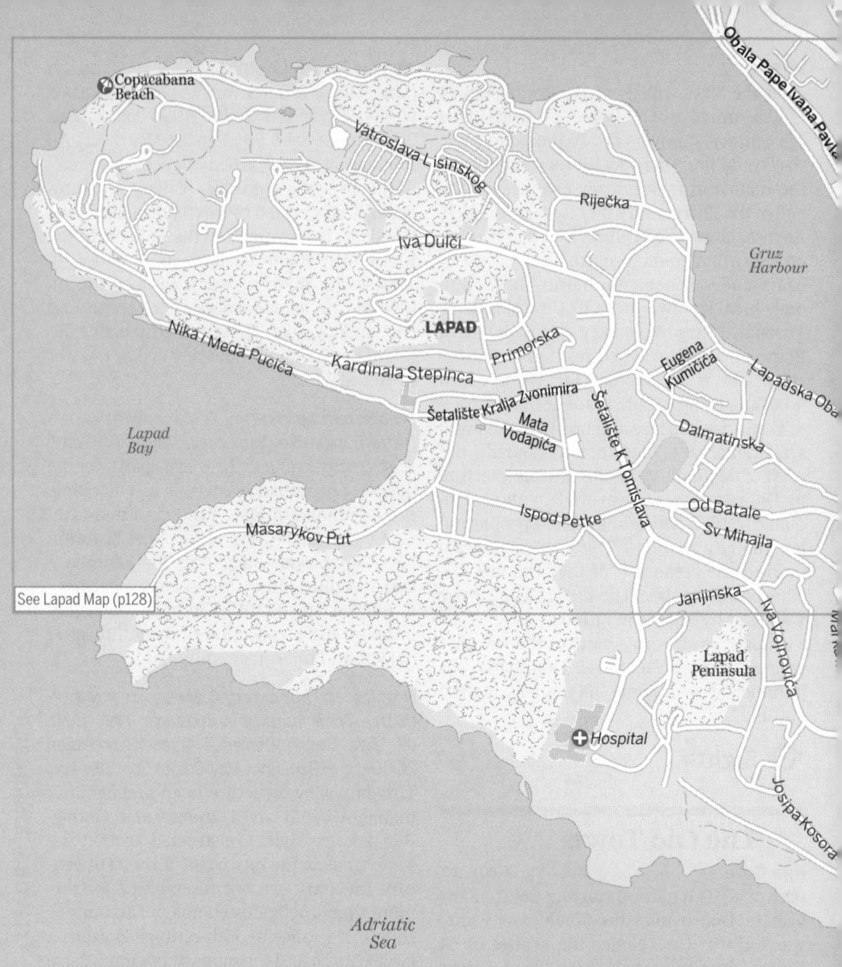

Dubrovnik Highlights

❶ Revelling in the most lovely and touristy of activities: gazing down on Dubrovnik from its **city walls** (p123).

❷ Visiting the excellent **War Photo Limited** (p123) gallery and putting recent Balkan history in perspective.

❸ Enjoying a sundowner from one of the **Buža** (p132) bars.

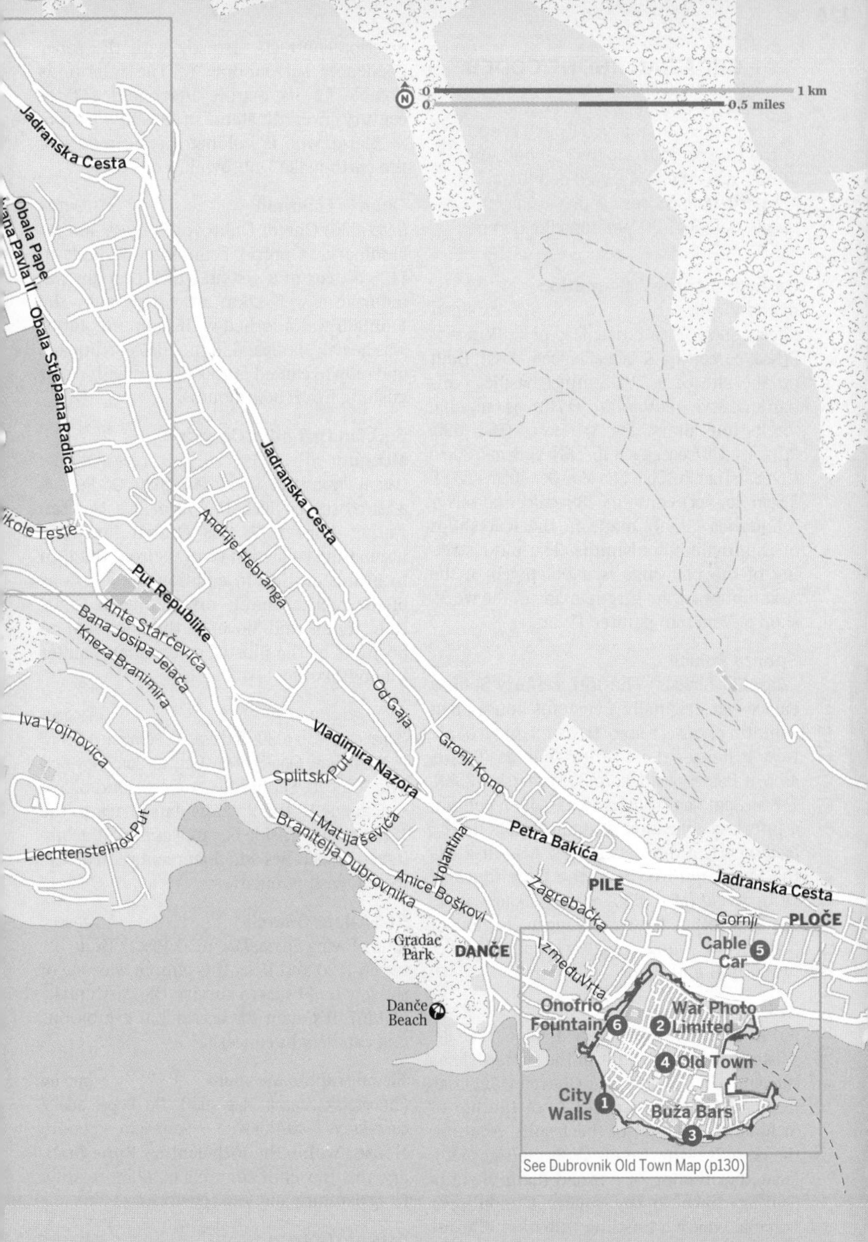

4 Exploring the marbled streets of the **Old Town** (p123) early in the morning or late at night, free from the cruise-ship crowds.

5 Taking the revamped **cable car** (p127) up to Mt Srđ for expansive views and an interesting display on Dubrovnik's bombardment.

6 Quenching your thirst in the time-honoured way, at the **Onofrio Fountain** (p126).

CROATIAN PHONE CODES

To call the numbers in this chapter from within Croatia, you'll need to add the area code 020 to the number. From outside Croatia, dial your country's international access code (usually 00) and then 385-20, and then the number.

Cathedral of the Assumption of the Virgin CATHEDRAL
(Stolna Crkva Velike Gospe; Map p130; Poljana M Držića; ⏲morning & late-afternoon Mass) Built on the site of a 7th-century basilica, this baroque-style cathedral (1713) is notable for its fine altars. The **treasury** (Map p130; Riznica; adult/concession 10/5KN; ⏲8am-5.30pm Mon-Sat, 11am-5.30pm Sun May-Oct, 10am-noon & 3-5pm Nov-Apr) contains 138 gold and silver reliquaries largely made in the workshops of Dubrovnik's goldsmiths. The most striking of the paintings is a polyptych of the Assumption of the Virgin, made in the workshop of Venetian painter Titian.

Sponza Palace PALACE
(Map p130; Stradun) The 16th-century Sponza Palace was originally a customs house, then a minting house, a state treasury and a bank. Now it houses the **State Archives** (Državni Arhiv u Dubrovniku; Map p130; admission 20KN; ⏲8am-3pm Mon-Fri, to 1pm Sat), which contain a priceless collection of manuscripts dating back nearly a thousand years. Also inside is the **Memorial Room of the Defenders of Dubrovnik** (Map p130; ⏲10am-10pm Mon-Fri, 8am-1pm Sat), a heartbreaking collection of portraits of young people who perished between 1991 and 1995.

St Ignatius Church CHURCH
(Crkva Svetog Ignacija; Map p130; Uz Jezuite; ⏲late-evening Mass) Built in the same style as the cathedral, St Ignatius Church (1725) has frescoes displaying scenes from the life of St Ignatius, founder of the Jesuits. Abutting the church is the **Jesuit College** (Map p130), located at the top of a broad flight of stairs leading down to the square Gundulićeva Poljana, where a bustling **morning market** is held.

St Blaise's Church CHURCH
(Crkva Svetog Vlahe; Map p130; Luža Sq; ⏲morning & late-afternoon Mass Mon-Sat) Built in 1715 in a baroque style, this imposing church's ornate exterior contrasts strongly with the sober residences surrounding it. The interior is notable for its marble altars and a 15th-century silver gilt statue of the city's patron, St Blaise, who is holding a scale model of pre-earthquake Dubrovnik.

Onofrio Fountain FOUNTAIN
(Map p130) One of Dubrovnik's most famous landmarks, Onofrio Fountain was built in 1438 as part of a system which brought water from a well 12km away. Originally the fountain was adorned with sculpture, but it was heavily damaged in the 1667 earthquake and only 16 carved masks remain with water gushing from their mouths.

Serbian Orthodox Church & Museum CHURCH, MUSEUM
(Muzej Pravoslavne Crkve; Map p130; Od Puča 8; adult/concession 10/5KN; ⏲9am-2pm Mon-Sat) Dating from 1877, this church houses a fascinating collection of icons from the 15th to 19th centuries. In addition to depictions of the biblical family originating in Crete, Italy, Russia and Slovenia, there are several portraits by the illustrious Croatian painter Vlaho Bukovac.

Synagogue SYNAGOGUE
(Sinagoga; Map p130; Žudioska 5; admission 20KN; ⏲10am-8pm Mon-Fri May-Oct, to 3pm Nov-Apr) The oldest Sephardic and second-oldest synagogue in the Balkans dates back to the 15th century. Inside is a museum that exhibits religious relics and documentation on the local Jewish population.

St Saviour Church CHURCH
(Crkva Svetog Spasa; Map p130; Placa) Built between 1520 and 1528, this church was one of the few buildings to survive the earthquake of 1667. It's open for occasional exhibitions and candlelight concerts.

Ethnographic Museum MUSEUM
(Etnografski Muzej; Map p130; Od Rupa; adult/concession 40/20KN; ⏲9am-4pm Sun-Fri) Housed within the 16th-century Rupe Granary, this museum contains exhibits relating to agriculture and local customs.

Orlando Column MONUMENT
(Map p130; Luža Sq) This popular meeting place is the spot where edicts, festivities and public verdicts were announced. Carved in 1417, the forearm of this medieval knight

was the official linear measure of the republic (51.1cm).

Maritime Museum MUSEUM
(Map p130; adult/concession 40/20KN; 9am-6pm May-Sep, to 4pm Oct-Apr) Inside St John Fort, this museum traces the history of navigation in Dubrovnik with ship models, maritime objects and paintings.

East of the Old Town

★Cable Car CABLE CAR
(Map p130; www.dubrovnikcablecar.com; Petra Krešimira IV; adult/concession 87/50KN; 9am-10pm Tue-Sun May-Oct, shorter hours rest of year) Dubrovnik's cable car whisks you from just north of the city walls up to Mt Srđ in under four minutes. At the end of the line there's a stupendous perspective of the city and islands from a lofty 405m.

Homeland War Museum MUSEUM
(www.tzdubrovnik.hr; admission 20KN; 8am-6pm Apr-Oct, 9am-4pm Nov-Mar) Dedicated to the 'Homeland War' – as the 1990s war is dubbed in Croatia – this museum is set inside a Napoleonic Fort, just above where the cable car drops you off. It provides a detailed account of the damage wreaked on the city, as well as videos of the bombardment.

Museum of Modern Art MUSEUM
(Frana Supila 23; 10am-7pm Tue-Sun) FREE Features contemporary Croatian artists, particularly the local painter Vlaho Bukovac.

Activities

Swimming

Banje Beach (outside Ploče Gate), around 600m east of the Ploče Gate, is the most popular city beach. Just southeast of here is **Sveti Jakov**, a good local beach that doesn't get rowdy and has showers, a bar and a restaurant. Buses 5 and 8 will get you there.

In the Old Town, you can swim below the two Buža bars, on the outside of the city walls. Steps help swimmers get in and out, and sunbathers can make use of a cemented space between the rocks.

On the west side of the city, beaches include the pebbly **Šulići** and the rocky **Danče**. The nicest beach that's walkable from the old town is below Hotel Bellevue, where you'll find a sheltered cove backed by high cliffs (which cast a shadow over its pebbled shore by late afternoon).

Diving & Kayaking

Navis Underwater Explorers (Map p128; 099 35 02 773; www.navisdubrovnik.com; Copacabana Beach) and **Blue Planet Diving** (Map p128; 091 89 90 973; www.blueplanet-diving.com; Masarykov Put 20, Hotel Dubrovnik Palace) offer recreational dives (including the wreck of the *Taranto*) and courses.

Contact **Adriatic Kayak Tours** (Map p130; 091 72 20 413; www.adriatickayaktours.com; Zrinsko Frankopanska 6) for kayak excursions (from a half-day paddle to a weeklong trip).

Sleeping

Dubrovnik is the most expensive city in Croatia. Lots of midrange hotels are in Lapad, 4km west of the centre, which has regular buses to the Old Town. Book all accommodation well in advance, especially in the summer season.

Private accommodation is a good alternative, but beware the scramble of owners at the bus station and ferry terminal. Try to pin down the location in advance if you want to be able to walk to the Old Town. Note that if you stay in unlicensed accommodation you are unprotected in case of a problem; all registered places should have a blue *sobe* (rooms available) sign. In high season, expect to pay from 300KN for a double room, or from 500KN for an apartment.

★Fresh Sheets HOSTEL €
(Map p130; 091 79 92 086; www.igotfresh.com; Sv Šimuna 15; dm/d 210/554KN; @) This classic backpackers is warm and welcoming, with a lively atmosphere. It's in a quiet location tight by the city walls, close to Buža bar. Downstairs there's space for socialising and cold beers in the fridge. Upstairs you'll find two clean and simple eight-bed dorms with lockers and fans, a four-bed dorm and a cosy double with a sea view.

★Begović Boarding House PRIVATE ACCOMMODATION €
(Map p128; 435 191; www.begovic-boarding-house.com; Primorska 17; dm/r/apt 150/320/385KN; P @) A steep walk uphill from Lapad, this is a popular and welcoming family-run place where the English-speaking owners go to a lot of trouble to make sure their guests are happy. Pine-trimmed rooms are smallish but clean, and some open out onto a wonderful communal garden with amazing views.

Lapad

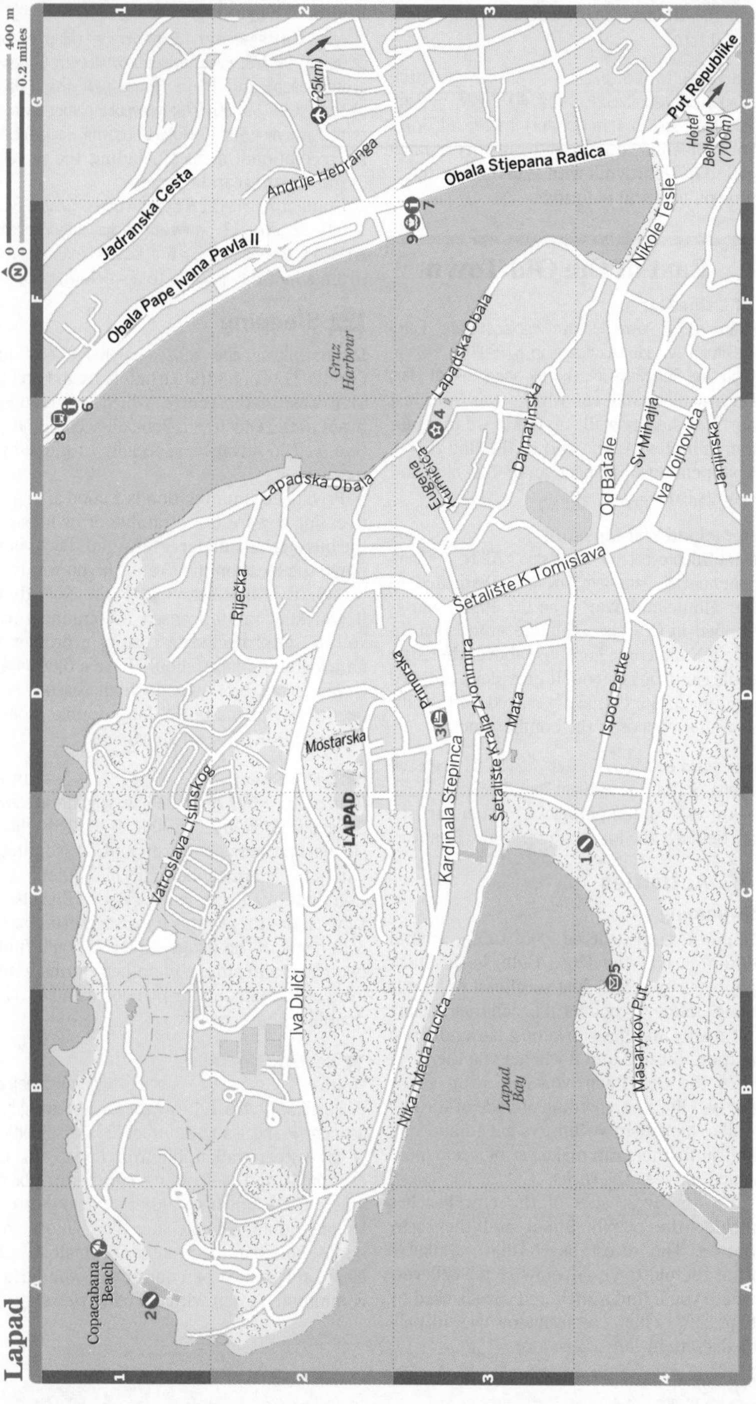

0 400 m
0 0.2 miles

Copacabana Beach
2
Vatroslava Lisinskog
Riječka
Iva Dulči
Mostarska
LAPAD
Nika i Meda Pucića
Primorska
3
Kardinala Stepinca
Šetalište Kralja Zvonimira
Mata
Šetalište K Tomislava
Lapad Bay
1
5
Masarykov Put
Ispod Petke
Od Batale
Sv Mihajla
Iva Vojnovića
Janjinska
Lapadska Obala
Eugena Kumičića
4
Dalmatinska
Gruz Harbour
8
6
Obala Pape Ivana Pavla II
Jadranska Cesta
Andrije Hebranga
(25km)
9
7
Obala Stjepana Radica
Nikole Tesle
Put Republike
Hotel Bellevue (700m)

Lapad

Apartments & Rooms Biličić APARTMENTS €
(Map p130; ☎417 152; www.dubrovnik-online.com/apartments_bilicic; Privežna 2; r/apt 450/870KN; ❄) A highly atmospheric place to stay within walking distance of the Old Town (via some vertiginous steps). Offers bright, clean and pleasant rooms with a homely touch and TVs (though bathrooms are not en suite). There's a gorgeous garden with subtropical plants and a guests' kitchen.

★ **Karmen Apartments** APARTMENTS €€
(Map p130; ☎098 619 282, 323 433; www.karmendu.com; Bandureva 1; apt 450-1200KN; ❄ 📶) Run by an Englishman who has lived in Dubrovnik for decades, these four inviting, homely apartments enjoy a great location a stone's throw from Ploče harbour. All have plenty of character and are individually styled with art, splashes of colour, tasteful furnishings and books to browse. Apartment 2 has a little balcony while Apartment 1 enjoys sublime port views.

★ **Villa Klaić** PRIVATE ACCOMMODATION €€
(☎411 144; Šumetska 11; s/d 288/492KN; P ❄ @ 🏊) In terms of service, five-star hotels could learn a lot from Milo Klaić, a worldly, hospitable character who takes a lot of trouble to make sure his guests are happy. Free pick-ups are offered and there's a private outdoor swimming pool. The location is just off the main coast road, high above town, but free bus tickets are included.

Apartments Amoret APARTMENTS €€
(Map p130; ☎091 53 04 910; www.dubrovnik-amoret.com; Dinke Ranjine 5; apt 755-1423KN; ❄ 📶) Spread over three historic buildings in the heart of the Old Town, Amoret offers 11 high-quality renovated studio apartments. Elegant decor, tasteful furniture, a dash of art and parquetry flooring feature throughout. Cooking facilities are kitchenette-style. Amoret 1 has a pleasant guests' terrace.

★ **Hotel Bellevue** HOTEL €€€
(☎330 000; www.hotel-bellevue.hr; Petra Čingrije 7; d from 1900KN; P ❄ @ 📶 🏊) Ignore the slightly dated tinted-glass frontage, this is a very classy hotel indeed. Positioned on a cliff overlooking the Adriatic, all rooms boast balconies that make the most of the inspirational views. The decor is modern and the facilities are excellent. Best of all, there's a gem of a cove below. It's a 15-minute walk west of the Pile Gate.

Hotel Excelsior HOTEL €€€
(☎353 353; www.hotel-excelsior.hr; Frana Supila 12; s/d from 1640/1960KN; P ❄ @ 📶 🏊) Dubrovnik's best address had an impressive €22 million renovation in 2008, and it wasn't in vain. There's a sense of occasion about this hotel, the haunt of royalty and Hollywood stars. Rooms are simply wonderful and many have remarkable views of the walled city. It's a short stroll from the Old Town.

Eating

You have to choose carefully when dining out in the Old Town. Prices here are the highest in Croatia and many places ride on the assumption that you're here just for a day and you won't be coming back. The two streets where average fodder is the norm are Placa and Prijeko; head to the back streets for more interesting restaurants. Lapad's main drag, Šetalište Kralja Tomislava, is packed with cafes, bars and restaurants.

★ **Sugar & Spice** CAFE, BAKERY €
(Map p130; Sv Josipa 5; cakes from 8KN) A gorgeous little cafe-bakery whose owner is a master of cheesecake, carrot cake, banana pie and divine chocolate torte. She also makes her own jams and marmalades, and on a hot summer's day her cool mint and lemon juice hits the spot. Everything has a cute vintage look. An original place in a sea of traditional patisseries.

Dubrovnik Old Town

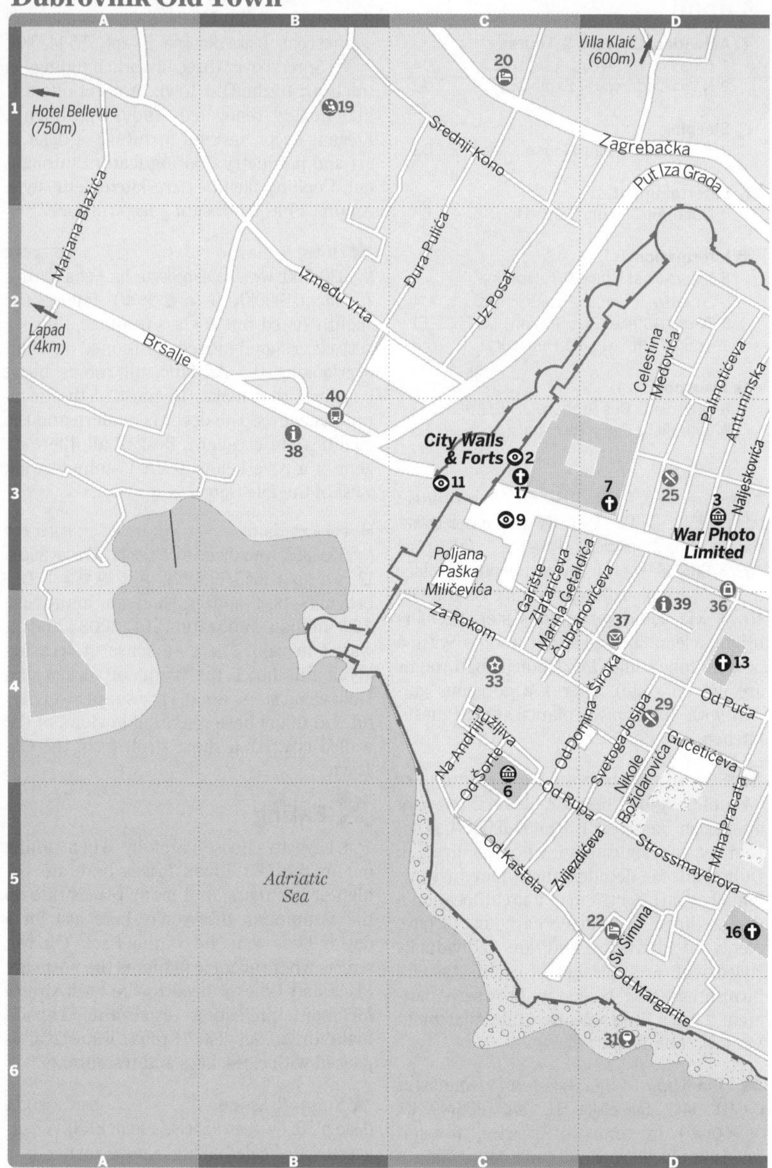

★ **Oyster & Sushi Bar Bota Šare** SUSHI €€
(Map p130; ☎324 034; www.bota-sare.hr; Od Pustijerne bb; oysters/sushi from 12/15KN per piece) Not only is this place a treat for its offerings of fresh Ston oysters and the best sushi in Dalmatia, the setting is absolutely divine, with views of the Cathedral from its terrace tables. And it all goes wonderfully with a chilled Croatian white. The service is friendly and professional.

★ **Lucin Kantun** CROATIAN €€
(Map p130; ☎321 003; Od Sigurate bb; mains from 80KN) Lucin Kantun is a modest-looking

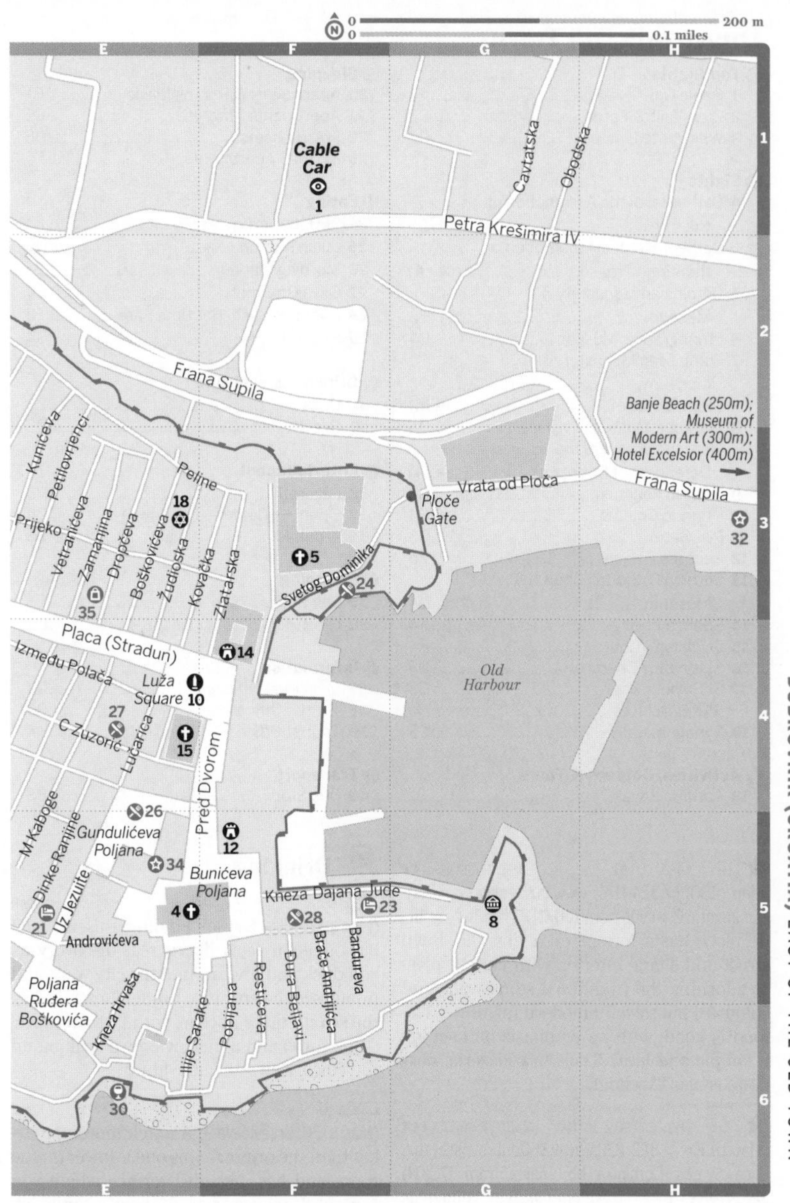

establishment with shabby-chic decor and a few pavement tables, but appearances can be deceptive – this restaurant serves up some of the most creative food in Dubrovnik. Virtually everything on the short mezze-style menu is excellent. It's all freshly cooked from an open kitchen so you may have to wait a while at busy times.

Dubrovnik Old Town

Top Sights
1 Cable Car ... F1
2 City Walls & Forts ... C3
3 War Photo Limited ... D3

Sights
4 Cathedral of the Assumption of the Virgin ... E5
Cathedral of the Assumption of the Virgin Treasury ... (see 4)
5 Dominican Monastery & Museum ... F3
6 Ethnographic Museum ... C4
7 Franciscan Monastery & Museum ... D3
Jesuit College ... (see 16)
8 Maritime Museum ... G5
Memorial Room of the Defenders of Dubrovnik ... (see 14)
9 Onofrio Fountain ... C3
10 Orlando Column ... E4
11 Pile Gate ... C3
12 Rector's Palace ... F5
13 Serbian Orthodox Church & Museum ... D4
14 Sponza Palace ... F4
15 St Blaise's Church ... E4
16 St Ignatius Church ... D5
17 St Saviour Church ... C3
State Archives ... (see 14)
18 Synagogue ... E3

Activities, Courses & Tours
19 Adriatic Kayak Tours ... B1

Sleeping
20 Apartments & Rooms Biličić ... C1
21 Apartments Amoret ... E5
22 Fresh Sheets ... D5
23 Karmen Apartments ... F5

Eating
24 360° by Jeffrey Vella ... F3
25 Lucin Kantun ... D3
26 Morning Market ... E5
27 Oliva Gourmet ... E4
28 Oyster & Sushi Bar Bota Šare ... F5
29 Sugar & Spice ... D4

Drinking & Nightlife
30 Buža ... E6
31 Buža II ... D6

Entertainment
32 Lazareti ... H3
33 Open-Air Cinema (Old Town) ... C4
34 Troubadur ... E5

Shopping
35 Lega-Lega ... E3
36 Uje ... D3

Information
37 Main Post Office ... D4
38 Tourist Office ... B3
39 Tourist Office (Old Town) ... D4

Transport
40 Bus Stop ... B3

★Oliva Gourmet MEDITERRANEAN €€
(Map p130; ☎324 076; www.pizza-oliva.com; Cvijete Zuzorić 2; mains from 100KN) This lovely little place has a terrace on a tiny Old Town street and a cute interior, with vintage pieces adorning the traditional stone walls and colourful but tasteful modern furniture. The food is good, with an emphasis on keeping it simple and local. The Oliva Pizzeria, next door, is also excellent.

★360° by Jeffrey Vella MEDITERRANEAN €€€
(Map p130; ☎322 222; www.360dubrovnik.com/; Ulica Svetog Dominika bb; mains from 170KN) Taken over by Maltese chef Jeffrey Vella, this is fine dining at its highest, with small, refined, flavour-bursting (and wallet-busting) parcels of creative food resting on your plate like jewels. The setting is unmatched, on top of the city walls with tables positioned so you can peer through the battlements over the harbour.

Drinking

★Buža BAR
(Map p130; Ilije Sarake) Finding this isolated bar-on-a-cliff feels like a real discovery as you duck and dive around the city walls and finally see the entrance tunnel. Emerging by the sea it's quite a scene, with tasteful music (soul, funk) and a mellow crowd soaking up the vibes, views and sunshine.

Buža II BAR
(Map p130; Crijevićeva 9) A notch more upmarket than the original, this one is lower on the rocks and has a shaded terrace where you can snack on crisps, peanuts or a sandwich and lose a day quite happily, mesmerised by the vistas.

Entertainment

★Lazareti PERFORMING ARTS
(Map p130; ☎324 633; www.lazareti.com; Frana Supila 8) Dubrovnik's best cultural centre,

GETTING TO MONTENEGRO

Airport Transfer

There are no buses from Dubrovnik Airport to Montenegro, but you should be able to pre-arrange a transfer through a Herceg Novi travel agent or accommodation provider for about €40.

Bus

At least two buses head to Herceg Novi (€10) and Kotor (€14) from Dubrovnik bus station each day. The duration of the trip depends entirely on how busy the border is; allow two hours for Herceg Novi.

Car

The distance between the Old Towns of Herceg Novi and Dubrovnik is only 47km but the border crossing can cause major delays, particularly on the Croatian side; to be safe, allow an hour for the crossing during the peak season. There are worries that when Croatia enters the EU it may take even longer. There's a smaller, lesser-known border crossing on the tip of the Preklava peninsula. We have been told that it's only supposed to be for locals, but we've never had any problem crossing there.

Lazareti hosts cinema nights, club nights, live music, gigs and pretty much all the best things in town.

Open-Air Cinema (Lapad) CINEMA
(Map p128; Kumičića, Lapad) Screens movies after sundown, nightly in July and August. There's also an **old town branch** (Map p130; Za Rokom).

Troubadur LIVE MUSIC
(Map p130; ☎412 154; Bunićeva Poljana 2) This corner bar looks pretty nondescript in the day, but on summer nights things get far more lively with live jazz concerts, often (though not always) featuring Marko, the owner, and his band.

Shopping

Placa is mostly lined with tacky souvenir shops; the best boutiques are down its side lanes. Check out the **morning market** (Map p130; Gundulićeva Poljana; ⏰7am-1pm) for local crafts and produce.

★**Lega-Lega** GIFTS
(Map p130; www.lega-lega.com; Dropčeva 3; ⏰9am-7pm Mon-Sat) A hip place to shop for gifts with a difference, including T-shirts, notebooks, coasters and badges. Lega-Lega is a Croatian design collective originating in the northern town of Osijek.

Uje FOOD
(Map p130; www.uje.hr; Placa 9; ⏰9am-9pm Mon-Sat, 9am-3pm Sun) The best place in town to stock up on quality Croatian produce. It specialises in olive oils and sells excellent jams (the lemon spread is divine), pickled capers and local herbs and spices.

Information

Hospital (☎431 777; Dr Roka Mišetića)

Tourist Office (www.tzdubrovnik.hr; ⏰8am-8pm Jun-Sep, 8am-3pm Mon-Fri & 9am-2pm Sat Oct-May) Bus Station (Map p128; ☎417 581; Obala Pape Ivana Pavla II 44a); Gruž Harbour (Map p128; ☎417 983; Obala Stjepana Radića 27); Lapad (Map p130; ☎437 460; Šetalište Kralja Zvonimira 25); Old Town (Map p130; ☎323 587; www.tzdubrovnik.hr; Široka 1; ⏰8am-8pm Jun-Sep, 8am-3pm Mon-Fri, 9am-2pm Sat Oct-May); Old Town 2 (☎323 887; Ulica Svetog Dominika 7) Maps, information and the indispensable *Dubrovnik Riviera* guide. The smart new head office that's under construction just west of the Pile Gate should open by the time you read this.

Getting There & Away

AIR

Dubrovnik Airport is served by over 20 airlines from across Europe. See p169 for details.

BOAT

A twice-weekly **Jadrolinija** (Map p128; ☎418 000; www.jadrolinija.hr; Gruž Harbour) coastal ferry heads north to Korčula, Hvar, Split, Zadar and Rijeka. Ferries also go from Dubrovnik to Bari, in southern Italy; there are six per week in the summer season (300KN to 450KN, nine hours) and two in the winter months. Local ferries head to nearby islands.

BUS

Buses out of **Dubrovnik bus station** (Map p128; ☎060 305 070; Obala Pape Ivana Pavla II 44a) can be crowded, so book tickets ahead in summer. For those who need to store bags, there's a **garderoba** (1st hr 7KN, then per hr 2KN; ⏲4.30am-10pm). Destinations include Split (140KN, 4½ hours, 14 daily), Zadar (230KN, eight hours, eight daily), Zagreb (270KN, 11 hours, nine daily), Mostar (130KN, three hours, three daily) and Sarajevo (230KN, five hours, two daily). All bus schedules are detailed at www.libertasdubrovnik.hr.

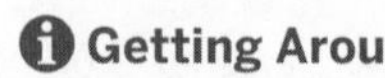

Getting Around

TO/FROM THE AIRPORT

Dubronik Airport (www.airport-dubrovnik.hr) is 24km southeast of the Old Town; a taxi costs about 250KN. Buses (35KN) leave the airport for Dubrovnik bus station (via Pile Gate) several times a day.

BUS

Buses run frequently and, on the key tourist routes, until after 2am in summer. The fare is 15KN if you buy from the driver, and 12KN if you buy a ticket at a *tisak* (news-stand). Timetables are available at www.libertasdubrovnik.hr. From the bus station, take buses 1a, 1b, 3 or 8 to the Old Town, and bus 7 to Lapad. From the Pile Gate, bus 6 heads to Lapad.

CAR

The entire Old Town is a pedestrian area. Cars with Montenegrin plates are targets for vandals if they're left on the street, so you're best to park in a monitored car park. The best-located **car park** (Ilijina glavica; per day 80KN ; ⏲24hr) for the centre is a 10-minute walk above the Pile Gate.

Understand Montenegro

Montenegro Today

When Montenegro chose to part ways from Serbia in 2006, it was a brave move – especially given its tiny population. But toughing it out is something these gutsy people have had plenty of experience with. Montenegro's national identity was built around resisting the Ottoman Empire for hundreds of years in a mountainous enclave much smaller than the nation's current borders. Determined to hold on to its regained independence, Montenegro has set a course towards the European Union.

Best on Film

Casino Royale (2006) James Bond plays poker in a casino in Montenegro; suspend your disbelief, as the Montenegro scenes were actually filmed in Italy and the Czech Republic.

The Battle of Neretva (1969) Featuring a stellar cast including Yul Brynner and Orson Welles, this movie garnered an Academy Award nomination. It's set and filmed across the border in Bosnia, but director Veljko Bulajić was born in (what is now) Montenegro.

Best in Print

The Son (Andrej Nikolaidis; 2011) Set in Ulcinj over the course of a single night, this novel won a European Union Prize for Literature.

Realm of the Black Mountain (Elizabeth Roberts; 2007) An interesting and detailed dissection of Montenegro's convoluted history.

Montenegro: A Novel (Starling Lawrence; 1997) An entertaining tale of politics, bloodshed and romance set at the dawn of the 20th century.

Black Lamb and Grey Falcon (Rebecca West; 1941) One of the classics of travel literature.

The Never-Changing Goverment

In the 2012 general election, the Democratic Party of Socialists (DPS) fell two seats short of ruling in their own right but quickly formed a coalition with ethnic Bosniak (South-Slav Muslim), Albanian and Croat parties to form a government (ethnicity still plays a large role in political affiliation here). What's extraordinary about this is that the DPS has won every single vote since multiparty elections were established in 1990, marking the end of communism in Yugoslavia.

It's even more extraordinary if you consider that the DPS was born out of Montenegro's Communist Party – so you could argue that it's been in power continuously since 1945 in one form or other. However, today's DPS is a long way from communist, having embarked on an enthusiastic and often controversial campaign of privatisations since the demise of Yugoslavia.

One factor in the DPS's success is the charismatic figure of returning Prime Minister Milo Đukanović. As a tall (198cm), handsome 26-year-old he was part of the 'anti-bureaucratic revolution' that took control of the Community Party in 1989. At the age of 29 he became the first prime minister of post-Communist Montenegro and apart from a few years of 'retirement' he has been prime minister or president ever since. However, Đukanović remains a controversial figure. While still president he was investigated by an Italian anti-mafia unit and charged for his alleged role in a billion dollar cigarette-smuggling operation; the charges were dropped in 2009.

Part of the DPS's continued popularity is the role it played in gaining Montenegro its independence. Several of the main opposition parties, especially the Serb-aligned parties, were strongly opposed to the break with Serbia, and although most have publicly dropped their anti-independence stance, many voters remain wary of their intentions. In the latest election a new non-ethnic, pro-independence party Pozitivna Crna Gora won 8% of the vote, and arguably it's parties such as these that will provide a new form of political choice for the electorate in the future.

The Big Issues

In 2012, thousands of people took to the streets of Podgorica in a series of marches protesting against corruption, organised crime and the worsening economy. Montenegro hasn't been spared the effects of the international economic crisis. The rapid growth that followed independence has slowed, unemployment has shot up and average incomes remain low.

Foreign Affairs magazine recently published an essay describing Montenegro as a 'mafia state'. While that might be overdramatising the situation, the European Commission noted in its 2012 Montenegro Progress Report that 'corruption remains widespread and continues to be a serious cause for concern, hindering law enforcement investigations of organised crime'. The commission did, however, note that 'some progress has been made on fighting corruption' since its previous report.

NATO & the EU

Meanwhile, Montenegro has been pushing ahead with its goal to join both the North Atlantic Treaty Organisation (NATO) and the European Union (EU). Shortly after independence Montenegro applied to join them and in June 2012 it opened formal accession negotiations with the EU.

While most Montenegrins strongly favour EU membership, joining NATO is much more contentious. Memories of the NATO bombing of Serbia during the Kosovo conflict are still fresh. In a recent interview with *Dan* newspaper, Metropolitan Amfilohije of the Serbian Orthodox Church spoke out against joining, describing NATO as an organisation that 'exerts violence on the entire world'. However, the Montenegrin government has stood firm in its resolve, publicly stating that it expects to be invited to join the alliance in 2014.

POPULATION: **626,000**

AREA: **13,812 SQ KM**

GDP PER CAPITA: **€5211**

ECONOMIC GROWTH: **0.5% (2012 ESTIMATE)**

UNEMPLOYMENT: **20%**

AVERAGE MONTHLY WAGE: **€491**

if Montenegro were 100 people

45 would identify as Montenegrin
29 would identify as Serb
12 would identify as Bosniak/Muslim
5 would identify as Albanian
9 are undeclared or another ethnicity

belief systems

(% of population)

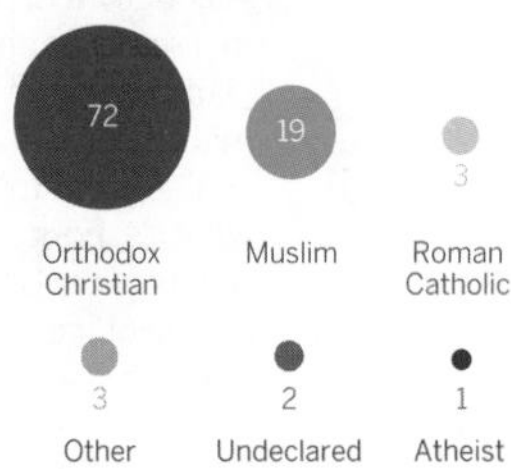

population per sq km

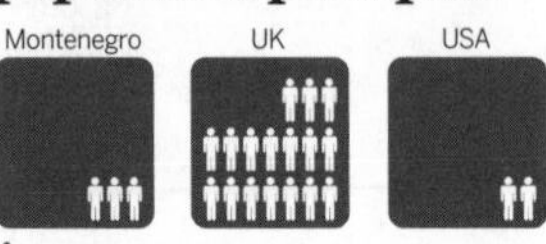

History

Nothing about Balkan history is straightforward. Yet in this part of the world, events that are centuries old factor heavily in the national consciousness and public discourse. State boundaries have changed continuously through the ages, so what is now Montenegro has many distinct histories. This chapter focuses on the story of Montenegro and its direct antecedents; the history of the coastal regions is covered in more depth within their respective chapters.

The Romans took advantage of the beautiful Adriatic coastline to build lavish seaside villas complete with mosaic floors, the remains of which are displayed in both Risan and Petrovac. Other Roman ruins can be seen at the site of Doclea, on the northern edge of Podgorica.

The Illyrians & the Romans

The Illyrians were the first known people to inhabit the region, arriving during the late Iron Age. By 1000 BC a common Illyrian language and culture had spread across much of the Balkans. Interaction amongst groups was not always friendly – hill forts were the most common form of settlement – but distinctive Illyrian art forms such as amber and bronze jewellery evolved. In time the Illyrians established a loose federation of tribes centred in what is now Macedonia and northern Albania.

Maritime Greeks created coastal colonies on the sites of some Illyrian settlements around 400 BC. Thereafter Hellenic culture gradually spread out from Greek centres, particularly from Bouthoe (Budva). The Romans eventually followed, initially at the behest of the Greeks who sought protection from the Illyrian Queen Teuta. The Illyrians continued to resist the Romans until 168 BC, when the last Illyrian king, Gentius, was defeated. The Romans fully absorbed the Balkans into their provinces and established networks of forts, roads and trade routes from the Danube to the Aegean. However, outside the towns Illyrian culture remained dominant.

The Romans established the province of Dalmatia, which included what is now Montenegro. The most important Roman town in this region was Doclea (present-day Podgorica), founded around AD 100. Archaeological finds indicate that it was a hub in an extensive trade network.

TIMELINE

300 BC

Illyrian tribes achieve supremacy in the Balkans, founding city states (including one at Lake Skadar near the modern Montenegro–Albania border) and establishing themselves as maritime powers in the Adriatic.

231–228 BC

Illyrian Queen Teuta establishes her base at Risan and pirates under her command roam the Adriatic, harrying the Romans, among others. Eventually the Romans bring her reign to an end.

AD 100

Doclea (present-day Podgorica), a settlement established by the Illyrians, grows to become a significant city under Roman rule. It is home to up to 10,000 people.

Over the centuries the Roman Empire gradually declined. Invaders from the north and west began encroaching on Roman territory and in 395 the empire was formally split, the western half retaining Rome as capital and the eastern half (which eventually became the Byzantine Empire) choosing Constantinople (present-day Istanbul). What is now Montenegro lay on the fault line between these two entities.

In the 6th century the Byzantine Emperor Justinian took control of the previously Roman-ruled parts of the Balkans, pushing out the Ostrogoths who had bowled through the region. He brought with him Christianity.

For all their ferocity, the Avars disappeared swiftly from the annals of history. To 'die away like Avars' is a common Balkan saying.

The Slavs Arrive

In around the early 6th century a new group, the Slavs, began moving south from the broad plains north of the Danube. It is thought that they moved in the wake of a nomadic Central Asian people, the Avars, who were noted for their ferocity. The Avars tangled with the Byzantines, razing Doclea while roaring through the Balkans. They had too much momentum, however, rolling on and besieging the mighty Byzantine capital at Constantinople in 626. The Byzantines duly crushed them and the Avars faded into history.

Controversy remains as to the role the Slavs played in the demise of the Avars. Some claim that Byzantium called on the Slavs to help stave off the Avar onslaught, while others think that the Slavs merely filled the void left when the Avars disappeared. Whatever the case, the Slavs spread rapidly through the Balkans, reaching the Adriatic by the early 7th century.

Two closely related Slavic groups settled along the Adriatic coast and its hinterland, the Croats and the Serbs. Byzantine culture lingered on in the towns of the interior, thus fostering the spread of Christianity amongst the Slavs.

It seems that the Byzantines' first impressions of the Slavs weren't entirely positive. The Byzantine historian John of Ephesus remarked that they were 'rude savages'.

First Slavic Kingdoms

In the 7th centry the Bulgarians created the first Slavic state in the Balkans. By the 9th century the Bulgarian Prince Boris was advocating that the Slavonic language be used for the church liturgy. The subsequent spread of the Cyrillic script allowed various other Slavic kingdoms to grow as entities separate from Byzantium.

One such polity was Raška, a group of Serbian tribes that came together near Novi Pazar (in modern Serbia) to shake off Bulgarian control. This kingdom was short-lived, being snuffed out by Bulgarian Tsar Simeon around 927, but not before Raška recognised the Byzantine emperor as sovereign, further speeding the spread of Christianity in the region.

395

The Roman Empire is divided into two. Present-day Croatia and Bosnia land in the western half and Serbia in the eastern Byzantine Empire, while Montenegro sits on the dividing line.

614

The Avars sack the Roman cities of Salona (Split) and Epidaurum (Cavtat). The Slavic tribes follow in their wake, either as invited defenders or as opportunistic vacuum-fillers.

800s

The first Serbian entity, Raška, arises near what is now the Serbian city of Novi Pazar. It is squeezed between the Byzantine and Bulgarian Empires.

869

At the behest of Byzantium, Macedonian monks Methodius and Cyril create the Glagolitic alphabet, precursor of the Cyrillic alphabet, to help speed the spread of Christianity among the Slavic peoples.

Soon another Serbian state, Duklja, sprang up on the site of the Roman town of Doclea. Under its leader Vladimir, Duklja swiftly expanded its territory to take in Dubrovnik and what remained of Raška. By 1040 Duklja was confident enough to rebel against Byzantine control, expand its territory along the Dalmatian coast and establish a capital at Skadar (modern Shkodra in Albania). Around 1080 Duklja achieved its greatest extent, absorbing present-day Bosnia. This zenith was temporary, however, as civil wars and various intrigues led to its downfall and power shifted back to Raška during the 12th century.

The Nemanjići & the Golden Age

Stefan Nemanja (born near present-day Podgorica) was to establish the dynasty that saw Raška (which came to be known as Serbia) reach its greatest territorial extent. By 1190 he had regained Raška's independence from Byzantium, also claiming present-day Kosovo and Macedonia for his kingdom. Nemanja later retired as a monk to Mt Athos in Greece, while his sons conquered further territory. After his death he was canonised by the Orthodox church and became St Simeon.

The legacy of the Raška state can be seen in the Church of the Dormition in Reževići Monastery, founded by Stefan Nemanja, and Morača Monastery, founded by his grandson. Raškan royals feature in church frescoes throughout the country.

Meanwhile, the Fourth Crusade in 1204 had hobbled the Byzantines and Venetian influence began spreading through the Adriatic. In 1219, Sava, one of Nemanja's sons, made an agreement with a weakened Byzantium that the Serbian church should be autocephalous (self-ruling), and appointed himself its first archbishop; he too was eventually sainted.

Around 1331 Dušan was proclaimed the 'young king'. He was to prove a towering figure in Serbian history, both physically (he was around 2m tall) and historically. He swiftly confirmed he was in control by chasing the Bulgarians out of Macedonia and capturing territory from the Byzantines. In expanding so rapidly under Dušan, Serbia became an 'empire', its territory doubled taking in Serbs, Albanians, Bulgarians and Greeks. More than just an aggressive campaigner, Dušan also codified the Serbian law (known as the *Zakonik*) and established the Serbian Patriarchate. In linking the Orthodox church with the Serbian royal line, Dušan also created a sense of cohesion amongst previously fractious Serbian tribes.

Nonetheless, throughout this period Zeta (as Duklja was now called) remained distinct from Serbia. Zetan nobles displayed a reluctance to submit to the Raškan rulers of Serbia, while the Raškan rulers generally appointed their sons to oversee Zeta, further indicating the separation of the two entities. As Raška became Serbia, so Duklja/Zeta is seen as the antecedent of Montenegro.

1015

With the decline of the Bulgarian Empire, following the death of Tsar Samuil, Duklja arises as a Serb-controlled principality in the place of the recently departed Raška.

1166

Stefan Nemanja establishes the Nemanjić dynasty, a Serbian line which is to reign for over 200 years. He is later recognised as an Orthodox saint.

1331

Allegedly the tallest man alive at the time, Dušan assumes the leadership and raises Serbia to be one of the largest kingdoms in Europe during that period.

1355

The Balšići come to the fore. Although they assume a position amongst the Serbian nobility, it is likely that the family actually came from a Vlach background.

The Arrival of the Turks

During the reign of Dušan's son, Uroš, various factions tussled for power and the Balšić family rose to prominence in Zeta. The Balšići established a base near Skadar and began claiming territory along the Adriatic coast. In the north the Venetians reappeared. By the time Uroš died, Serbian barons were busy squabbling amongst themselves, oblivious to a greater threat that was steadily advancing through the Balkans: the Ottoman Turks.

By 1441 the Ottomans had rolled through Serbia and in the late 1470s they lunged at the previously unbowed region of Zeta. Ivan Crnojević led a beleaguered group of Zetan survivors to the easily defensible and inaccessible heights near Mt Lovćen and in 1482 established a court and a monastery at what was to become Cetinje. Around this time Venetian sailors began calling Mt Lovćen the Monte Negro (meaning 'black mountain'). Meanwhile, the Ottomans continued assailing Cetinje and succeeded in overrunning it in 1514.

Sites related to Ivan Crnojević include the ruins of his abandoned fortress, Žabljak Crnojevića, and Cetinje Monastery, which he founded.

Ottoman Control of the Balkans

Despite taking Cetinje, the Ottomans withdrew. This remote corner was inhospitable and barren, and in any case the Turks were more intent on controlling the Adriatic. Under Süleyman the Magnificent, the Turks took Belgrade in 1521, putting beyond doubt their dominance of the Balkans. That one rocky eyrie, Mt Lovćen, and its environs became the last redoubt of Serbian Orthodox culture holding out against the Ottomans.

Despite being barely known in the rest of Europe, the Montenegrins retained a degree of autonomy. Innately warlike and uncontrollable,

THE BATTLE OF KOSOVO POLJE

In 1386 the Ottoman Turks took the Serbian stronghold at Niš, then in 1389 at Kosovo Polje the amassed armies of Serbian Prince Lazar and Ottoman Sultan Murat met. This proved to be one of the most pivotal events in Balkan history. Both leaders were killed and while neither side could conclusively claim victory, the Serbian empire was emphatically brought to an end and the Ottomans were free to continue their march into central Europe. Lazar's widow accepted Ottoman suzerainty and the battle entered Serbian legend, portrayed as a noble and ultimately hopeless act of Serbian bravery in the face of overwhelming odds.

The battle remains a defining part of Serbian identity to this day and partly explains Serb hostility to the notion of an independent Albanian-dominated Kosovo. You'll see '*Kosovo je Srbija*' (Kosovo *is* Serbia) graffiti throughout Serbia and the Serb-identified parts of Montenegro, often accompanied by '1389', the date of the battle.

1389

At the battle of Kosovo Polje much of the Serbian nobility is killed by the invading Ottoman Turks. In time the Ottomans regroup and expand further into the Balkans.

1482

After a series of Ottoman attacks against Zeta during the late 1470s, Ivan Crnojević leads the remaining nobility to Cetinje, which will become the kernel of the Montenegrin state.

PATRICK HORTON / GETTY IMAGES ©

➡ Statue of Ivan Crnojević

1521

The Ottomans take Belgrade, thereby confirming their control of Serbia. The Venetians have been expanding along the Adriatic coast for over a century and now control most of it.

their behaviour was such that the Ottomans opted for pragmatism and largely left them to their own devices. With the Venetians extending their control in the Adriatic, taking Kotor and Budva, the Montenegrins found themselves at the fault line between the Turkish and Venetian empires.

Through the 17th century a series of wars in Europe exposed weaknesses in the previously invincible Ottoman war machine. At one stage the Ottomans determined to remove the concessions which the Montenegrins had long enjoyed and which they now considered rightfully theirs. Montenegrin resistance to the Turkish attempt to enforce a tax regime was violent and the Turkish retribution horrific. As Turkish reactions grew more violent, the bonds between previously unruly Montenegrin clans became stronger.

During the 1690s the Ottomans took Cetinje several times, but each time they were forced to retreat due to persistent harrying from Montenegrin tribesmen. At the conclusion of the Morean War in 1699 the Ottomans sued for peace for the first time ever, ceding territory at Risan and Herceg Novi to Venice. The Montenegrins' enthusiastic and effective participation in the war had brought them – and their martial virtues – to the attention of the Habsburgs and the Russians while also furthering a sense of common purpose amongst the previously squabbling tribes.

It was then that the Ottomans finally realised they would not be able to control Montenegro; nonetheless they were clearly reluctant to give up their claim. To encircle it, they built a string of fort towns that attracted the Muslim population of the region. In the countryside remained the Orthodox tribes and peasants, who developed a sense of solidarity and separateness from the relatively well-off town populations. For the locals, identity was tied to the notion of tribe and the Serbian Orthodox Church, rather than Serbia or Montenegro. Nonetheless, distinct Serbian and Montenegrin identities were evolving: the Serbs were directly ruled by the Ottomans, while the Montenegrins retained a degree of autonomy in their mountain fastness and had managed to avoid being entirely weighed down by the Ottoman 'yoke'.

ŠĆEPAN MALI

One of the more bizarre characters in Montenegrin history is Šćepan Mali, who emerged in 1767 claiming to be the murdered Russian Tsar Peter III. Šćepan hoodwinked the Montenegrins and succeeded in being elected to lead the *zbor* (council). His luck run out when he was murdered in 1773.

The Vladikas

In 1696 Danilo Petrović-Njegoš was elected *vladika,* the equivalent of a bishop within the Orthodox church hierarchy. Ambitious and warlike, he declared himself 'Vladika of Cetinje and Warlord of all the Serb lands'. In so doing, Danilo presumed a role as the leader of the Serbs, perhaps a reflection of Montenegrins dubbing themselves 'the best of the Serbs' during their years of battles against the Turks. Beyond this, Danilo succeeded in elevating the *vladika* role into that of a hereditary 'prince-bishop' – a political (and military) leader as well as a church leader – and founded the Petrović dynasty, which would rule Montenegro until WWI.

1593–1606

During the Austrian-Ottoman wars the pope attempts to incite the Montenegrins, as fellow Christians, to fight against the Ottomans, but with limited success. The Ottomans have control of Bar and Ulcinj.

1667

A devastating earthquake hits the Adriatic coast, destroying much of Kotor, which is under Venetian control. The city has also recently endured an outbreak of plague.

1697

Danilo becomes *vladika* (prince-bishop) and establishes the Petrović dynasty. He mediates disputes between tribes and clans and within 15 years begins the fight back against the Ottomans.

1784

Petar I is consecrated as *vladika*, eventually becoming an enduring military and spiritual hero. In 1796 he defeats the Ottoman renegade Kara Mahmud and expands Montenegrin territory considerably.

MONTENEGRO & RUSSIA'S SPECIAL RELATIONSHIP

In the early 18th century a newly assertive Russia, under Peter the Great, was looking to modernise. Peter's agents appeared in the Adriatic and encountered the Montenegrins. As well as being fellow adherents of the Orthodox faith and fellow combatants against the Ottomans, the Russians immediately recognised the fighting abilities of the Montenegrins. Vladika Danilo, realising his small realm needed larger allies, approached the Russian tsar for support in the struggle against the Turks. Travelling to St Petersburg, Danilo established an alliance with Russia that was to prove significant for Montenegro.

Subsequent *vladika*s, upon achieving office, made a point of visiting Russia to cement their relationships with the tsar. In 1833 Petar II Petrović Njegoš went so far as to travel to St Petersburg to have himself consecrated by Tsar Nicholas I. Several *vladika*s were educated in Russia, primarily as there were virtually no teaching institutions in Montenegro; *vladika*s invariably returned to Montenegro with new ideas to modernise their relatively undeveloped state.

Throughout the Montenegrins' struggle against the Ottomans, Russia provided tactical and financial support, although Montenegrin independence always took a back seat to Russia's wider strategic interests.

In 1766 the Ottomans established the Ecumenical Patriarchate in Constantinople responsible for all of the Orthodox churches in the Ottoman domain. The Serbs later set up their own patriarchate in Habsburg territory, beyond the reach of Ottoman authorities. These moves effectively led to the creation of separate Montenegrin and Serbian Orthodox churches, and while the Montenegrins retained some sense of community with the Serbs this was another factor in the divergent experience and the evolution of a separate national consciousness amongst the Montenegrins.

Dealing with the Great Powers

Napoleon appeared in 1797 claiming Venice's Adriatic territories, thus removing Montenegro's main rival for power in the Adriatic. The years to come saw Napoleon tangling with the Montenegrins, British and Austrians in the Adriatic. The Montenegrins operated with military support from the Russians and briefly captured Herceg Novi, a long-hoped-for Adriatic coastal town, but in the aftermath they were forced to abandon it due to diplomatic horse-trading.

Petar I was not only a social and ecclesiastical leader; he is also credited with introducing the potato to Montenegro.

In 1830 Petar II Petrović Njegoš became *vladika* upon the death of his uncle. Two meters tall, Njegoš fulfilled the requirement that the *vladika* be striking, handsome and dashing. Njegoš made further unsuccessful attempts to gain access to the sea, but in other aspects of nation-building

1797–1815

Napoleon brings the Venetian Republic to an end; Venetian dominions are initially given to the Habsburgs, but in 1806 Napoleon gains the Adriatic coast, which he dubs the Illyrian Provinces.

1800s

Petar I courts Russia in the hope of military and financial support in the struggle against the Ottomans. Russia's interest waxes and wanes in the wake of other diplomatic priorities.

1830

Petar II Petrović Njegoš rules as the last *vladika* and becomes one of the nation's most acclaimed leaders. His epic poem *The Mountain Wreath* is regarded as Montenegro's greatest literary work.

1851

Njegoš' nephew Danilo becomes the country's first secular leader, taking the title 'prince'. He is assassinated in 1860, a victim of a blood feud with a rival Montenegrin clan.

he was more successful. He increased the role of government and developed a system of taxation for Montenegro. He also canonised his predecessor Petar I, thus bringing a saintly aspect to the role of *vladika,* in emulation of the saintly kings of medieval Serbia.

Njegoš made the now traditional trip to St Petersburg in search of military and monetary support from the Russian tsars and set about modernising his nation, which was primitive and undeveloped. Succeeding Petrović rulers continued the process of modernisation, albeit gradually. Danilo came to power in 1851 and promptly declared himself prince, thus bringing an end to the ecclesiastical position of *vladika* as leader of the Montenegrins. In 1855 he won a great victory over the Ottomans at Grahovo and he skilfully steered a course between the interests of the Great Powers – Austria-Hungary, Russia, France and Britain – all of whom had designs on Montenegro and the broader Balkan region.

Nikola, who became prince after Danilo, pressed on with a road-building program and introduced the telegraph to Montenegro. He was also responsible for founding a school for girls in Cetinje, the first-ever such institution in Montenegro. During the 1860s Nikola established contact with Mihailo Obrenović, ruler of the Serbian principality (by then de facto independent from the Ottoman rule). The two leaders signed an agreement to liberate their peoples and create a single state. Most significantly, Nikola reorganised the Montenegrin army into a modern fighting force.

BLACK MOUNTAIN

Elizabeth Roberts' lively and detailed history of Montenegro, *Realm of the Black Mountain*, is a must for anyone interested in the goings-on of this fascinating country.

Freedom from the Ottomans

A rebellion against Ottoman control broke out in Bosnia and Hercegovina (BiH) in 1875. Both Serbs and Montenegrins joined the insurgency, Montenegrins (under Nikola) again excelling themselves and making significant territorial gains. In the wake of the struggle for Bosnia, the Congress of Berlin in 1878 saw Montenegro and Serbia officially achieve independence from the Ottomans. Montenegro won control of upland territories in Nikšić, Podgorica and Žabljak and territory around Lake Skadar and the port of Bar, effectively tripling in size. The expansionist Austrians annexed BiH, thus stymying any further Montenegrin expansion to the north. The Montenegrins, however, managed to take control of the Ulcinj region of the Adriatic coast.

After 1878 Montenegro enjoyed a period of ongoing peace. Nikola's rule, however, became increasingly autocratic. His most popular move during these years was marrying off several of his daughters to European royalty. In 1910, on his 50th jubilee, he raised himself from the role of prince to king.

In the early years of the 20th century there were increasing calls for union with Serbia and rising political opposition to Nikola's rule. The

1876–78

Wars of independence see Serbia, Bulgaria and Montenegro win their freedom from the rapidly shrinking Ottoman Empire. Montenegro triples in size, gaining Nikšić, Podgorica, Žabljak and Bar.

1910

Prince Nikola takes the title of king, raising eyebrows across Europe that such a diminutive and impoverished territory, home to only 200,000 souls, could really qualify as a kingdom.

1918

The Kingdom of Serbs, Croats and Slovenes is created in the aftermath of WWI. Serbia's King Petar I Karađorđević assumes the monarchy. Montenegro is included within his domains.

1920–39

The interwar years are an unhappy time for Montenegro, marked by the dismantling of Montenegrin institutions, squabbles about organisation of the Yugoslav entity and socio-economic stagnation.

Serbian King Petar Karađorđević (whose late wife was one of Nikola's daughters) was suspected of being involved in attempts to overthrow King Nikola, and Montenegrin-Serbian relations reached their historical low point.

The Balkan Wars of 1912–13 saw the Montenegrins patching things up with the Serbs to join the Greeks and Bulgarians in an effort to throw the Ottoman Turks out of Europe once and for all. During the wars the Montenegrins gained Bijelo Polje, Berane and Plav and in so doing bordered Serbia for the first time in over 500 years. The idea of a Serbian-Montenegrin union gained more currency, and in the elections of 1914 many voters opted for union. King Nikola pragmatically supported the idea on the stipulation that both the Serbian and Montenegrin royal houses be retained.

WWI & the First Yugoslavia

Before the union could be realised, WWI intervened. Montenegro entered the war on the side of Serbia and the Allies. Austria-Hungary invaded shortly afterwards and swiftly captured Cetinje, sending King Nikola into exile in France. In 1918 the Serbian army entered Montenegro and the French, keen to implement the Serbian-Montenegrin union, refused to allow Nikola to leave France, formally bringing an end to the Petrović dynasty. The same year Montenegro ceased to exist after being subsumed into the newly created Kingdom of Serbs, Croats and Slovenes – the first Yugoslavia.

Throughout the 1920s some Montenegrins, peeved at their 'little-brother' to Serbia status, as well as the loss of their sovereignty and distinct identity, put up spirited resistance to the union with Serbia. This resentment increased after the abolition of the Montenegrin church, which was subsumed into the Serbian Orthodox Patriarchate in Belgrade. Taking advantage of fears of a Serb-Croat civil war, on 6 January 1929 King Aleksandar proclaimed a royal dictatorship, abolished political parties and suspended parliamentary government, thus ending any hope of democratic change. In 1934, while on a state visit in Marseilles, King Aleksandar was assassinated by the fascist-inspired Croatian Ustaše.

Meanwhile, during the mid-1920s the Yugoslav Communist Party arose; Josip Broz Tito was to become leader in 1937. The high level of membership of the Communist Party amongst Montenegrins was perhaps a reflection of their displeasure with the status of Montenegro within Yugoslavia.

TITO

For a quirky, or perhaps reverent (who can tell) look at Tito visit www.titoville.com. Enjoy pictures of him striking statesman-like poses, scripts from his speeches, lists of his 'wives' and jokes about him.

WWII & the Second Yugoslavia

During WWII Hitler invaded Yugoslavia on multiple fronts. The Italians followed on their coat-tails. After routing the Yugoslav army, Germany

1941

Hitler invades Yugoslavia and divides it into areas of German and Italian control. Mussolini occupies Montenegro with plans to absorb it as an Italian protectorate.

1943

Tito's communist Partisans achieve military victories and build a popular antifascist front. They reclaim territory from retreating Italian brigades. The Partisans eventually take control of Yugoslavia.

1945–48

Founding of the Federal People's Republic of Yugoslavia. In time, Tito breaks with Stalin and steers a careful course between Eastern and Western blocs, including establishing the nonaligned movement.

1960s

Tourism takes off in Yugoslavia, with a particular focus on the Adriatic coast. Hot spots such as Sveti Stefan attract the international jet set right up until the Yugoslav wars.

and Italy divided the country into a patchwork of areas of control. The Italians controlled Montenegro and parts of neighbouring Dalmatia. Some anti-union Montenegrins collaborated with the Italians in the hope that the Petrović dynasty would be reinstated. Meanwhile, Tito's Partisans and the Serbian Četniks (royalists) engaged the Italians, sometimes lapsing into fighting each other. The most effective antifascist struggle was conducted by Partisan units led by Tito. With their roots in the outlawed Yugoslav Communist Party, the Partisans attracted long-suffering intellectuals and antifascists of all kinds. They gained wide popular support with an early manifesto which, although vague, appeared to envision a postwar Yugoslavia based on a loose federation.

Although the Allies initially backed the Serbian Četniks, it became apparent that the Partisans were waging a far more focused and determined fight against the Nazis. With the diplomatic and military support of Churchill and other Allied powers, the Partisans controlled much of Yugoslavia by 1943. The Partisans established functioning local governments in the territory they seized, which later eased their transition to power. Hitler made several concerted attempts to kill Tito and wipe out the Partisans, but was unsuccessful. As the tide of the war turned, the Italians surrendered to the Allies and, with the Partisans harassing them, the Germans withdrew. On 20 October 1944 Tito entered Belgrade with the Red Army and was made prime minister.

CAPITAL

In 1946 the Montenegrin capital was moved from Cetinje to Podgorica and renamed Titograd. In 1992 Titograd was changed back to Podgorica, which remained the capital.

The communist federation of Yugoslavia was established. Tito was determined to create a state in which no ethnic group dominated the political landscape. Montenegro became one of six republics – along with Macedonia, Serbia, Croatia, BiH and Slovenia – in a tightly configured union. Tito effected this delicate balance by creating a one-party state and rigorously stamping out all opposition whether nationalist, royalist or religious. The border of the modern state was set: Montenegro won Kotor, but lost some areas of Kosovo in the horse-trading that Tito undertook in order to establish a balance between the various Yugoslav republics.

In 1948 Tito fell out with Stalin and broke off contacts with the USSR. This caused some consternation in Montenegro given its historical links with Russia. Of all the Yugoslav republics, Montenegro had the highest per capita membership of the Communist Party, and it was highly represented in the army.

During the 1960s the concentration of power in Belgrade became an increasingly testy issue as it became apparent that money from the more prosperous republics of Slovenia and Croatia was being distributed to the other republics, and not always fairly. Unrest reached a crescendo in 1971 when reformers called for greater economic autonomy and the loosening of ties within the Yugoslav federation, but nationalistic elements manifested themselves as well. Tito's 1974 constitution afforded the re-

1980

Death of President Tito prompts a genuine outpouring of grief. Tributes flow, but Yugoslavia is beset by inflation, unemployment and foreign debt, setting the scene for the difficulties to come.

1991

Yugoslavia splits. As Slovenia, Croatia, BiH and Macedonia seek their independence, the question of Montenegrin independence is raised, but a year later Montenegrins vote to remain in Yugoslavia.

1997

Milo Đukanović wins a further election victory. Montenegro adopts a pro-Western stance and distances itself from the Serbian position during the NATO raids in defence of Kosovo in 1999.

2003

Yugoslavia expires and is replaced by the state union of Serbia and Montenegro. The union is intended to be an equal partnership but it rapidly proves unworkable.

publics more autonomy, but the stage was set for the rise of nationalism and the wars of the 1990s.

Tito left a shaky Yugoslavia upon his death in May 1980. A presidency rotating among the six republics could not compensate for the loss of his steadying hand at the helm. The authority of the central government sank with the economy, and long-suppressed mistrust among Yugoslavia's ethnic groups resurfaced.

Union with Serbia, then Independence

As communism collapsed throughout Eastern Europe, Slobodan Milošević used the issue of Kosovo to ride to power in Serbia on a wave of nationalism. Montenegrins largely supported their Orthodox co-religionists.

Božidar Jezernik's *Wild Europe* is a fascinating collage of travellers' impressions of the Balkans over 500 years. Two lively chapters record Western perceptions of Montenegro.

In 1991 Slovenia and Croatia declared independence from the federation and the Yugoslav wars commenced. There was no fighting in Montenegro, but Montenegrin paramilitary groups, in conjunction with the Serb-dominated Yugoslav army, were responsible for the shelling of Dubrovnik and parts of the Dalmatian littoral. These acts appeared to serve no strategic purpose and were roundly criticised in the international press. In 1992, by which point BiH and Macedonia had also opted for independence, the Montenegrins voted overwhelmingly to remain in the rump Yugoslav state with Serbia. Admittedly there was some Montenegrin edginess about their place within 'Greater Serbia', and the autocephalous Montenegrin church was revived in 1993.

As the bloody war in Bosnia wound down with the signing of the Dayton accords in 1995, Montenegrin Prime Minister Milo Đukanović began distancing himself from Milošević. Previously a Milošević ally, Đukanović, who had been elected in 1991, realised that in the face of declining living standards and rising discontent, Montenegro would fare better if it adopted a more pro-Western course. In doing so he became the darling of Western leaders, who were trying to isolate and bring down Milošević. As the Serbian regime became an international pariah, the Montenegrins increasingly moved to re-establish their distinct identity. Relations with Serbia rapidly cooled, with Đukanović winning further elections in Montenegro despite spirited interference from Belgrade.

In 2000 Milošević lost the election in Serbia and in 2001 he was arrested; he died in prison in The Hague while on trial for war crimes. In 2003 the name Yugoslavia was consigned to the dustbin of history and Montenegro entered into a state union with Serbia. In theory the union was based on equality between the two members but in practice Serbia was such a dominant partner that the union proved infeasible from the outset. Again, this rankled given the Montenegrins' historic self-opinion as the 'best of the Serbs'. In May 2006 a slim majority voted for independence and the modern state of Montenegro was formed.

2006

In May Montenegrins vote in a referendum for independence from Serbia. With a slim majority (55%) voting in the affirmative, Montenegro declares independence in June.

PRISMA ARCHIVO / ALAMY ©

➡ Montenegrin flag

2007

Having the previous year become a member of the UN, Montenegro is admitted to the IMF and, continuing its pro-Western stance, signs a 'stabilisation and association' agreement with the EU.

2011

Parliament grants French citizen Prince Nikola II Petrović Njegoš, King Nikola's great-grandson, dual Montenegrin citizenship and allows him to represent the country in certain non-political duties.

Montenegro's People

In this part of the world questions of ethnicity are so thickly embroiled with history, politics and religion that discussions of identity can be a minefield. This is, after all, where phrases like 'ethnic cleansing' were first invented. Yet to an outsider, the more you travel in the Balkans, the more you're struck by the similarities between its various peoples: the warm hospitality, the close family bonds, the social conservatism, the fiery temper, and the passionate approach to life.

Football (soccer), basketball, water polo and handball are the national sporting obsessions. Current big-name footballers include Mirko Vučinić (Juventus FC), Stevan Jovetić (ACF Fiorentina) and Simon Vukčević (Blackburn Rovers). Montenegrins playing in American NBA squads include Orlando Magic's Nikola Vučević and Minnesota Timberwolves' Nikola Peković.

Ethnicity vs Nationality

Throughout the Balkans people tend to identify themselves more by ethnicity than citizenship. This is hardly surprising as a family which has never left its ancestral village may have had children born in Montenegro, parents born in Yugoslavia, grandparents born in the Kingdom of Serbs, Croats and Slovenes, and great-grandparents born in the Ottoman or Austro-Hungarian Empires. Countries may come and go, but self-identity tends to stick around. It's understandable then that an Albanian, Bosniak (South Slav Muslim), Croat or Serb might not call themselves Montenegrin, even if their family has lived in the area that is now Montenegro for generations.

In the 2011 census the country's main ethnic groups were Montenegrins (45%), Serbs (29%), Bosniaks (9%) and Albanians (5%). Tellingly, the next major group was 'Does not want to declare' at 5%. To give you an idea of the kind of ethnic knots people tie themselves in, smaller categories represented in the census include Montenegrin Serbs, Serb Montenegrins, Montenegrin Muslims, Muslim Montenegrins, Muslims, Muslim Bosniaks, Bosniak Muslims, Bosnians and just plain Muslims.

In fact, these myriad ethnic identities have little to do with actual genetic heritage and despite the 29 ethnicities listed in the census, around 88% of the population could reasonably be labelled as some flavour of South Slav, with Albanians (5%) and Roma (1%) being the largest non-Slavic minorities. Scratch a little further and its even more complicated, as numerous armies have raped and pillaged their way through these lands over the millennia. One Montenegrin we spoke to was bemused to discover while volunteering for a scientific study that his genetic markers indicated a spectacular mishmash of ethnicities, including a significant proportion of Hun.

Montenegrins are in the majority in most of the country, while Albanians dominate in the southeast (Ulcinj), Bosniaks in the far east (Rožaje and Plav), and Serbs in Herceg Novi (due to a large influx caused by the Yugoslav wars) and parts of the north and east (Plužine, Pljevlja, Bijelo Polje, Berane and Andrijevica).

Religion and ethnicity broadly go together in these parts. Over 72% of the population is Orthodox (mainly Montenegrins and Serbs), 19% Muslim (mainly Bosniaks and Albanians), 3% Roman Catholic (mainly Albanians and Croats) and only 1% atheist.

A popular self-belief is that Montenegro has a better tolerance of ethnic and religious minorities than many of its neighbours. This is possibly true, although you may still hear some mutterings from locals about the threat of a Greater Serbia/Albania/Croatia.

The Warrior Spirit

It's no surprise that the areas where people most strongly identify as Montenegrin are those which were part of Montenegro before the dawn of the 20th century, especially in the old heartland around Cetinje. This is where the archetype of the noble Montenegrin warrior, fierce in battle and devoted to freedom and the Orthodox Church, had its origins.

A staple feature of nearly every museum in Montenegro is a display of weapons. These aren't any old guns and swords. Inlaid with mother-of-pearl and set with precious jewels, these are finely crafted objects that have been handled with obvious love and care. The period architecture was solid and perfunctory and the paintings largely devotional, but when it came to making guns, the Montenegrins were happy to indulge themselves. Men weren't properly dressed without a pair of fancy pistols protruding from their waistbands; one can only imagine what kind of accidental injuries were sustained.

The warrior spirit may traditionally have been at the heart of Montenegrin society but today most people are keen to get on with their lives and put the turbulence of the last 25 years behind them. Gunshots can still be heard here but only in celebration. It's the traditional accompaniment to weddings and other festivities, as a flight from Ljubljana to Podgorica discovered when it took an accidental hit during celebrations for Orthodox Christmas Eve in 2008. There were no casualties.

Tied in with the warrior culture is the importance of *čojstvo i junaštvo*, which roughly translates as 'humanity and bravery' – in other words,

It's said that the first prison in Cetinje didn't need to lock the doors: confiscating the prisoners' pistols was enough to keep them inside as it was considered shameful to walk around unarmed.

MONTENEGRIN VS SERB

The issue of identity is particularly thorny with regard to current Montenegrin-Serb relations. For centuries, Montenegrins considered themselves 'the best of the Serbs', keeping the flame of independent Serbian culture alive while their brethren elsewhere were under the Ottoman yoke. Pro-Serbian graffiti covers the country and while most Montenegrins feel a strong kinship to their closest siblings, this is coupled with a determination to maintain their distinct identity.

The main unifying factor has traditionally been the Serbian Orthodox Church (SOC), but even that was shaken with the formation of a new Montenegrin Orthodox Church (MOC) in 1993, claiming to revive the self-governing church of Montenegro's *vladikas* (prince-bishops) which was dissolved in 1920. Furthermore, they claim that all church property dating prior to 1920, and any churches built with state funds since, should be returned to it. The SOC doesn't recognise the MOC and neither do the other major Orthodox churches. The SOC still controls most of the country's churches and monasteries. Relations between the two churches have been acrimonious, to the say the least.

On a temporal level, things have been equally tense. After negotiating a reasonably amicable divorce from the unhappy state union with Serbia in 2006, relations took a turn for the worse. In 2008 Serbia expelled Montenegro's ambassador after Montenegro officially recognised the former Serbian province of Kosovo as an independent country, joining around 50 other nations that had already done so. Serbia has vowed never to recognise Kosovo, which many Serbs view as their spiritual heartland.

Diplomatic relations between Montenegro and Serbia have since improved. After his election in 2012, Serbian president Tomislav Nikolić, regarded as a nationalist, stated 'I recognise Montenegrin independence, but I don't recognise any difference between Serbs and Montenegrins, because it doesn't exist.'

chivalry. In the past it inspired soldiers to fight to the death rather than abandon their mates to the enemy or face the shame of being captured. While it might not have exactly the same practical application today, don't expect a Montenegrin to back down from a fight, especially if the honour of their loved ones is at stake. Luckily Montenegro doesn't (yet) attract stag-party groups – it doesn't take much to imagine the sort of reception that drunken louts would receive if they were stupid enough to be disrespectful to the local women.

The most common graffiti you'll spot in Montenegro is a cross with the letter 'c' in each of its quadrants. This is actually the Cyrillic version of the letter 's' and it stands for *samo sloga Srbina spasava*, meaning 'only unity saves the Serbs'.

Montenegrin Life

On a warm summer's evening the main street of every town fills up, as they do throughout the Balkans, with a constant parade of tall, beautiful, well-dressed people of all ages, socialising with their friends, checking each other out and simply enjoying life. In summer, life is lived on the streets and in the cafes.

The enduring stereotype of Montenegrins is that they are lazy, an accusation that they themselves sometimes revel in. Certainly the cafes and bars are always full, but perhaps no more so than in the neighbouring countries. As a popular local joke goes, 'Man is born tired and lives to rest'. This accusation of indolence probably derived from the era when occupations other than fighting and raiding the neighbouring Turks were seen to be beneath a man's dignity. It's certainly not true of Montenegrin women, to whom all the actual heavy labour fell.

Montenegrin society has traditionally been rigidly patriarchal and women were expected to kiss a man's hand as a sign of respect. In 1855 Prince Danilo caused a scandal by publicly kissing the hand of his beloved fiancé; one of his officials berated him, saying: 'I would never kiss the hand of a woman or a Turk'. Despite major advances in education and equality for women during the communist years, distinct gender roles remain. If you're invited to a Montenegrin home for dinner, for example, it's likely that women will do all the cooking, serving of the meal and cleaning up, and it's quite possible that an older hostess may not sit down and eat with you but spend her whole time fussing around the kitchen.

In his 1848 book *Dalmatia and Montenegro*, Englishman Sir John Gardner Wilkinson noted that Montenegrin men were akin to 'despots' with women as their 'slaves': 'She is the working beast of burden and his substitute in all laborious tasks'.

These days you'll see plenty of younger women out and about in cafes and bars. Literacy and employment levels are relatively equal, and basic rights are enshrined in law including (since 1945) the right to vote.

Montenegrin society has traditionally been tribal, with much emphasis placed on extended family-based clans. This can create the potential for nepotism; accusations that major employers and public officials favour family, friends or business associates are commonplace. Family ties are strong and people generally live with their parents until they are married. This makes life particularly difficult for gays and lesbians or anyone wanting a taste of independence. Many young people get a degree of this by travelling to study in a different town.

Although people have drifted away from the more remote villages, Montenegro isn't particularly urbanised, with about half of the populace living in communities of less than 10,000 people. Roughly a third of the population live in the two cities that have more than 20,000 people (Podgorica and Nikšić).

Art & Architecture

Montenegro's historic preoccupation with religion and war focused its earliest artistic endeavours on sumptuously painted churches, beautifully crafted weapons and epic poetry. The modern stereotype of the bed-wetting poet whimpering on about romantic failures or fields of daffodils had no place in macho Montenegrin society; traditionally the role of the warrior and the poet went hand in hand. Peacetime in communist Yugoslavia saw a flourishing of divergent artistic expression, particularly in the fields of painting, sculpture, cinema and architecture.

Literature

Towering over Montenegrin literature is Petar II Petrović Njegoš (1813–51); towering so much, in fact, that his mausoleum overlooks the country from the top of the black mountain itself. This poet and prince-bishop produced the country's most enduring work of literature, *Gorski vijenac* (The Mountain Wreath; 1847), a verse play romanticising the struggle for freedom from the Ottomans. It's not without controversy as the story glorifies the massacre of Muslims on Orthodox Christmas Eve in 1702, known as the Montenegrin Vespers. It's not certain whether it actually happened, but according to the story Vladika Danilo, Njegoš' great-granduncle, ordered the leaders of the Montenegrin tribes to kill all of their kinspeople (men, women and children) who had converted to Islam. Some commentators have drawn a parallel between this story of ethnic cleansing and the atrocities that took place in Bosnia in the 1990s.

The Montenegrin language lends itself to poetry and it was once commonplace to frame formal language in verse. A British diplomat from the time of King Nikola reported that a government minister once delivered an entire budget in verse.

Following in the same epic tradition was Avdo Međedović (1875–1953), a peasant from Bijelo Polje who was hailed as the most important *guslar* (singer/composer of epic poetry accompanied by the *gusle,* a one-stringed folk instrument) of his time. If you think that 'Stairway to Heaven' is too long, it's lucky you didn't attend the marathon performance over several days where Međedović is said to have recited a 13,331-line epic.

He may have been born a Bosnian Croat but Ivo Andrić (1892–1975), Yugoslavia's greatest writer, had a home in Herceg Novi. Andrić was awarded the Nobel Prize in 1961 for his brilliant *Bridge over the Drina* (1945). While you're rafting along the Tara River, it's worth remembering that the Tara becomes the Drina just over the Bosnian border.

Miodrag Bulatović (1930–91) was known for his black humour and graphic portrayals of dark subjects. His most famous books such as *Hero on a Donkey* (1967), *The Red Rooster Flies Heavenward* (1959) and *The Four-Fingered People* (1975) are available in English.

Danilo Kiš (1935–89) was an acclaimed author of the Yugoslav period who had several novels translated into English, including *Hourglass* (1972) and *A Tomb for Boris Davidovich* (1976). He was born in what is now Serbia but moved to Cetinje with his Montenegrin mother after his Hungarian Jewish father was killed in the Holocaust.

Montenegrin-born Borislav Pekić (1930–92) was another significant name in Yugoslav literature. His huge opus includes novels, dramas, science fiction, film scripts, essays and political memoirs. His work has

MUSIC, SACRED & PROFANE

Archbishop Jovan of Duklja was producing religious chants in the 10th century, making him the earliest-known composer in the region. Traditional instruments include the flute and the one-stringed *gusle* which is used to accompany epic poetry.

The most famous Montenegrin musician of the moment is 30-year-old classical guitarist Miloš Karadaglić, who won the Breakthrough Artist prize at the 2012 Classical BRIT Awards and has been touring the world on the back of number one recordings on the US, UK and Australian classical charts.

In the 1990s the excruciatingly named Monteniggers carried the torch for home-grown hip hop. Continuing on the unfortunate name theme, Rambo Amadeus is Montenegro's answer to Frank Zappa. He's been releasing albums since the late 1980s, flirting with styles as diverse as turbofolk, hip hop and drum and bass – all with a large serving of laughs. In 2012 he created one of the more memorable Eurovision Song Contest moments, performing his song 'Euro Neuro' backed by a wooden 'Trojan donkey' and breakdancers. The lyrics, while topical ('monetary breakdance, give me time to refinance') included such inspired rants as 'I don't like snobism, nationalism, puritanism. I am different organism. My heroism is pacifism, altruism. I enjoy bicyclism, liberalism, tourism, nudism...'.

If anyone doubts the relevance of Eurovision they should travel through Montenegro. Montenegrins love their local pop, particularly if it's a gut-wrenching power ballad or a cheesy ditty played loud and accompanied by a thumping techno beat.

been translated into many languages but at present only the early novels *The Time of Miracles* (1965), *The Houses of Belgrade* (1970) and *How to Quiet a Vampire* (1977) are available in English.

Visual Arts

Montenegro's fine-arts legacy can be divided into two broad strands: religious iconography and Yugoslav-era painting and sculpture.

The nation's churches are full of wonderful frescoes and painted iconostases (the screen that separates the congregation from the sanctuary in Orthodox churches). A huge number were produced by members of the Dimitrijević-Rafailović clan from Risan in the Bay of Kotor, who turned out 11 painters between the 17th and 19th centuries.

One of the rising stars of Montenegrin literature is Andrej Nikolaidis, whose novel *Sin* (The Son; 2011) won the European Union Prize for Literature and has been translated into English, alongside *Dolazak* (The Coming; 2009). Another one to watch is Ognjen Spahić, whose *Hansenova djeca* (Hansen's Children; 2004) won a regional award.

Earlier Serbian masters (predating Montenegro) include Longin, a monk from 16th-century Peć (in present-day Kosovo), whose unique approach to colour created otherworldly scenes of saints and Serbian royalty backed by blue mountains and golden skies. You'll find his work at Piva Monastery. Following him half a century later was Đorđe Mitrofanović from Hilandar (now in northern Greece), whose accomplished icons and frescoes feature in the Morača and Pljevlja monasteries. A talented contemporary of his was Kozma, who also worked at Morača.

Yugoslavia proved to be something of a golden age for the arts. Among the modern painters, an early great was Petar Lubarda (1907–74) whose stylised oil paintings included themes from Montenegrin history. Miodrag (Dado) Đurić (1933–2010) was known for his accomplished surrealist paintings and drawings, but he also produced engravings, sculpture and, in later years, digital work. In 2012 an offshoot of the Montenegrin Art Gallery devoted to 20th-century and contemporary art was opened in Cetinje and named in his honour.

Other names to look out for include Milo Milunović (1897–1967), Jovan Zonjić (1907–61), Vojo Stanić (born 1924), Filip Janković (born 1935), Dimitrije Popović (born 1951) and sculptor Risto Stijović (1894–1974). The best places to see the works of these and others are at Cetinje's Montenegrin Art Gallery and the museums and galleries of Podgorica.

Of the contemporary crop, one to watch is Jelena Tomašević, whose paintings and video installations have been exhibited in New York, Berlin, Milan and Venice. Born in Belgrade to Montenegrin parents, performance artist Marina Abramović won the Golden Lion in the Venice Biennale in 1997. One of her most well-known pieces was *The Artist Is Present*, where she sat for 75 days immobile in a chair in New York's Museum of Modern Art while museum visitors took turns to sit opposite her.

The unusual *oro* is a circle dance accompanied by the singing of the participants as they tease each other and take turns to enter the circle and perform a stylised eagle dance. For a dramatic conclusion, the strapping lads form a two storey circle, standing on each other's shoulders.

Cinema

In the few years since independence, Montenegrin cinema has yet to set the world alight. Someone that's working hard to change that is Marija Perović, who is credited with being the country's first female film and TV director. She followed up her 2004 debut *Opet pakujemo majmune* (Packing the Monkeys, Again!) with *Gledaj me* (Look at Me) in 2008.

Montenegro-born Veljko Bulajić has been directing movies since the 1950s, with his most recent being *Libertas* in 2006. His *Vlak bez voznog reda* (Train Without a Timetable) was nominated for the Golden Palm at Cannes in 1959, while *Rat* (War) was nominated for the Golden Lion at the 1960 Venice Film Festival. In 1969 he wrote and directed *Bitka na Neretvi* (The Battle of Neretva), which was nominated for the Academy Award for Best Foreign Language Film.

Another noteworthy Yugoslav-era director was Živko Nikolić (1941–2001), who directed 24 features from the 1960s to 1990s.

Montenegro's biggest Hollywood success is cinematographer Bojan Bazelli, whose titles include *King of New York* (1990), *Kalifornia* (1993), *Mr & Mrs Smith* (2005), *Hairspray* (2007) and *Rock of Ages* (2012).

Ironically, the movie that springs to most people's minds when they think of Montenegro is the 2006 James Bond flick *Casino Royale;* the Montenegrin scenes were actually shot in the Czech Republic. The Golden Palm–nominated *Montenegro* (1981), directed by Serb Dušan Makavejev, was set in Sweden.

STEĆCI

Northern Montenegro and other parts of the Western Balkans are a treasure trove of carved medieval tombstones known as *stećci*. Their origins and symbolism continue to puzzle archaeologists.

Architecture

Traditional Montenegrin houses are sturdy stone structures with small shuttered windows and terracotta-tiled pitched roofs. In the mountainous regions a stone base is topped with a wooden storey and a steeply pitched cut-gable roof designed to let the snow slide off. The *kula* is a blocky tower-like house built for defence that's most common in the country's far eastern reaches. They are usually three to four stories tall with no windows on the lowest floor, and they sometimes have ornate overhanging balconies in wood or stone on the upper level.

The influence of Venice is keenly felt in the walled towns of the coast, which echo the spirit of Dubrovnik and other Dalmatian towns. Cetinje's streets include late-19th-century mansions and palaces remaining from its days as the royal capital.

It's easy to be dismissive of the utilitarian socialist architecture of the Yugoslav period, yet there are some wonderfully inventive structures dating from that time. James Bond would have been quite at home settling in with a martini beneath the sharp angles and bubbly light fixtures of some of the 1970s hotels. It would be a shame if those that haven't already been bowled over or modernised aren't restored to their period-piece glory.

As for the concrete apartment blocks of the cities, they may look grim but they're hardly the slums you'd expect of similar-looking housing projects in the West. While nobody seems to be charged with the upkeep of the exteriors, inside they're generally comfortable and well looked after.

The Montenegrin Kitchen

Loosen your belt, you're in for a treat. Eating in Montenegro is generally an extremely pleasurable experience. By default, most of the food is local, fresh and organic, and hence very seasonal. Despite its small size, Montenegro has at least three distinct regional styles: the food of the old Montenegrin heartland, mountain food and coastal cuisine.

In 1951, when acclaimed Croatian sculptor Ivan Meštrović was commissioned to create the models for the magnificent statues in the Njegoš Mausoleum on the top of Mt Lovćen, it's said that all he asked for by way of payment was cheese and *pršut* from Njeguši.

Montenegrin Heartland Specialties

The village of Njeguši on the edge of Lovćen (the black mountain) is famous for its *pršut* (smoke-dried ham) and *sir* (cheese). Anything with 'Njeguški' in its name is going to be a true Montenegrin dish stuffed with these two goodies; this might be pork chops, veal, steak or spit-roasted meat *(Njeguški ražanj).*

Old Montenegro extended to the Crnojević River and the upper reaches of Lake Skadar, where the cuisine is dominated by three main freshwater fish: eel *(jegulja)*, bleak *(ukljeva)* and carp *(krap).*

Mountain Food

In the northern mountains, the food was traditionally more stodgy, meaty and Serb-influenced, providing comfort and sustenance on long winter nights. A traditional method of cooking is *ispod sača*, where meat and vegetables are roasted under a metal lid covered with hot coals, usually set in a hearth in the middle of the room for warmth. Lamb may also be slowly poached in milk with spices and potato *(brav u mljeku)* in a dish that's particularly popular in the Albanian areas. Beef is cooked with cabbage-like *raštan*, rice and red peppers to make a rich stew called *japraci*. You might eat it with *cicvara* (a cheesy, creamy polenta or buckwheat dish) or *kačamak* (similar but with potato). The best honey *(med)* is also produced in the mountains.

Coastal Cuisine

For most sun-seeking holidaymakers, this is the food they'll mainly encounter – and it's absolutely delicious. The food on the coast is indistinguishable from Dalmatian cuisine: lots of grilled seafood, garlic, olive oil and Italian-style dishes.

Be sure to try the fish soup *(riblja čorba)*, a tasty clear broth that usually includes rice. Grilled squid *(lignje na žaru)* is always an excellent choice, the crispy tentacles coated in garlic and olive oil; *punjene lignje* is served stuffed with *pršut* and *sir*. Nearly 400 years of Venetian rule has left a legacy of excellent risotto and pasta dishes. Black risotto *(crni rižoto)* gets its rich colour and subtle flavour from squid ink and includes pieces of squid meat. Seafood risotto can also be white or red (made with a tomato-based sauce) and served hot or cold.

While all of these dishes make filling mains, at a formal dinner they're just a precursor to the grilled fish. In most fish restaurants, whole fish

MONTENEGRIN WINE

Montenegro's domestic wine is eminently drinkable and usually the cheapest thing on the menu. *Vranac* is the indigenous red grape, producing excellent, full-bodied wines. It's traditionally aged in walnut rather than oak barrels and its history goes back an extremely long way. Illyrian Queen Teuta is said to have been particularly fond of the drop and encouraged its production in the 3rd century BC. Locally produced whites include chardonnay, sauvignon blanc and the native *krstač*.

(ribe) are presented to the table for you to choose from and sold by the kilogram according to a quality-based category. Local varieties tend to be small but tasty; the bigger ones are probably fresh but imported. Fish dishes are flavoured with wild herbs such as laurel and parsley as well as lemon and garlic. The traditional accompaniment is a delicious mixture of silverbeet *(blitva)*, mushy boiled potato, olive oil and garlic, often referred to on English menus as a 'Dalmatian garnish'.

Many people distil their own *rakija* (brandy). The most common variety in Montenegro is *loza*, made out of grapes, but it can be made from just about anything. It's offered as a sign of hospitality, so brace yourself – it typically ranges from 40% to 60% alcohol.

Regional Dishes

Various types of grilled meat are common throughout the former Yugoslavia, including *ćevapčići* (pieces of minced meat shaped into small skinless sausages), *pljeskavica* (spicy hamburger patties) and *ražnjići* (pork or veal kebabs). Grills are often served with fried chips and salad.

For dishes that have more than just meat try *musaka* (layers of aubergine, potato and minced meat), *sarma* (minced meat and rice rolled in sour-cabbage leaves), *kapama* (stewed lamb, onions and spinach with yogurt) and *punjene tikvice* or *paprike* (courgettes or capsicum stuffed with minced meat and rice). Other regional dishes include spicy Hungarian goulash *(gulaš)* and Turkish kebabs *(kebap)*.

The cheapest and most ubiquitous Balkan snack is *burek*, a greasy filo-pastry pie made with cheese, meat *(meso)*, potato *(krompir)* or occasionally mushrooms *(pečurke)*, most commonly consumed with yogurt. Savoury or sweet pancakes *(palačinke)* are served from kiosks in busy areas. Toppings include chopped walnuts and almonds, jam and banana. For a major artery clog, go for a *slane* (salty) *palačinke* – a heart attack disguised as a crumbed, deep-fried, cheese-filled pancake.

There isn't a lot of comprehension about vegetarianism in these parts, so expect to get a few confused or incredulous looks. Pasta, pizza and salad are the best fallback options. Beware of ordering stuffed vegetables as they're likely to be stuffed with meat.

The Main Meals

Breakfast *(doručak)* usually consists of fresh bread with slices of cheese and cured meat (salami or *pršut*) or perhaps a sweet pastry. Locals often skip breakfast and grab something like *burek* on their way to work. Omelette *(omlet)* is the most common cooked breakfast.

Lunch *(ručak)*, served mid-afternoon, has traditionally been the main family meal, but with Western working hours catching on, this is changing. A family lunch might consist of soup followed by salad and a cooked meat or fish dish of some description. Dinner *(večera)* would then be lighter, possibly just bread with cured meats, cheese and olives. However, if you're heading out for a proper sit-down evening meal, you'll probably start late (after 8pm) and eat a meal similar to the typical lunch.

Fresh seasonal fruit is the usual closer to a meal. The most typical Montenegrin sweet dish is *priganice* (fritters) served with honey, cheese and jam *(džem)*. Incredibly sweet cakes and tortes are offered with coffee, including delicious baklava. The local ice cream *(sladoled)* is also excellent.

National Parks & Wildlife

'Wild Beauty', crows Montenegro's enduring tourism slogan, and indeed the marketing boffins are right to highlight the nation's extraordinary natural blessings. In the mountainous interior are pockets of virgin forest and large mammals, long since hunted out of existence on most of the continent, are still hanging on – just.

Montenegro has 500 types of herbs with medicinal properties, many of which are harvested for essential oils and ingredients for natural remedies. Wormwood is an ingredient of absinthe and was once exported to Italy to make the bitter liqueur Amaro Montenegro.

Durmitor National Park

Montenegro's first three national parks were declared in 1952: Lovćen, Biogradska Gora and Durmitor. The most interesting and popular of the three is Durmitor, a magnificent place for nature-lovers, blessed with springs of clear mountain water and glacial lakes that mirror the heavens. In 1980 it was recognised by Unesco as a World Heritage Site.

The 39,000-hectare park is comprised of the Durmitor mountain range and a narrow strip forming an elephant's trunk along the Tara Canyon. The Durmitor range has 48 peaks over 2000m high including Bobotov Kuk (2523m), which is often referred to as the country's highest mountain. In actual fact there is a higher peak in the Prokletije Mountains bordering Albania, but Bobotov Kuk is the highest mountain entirely within Montenegro. The Tara River is hidden in the deepest canyon in Europe (1300m at its apogee). It's not sheer force of water which has gouged such an impressive rift through the mountains but rather the carbon dioxide in the water reacting with the hard limestone (calcium carbonate) to form soluble calcium bicarbonate.

Popular activities in the park include rafting (between April and October), skiing (from January to March), hiking, rock climbing and jeep safaris (best in summer). These can all be organised from Žabljak, the park's gateway town.

Lovćen National Park

Lovćen National Park's 6220-hectare offering is cultural as well as natural, encompassing the old Montenegrin heartland and the impressive mausoleum of the national hero, Njegoš. Like many of Montenegro's mountains, Lovćen is karstic in nature with craggy grey-white outcrops, sparse vegetation and, beneath, caves. Water disappears into the rock and bubbles up elsewhere to form springs.

Heading up Mt Lovćen (1749m), the lower slopes are covered in forests of black beech. Once these deciduous trees lose their leaves and their distinctive black trunks are bared, you'll understand why the Venetians named it the 'black mountain'. Higher up, the beech is joined by an endemic pine called munika. Healing and sweet-smelling herbs poke out from the rocky slopes, including sage, rosemary, balm, mint, chamomile and St John's wort.

Cetinje, Montenegro's historic capital, is a great place to base yourself while tackling the park's hiking and mountain-biking trails, although Kotor and Budva are also nearby.

Biogradska Gora National Park

The smallest of the national parks, Biogradska Gora covers a 5650-hectare chunk of the Bjelasica Mountains which includes 1600 hectares of virgin forest – one of the most significant untouched stands remaining in Europe. Here you'll find groves of juniper, wild rose, pine, beech, maple, fir and elm trees, the tallest of which reach 45m.

There are no settlements within this park but campsites and bungalows are available near the park office. Mojkovac is the nearest town, although Kolašin makes a better base. Hiking is great in summer but autumn is the best time to visit, when the leaves erupt in colour.

Over half of Montenegro is more than 1000m above sea level and 15% is higher than 1500m.

Lake Skadar National Park

In 1983 Lake Skadar became the country's fourth national park and the first nonmountainous one. Skadar is the largest lake in southern Europe, stretching between Montenegro and Albania, where it's called Shkodër. It's mainly fed by the Morača River in the northwest and drained into the Adriatic by the Bojana River at its opposite corner. The lake is what is known as a cryptodepression, meaning that the deepest parts are below sea level. The lake's marshy edges are carpeted with white and yellow water lilies, reeds, willows and edible water chestnuts. Rare endemic species of orchids may also be found.

Lake Skadar National Park protects 40,000 hectares on the Montenegrin side of the lake, but the whole lake is recognised by an international treaty, the Ramsar Convention, as a 'wetland of international importance'. It is home to a quarter of the world's population of pygmy cormorants and 262 other, mainly migratory, species including the great snipe and the great bustard (mind how you read that). Other glamorous flappers include the Dalmatian pelican, the largest of all pelicans, which is the spokesmodel of the park.

As well as birdwatching, activities include hiking, kayaking, swimming and boat trips to various island monasteries and fortresses. The weather's usually best in August. Virpazar is the main gateway, but other settlements include Murići, Vranjina and Rijeka Crnojevića.

The Bojana River occasionally performs the unusual trick of flowing upstream. This happens in winter when the swollen waters of its Albanian tributary, the Drim, cut across it and the volume of water forces part of the flow back into its source, Lake Skadar.

Prokletije National Park

Montenegro's newest national park was declared in 2009, covering 16,000 hectares of the mountainous region on the border with Albania and Kosovo. It contains the country's highest peak, Kolac (2534m); on the Albanian side of the border the Prokletije mountains soar to 2694m. There has long been talk of declaring the entire range a cross-border Balkan Peace Park, but the politics have yet to be ironed out.

ENVIRONMENTAL ISSUES

Much of the credit for Montenegro's 'wild beauty' lies with the terrain itself. Its rugged contours haven't just hindered foreign invaders, they've limited population spread and the worst excesses of development. The Montenegrin government has realised the value of this by declaring the country the world's first 'ecological state', yet it remains to be seen what this means in a country where hunting is popular, recycling is virtually unknown and people litter as a matter of course. Despite trumpeting the existence of bears, lynx and wolves, no one knows what numbers remain. With numbers so low, hunting (illegal or otherwise) is of real concern.

On the coast, development continues unabated. With most of the Budva Riviera now given over to hulking resort complexes attention has turn to the largely unspoiled Luštica Peninsula.

Ancient glaciers formed the Plav Valley on the edge of the mountains. Lake Visitor, in the mountain of the same name above Plav, has the unusual quirk of a floating island. Local legends say that it was once a raft used by the ancient shepherds to transport stock. Because it was well fertilised it developed soil and foliage and now drifts around the lake.

Tourist infrastructure is limited in the gateway towns of Plav and Gusinje, but that is bound to improve. The park holds plenty of potential for mountain biking, hiking and serious mountaineering.

Wildlife

Many species of animal and bird have managed to find solace in Montenegro's hidden nooks. Precisely because those nooks are so hidden you're unlikely to see any of the more dramatic mammals.

Birdwatchers are more likely to have their tendencies gratified with plenty of rare wetland birds congregating around Lake Skadar and flashy birds of prey swooping over the mountains. King of them all is the golden eagle. It has a wingspan of up to 240cm and can sometimes supplement its rodent diet with lambs and small goats.

The big mammals (brown bear, grey wolves, Eurasian lynx) tend to keep their heads down so as not to have them blown off. Brown bears like to hang out in the forests at altitudes of 900m and higher. In 2000 there were estimated to be less than 130 remaining in Montenegro, concentrated in the northern and eastern mountains. Despite the male bears weighing up to 200kg, they pose little threat to humans unless they're protecting a cub or are startled.

OLM

One of Montenegro's more curious species is the olm, a blind amphibian that can be found in Biogradska Gora National Park. Its Montenegrin name, *čovječja ribica*, means 'human fish' because of its human-like skin.

Likewise grey wolves don't pose much of a threat unless they're rabid or starving. They too fancy forest living but may venture out into the meadows to make closer acquaintance with the odd bit of livestock. For this reason there's still a price on their head in some areas.

Look out for European otters going about their unspeakably cute business around Lake Skadar and the Tara River. Badgers hang out in Durmitor and Biogradska Gora National Parks. Balkan chamois join roe deer in Durmitor, while the latter also wander the Lovćen and Bjelasica Mountains. Golden jackals are known to live around Bar and Ulcinj with three packs spotted on Ada Bojana. Foxes, weasels, moles, groundhogs, hares, shrews, bats, wild boar, red squirrels and dormice complete the diverse mammalian picture.

If you're wandering the remote trails you'll often catch sight of something reptilian scurrying off the path. Montenegro has an impressive collection of lizards, newts, frogs, turtles and snakes. The isolated glacial lakes of the karstic mountain ranges harbour species such as the serdarski triton, a type of alpine newt that only exists in one small lake in Durmitor. The European pond turtle is listed as near-threatened but can still be spotted in both Lovćen and Lake Skadar National Parks.

Of more interest or concern to most visitors are the snakes. Commonly spotted and often mistaken for a snake is the harmless slow-worm (sometimes called blindworm), a 50cm-long brown legless lizard. Rather less harmless is the horned viper. Reaching up to 95cm, this is the largest and most venomous snake in Europe. It likes rocky habitats (which doesn't rule out much in Montenegro) and has a zigzag stripe on its body and a distinctive scaly 'horn' on its nose. If you're close enough to spot the horn you're probably a little too close. The good news is that this guy isn't at all aggressive and will only bite with extreme provocation, so mind where you tread.

Survival Guide

Directory A–Z

Accommodation

Hotels and private accommodation (rooms and apartments for rent) form the bulk of the sleeping options, although hostels have been popping up in the more touristy areas in recent years. Camping grounds operate in summer and some of the mountainous areas have cabin accommodation in 'eco villages' or mountain huts.

In the peak summer season, some places require minimum stays (three days to a week). Many establishments on the coast, even some of the established hotels, close during winter.

Hotel tariffs usually include breakfast, towels, basic toiletries and (unless otherwise mentioned in the reviews) en suites. Most midrange rooms will also have a TV set, a fridge and air conditioning *(klima)* – except in the mountains where cooling isn't necessary and heaters are provided in winter. Top-end establishments will usually have direct-dial telephone access, minibars and, in the very best establishments, fluffy robes, slippers, safes, swimming pools, health spas and 24-hour room service. Free wireless internet connection is becoming the norm, although often the signal is only available in certain parts of the building.

We've included websites in our reviews where they're available, and, failing that, email addresses. Be warned that many Montenegrin businesses are not adept at keeping their websites up to date or replying to emails.

If you don't mind paying a commission in order to save yourself some hassle, specialist travel agencies will arrange things on your behalf. Try **Black Mountain** (☎067-640 869; www.montenegroholiday.com) ❧, **Montenegro Adventures** (Map p100; ☎020-208 000; www.montenegro-adventures.com; Jovana Tomaševića 35) or other recommended local agencies.

Camping & Caravan Parks

Facilities at camping grounds tend to be basic, often with squat toilets and limited water. Some national parks have cabin-style accommodation but most camping grounds don't. Charges are a combination of a nightly rate per vehicle, size of tent, number (and age) of guests and whether you require power or not. Camping grounds are most common along the coast (including the Bay of Kotor) and near Žabljak.

During summer, when shepherds in the mountainous areas take their flocks to the higher meadows, you can ask permission to pitch your tent next to one of their traditional *katun* dwellings.

Hostels

Hostels have made a relatively recent appearance on the scene, as they previously never fitted into tidy bureaucratic pigeonholes, not being either private accommodation or a traditional hotel. Thankfully, that battle has been fought and won, and some great places have sprung up –

PRACTICALITIES

- **Print Media:** *Vijesti* (The News), *Dan* (The Day) and *Pobjeda* (Victory) are all daily newspapers. *Monitor*, a weekly news magazine, joins local-language versions of international titles on the news-stands.
- **Radio & Television:** RTCG (Radio TV Montenegro) is the state broadcaster, with two radio stations and three TV channels. In total there are 11 more-or-less national TV channels and six regional channels. There are dozens of independent radio stations broadcasting around the country.
- **Weights & Measures:** the metric system is used.

SLEEPING PRICE RANGES

Prices are very seasonal, so in this book we've listed prices for the shoulder season (June and September). Discounts are often available for longer bookings. Expect to pay more if you're travelling in the absolute peak months (July and August) and less in the off-season. In the ski resorts the high season runs from January through to March, with the absolute peak around New Year.

All visitors are required to pay a small nightly tourist tax (usually less than €1 per person per night), which is sometimes included in the quoted rate but more often added to the bill at the end. This is almost always collected and paid by the accommodation provider, although some private operators leave it up to the guest to pay. The procedure varies from area to area and it can be nigh on impossible to find the right authority to pay it to. Theoretically you could be asked to provide white accommodation receipt cards (or copies of invoices from hotels) when you leave the country, but in practice this is rarely required.

The following price ranges refer to the cheapest option available for a couple.

€ less than €40

€€ €40 to €99

€€€ more than €99

particularly in Kotor and Budva. Some are little different from private rentals split into dorms. The better custom-built places have well thought out communal spaces and offer a roster of activities. Most have some sort of kitchen facilities; shared bathrooms are the norm.

Hotels

A tidal wave of development has seen hotels large and small spring up in the popular destinations. They usually have some form of restaurant attached and offer the option of half- or full-board (breakfast plus one or two meals). In Montenegro, a hotel spa centre is called a 'wellness centre' and a double bed is referred to as a 'French bed' *(francuski ležaj)*.

Podgorica hotels are consistently pricey (they're targeted at business people and government officials) but you'll find more of a range of establishments on the coast. Generally, the further you travel from Budva, the cheaper the average price. Tourist-focused Žabljak and Kolašin are the most expensive of the northern centres, but you'll find good deals in the other towns.

Private Accommodation

The cheapest options in any town are almost always private rooms and apartment rentals. These can be arranged through travel agencies or, in season, you may be approached at the bus stop or see signs hanging outside the houses (they often read '*Sobe/Zimmer/*Rooms'). Some tourist offices publish guides to private accommodation. Rooms in local homes shouldn't be difficult to find but some places will require minimum stays in high season (often a three-day minimum). Don't expect en suites.

Apartments will always have their own bathroom and at least a kitchenette. Generally speaking, you'll get what you pay for. Cheaper options are a bit rougher and further from the attractions, but there shouldn't be a problem with cleanliness. For luxurious apartments, some of which have swimming pools and cliff-top locations, try www.exploremontenegro.com.

If you're armed with a bit of charm, an adventurous spirit, an unfussy attitude and a few words in the local lingo, it should be possible to turn up in remote villages and ask if anyone has any rooms to rent for the night.

Children

Children are more likely to be fussed over than frowned upon in Montenegro. For many parents this is half the battle won. Hotels, restaurants and cafes warmly welcome children, and we've even seen the occasional young teenager boogying with parents at beachside nightclubs.

However, special facilities for children are more limited. Better hotels may have cots

BOOK YOUR STAY ONLINE

For more accommodation reviews by Lonely Planet authors, check out http://hotels.lonelyplanet.com/montenegro. You'll find independent reviews, as well as recommendations on the best places to stay. Best of all, you can book online.

Climate

Podgorica

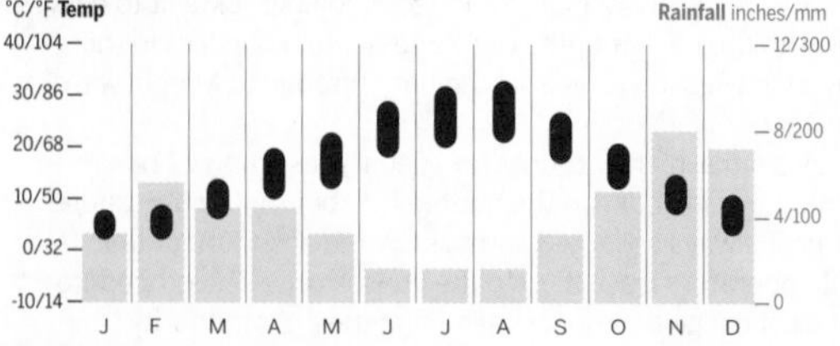

Kotor

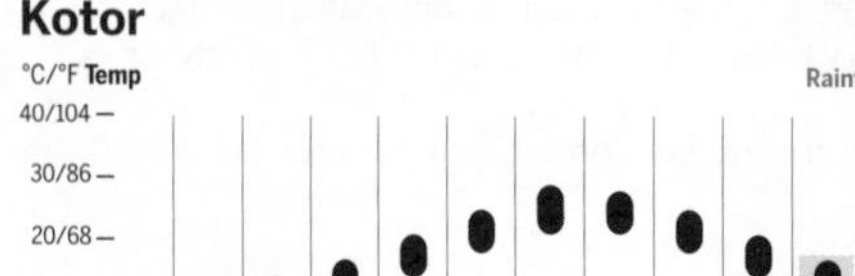

Bijelo Polje

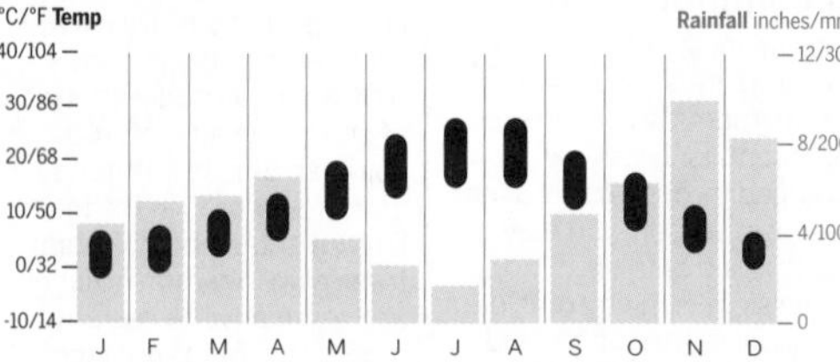

available, but it's best to check in advance. The same goes for car seats at rental car agencies or taxi companies. Car seats aren't legally required, but given the dangers on the roads you should consider bringing your own. Highchairs are the exception rather than the rule at restaurants.

You won't find children's menus but the ubiquity of kid-friendly favourites like pasta, pizza and hot chips (fries) makes mealtime easy. Babysitting services are only offered in the most exclusive five-star hotels.

Disposable nappies (especially Pampers and Huggies) are easy to find. Infant formula is available in the bigger supermarkets, but it's a good idea to bring a few days' supply with you. The main brands are Bebelac and Nestle; you can sometimes find Aptamil too.

You'll rarely see anyone breastfeeding in public, but given that this is encouraged here you're unlikely to strike negative reactions. You're best to bring sufficient breast pads with you, as they're hard to find in Montenegro.

Medical care is generally very good, but language difficulties can present problems. Every town has a medical centre *(Dom zdravlja)*. They generally have a separate section for children with two waiting rooms: one for kids with potentially contagious infections and one dealing with broken bones and the like.

Older offspring should have a blast in Montenegro, with the relatively safe environment allowing them off the leash a little. You may find that they're kicking a ball around with the local scallywags in no time. The opposite is true for toddlers and small children as a generally lower standard of safety regulations (missing railings, unfenced pools etc) means you'll have to keep a closer eye on them.

You'll struggle to get pushchairs along the cobbled lanes and stairways in the older towns and you'll often find yourself having to trundle them along dangerous roads due to parked cars blocking the footpaths. Still, bringing a pram is a good idea, if only so you can join the legions of parents promenading with their babies on summer nights.

Any hurdles you may strike will be insignificant compared to the wonderfully family-friendly atmosphere, fresh air and gently lapping Mediterranean waters that Montenegro provides. Lonely Planet's *Travel With Children* offers further tips for hitting the road with the brood in tow.

Customs Regulations

- To stop tourists from neighbouring countries bringing all their holiday groceries with them, Montenegro restricts the quantity of food which can be brought into the country to 1kg.
- Restrictions apply to entering with tobacco (200 cigarettes or 20 cigars or 250g tobacco), alcohol (1L of wine and 1L of spirits) and perfume (250ml).
- Amounts greater than €2000 of cash or travellers cheques must be declared when leaving the country. If you're entering with a large sum and think you might have more than €2000 left when you leave, complete a currency declaration form on arrival or you may find your money confiscated on departure.
- Drug laws are similar to most other European countries. Possession or trafficking of drugs could result in a lengthy jail sentence.

➡ When you enter the country you need to receive an entry stamp in your passport. If you don't, you may be detained or fined when you seek to leave for entering the country illegally.

Discount Cards

➡ The International Student Identity Card (ISIC; www.isic.org), issued to full-time students 12 years and over, entitles the bearer to discounts on train trips and some admission charges, shops, eateries, accommodation and other services in Montenegro. Get them from student unions, hostelling organisations and some travel agencies.

➡ The same organisation issues the International Youth Travel Card (IYTC; available to people who are between 12 and 26 years of age and not full-time students) and the International Teacher Identity Card (ITIC; available to teaching professionals), both of which give similar discounts to the ISIC.

Electricity

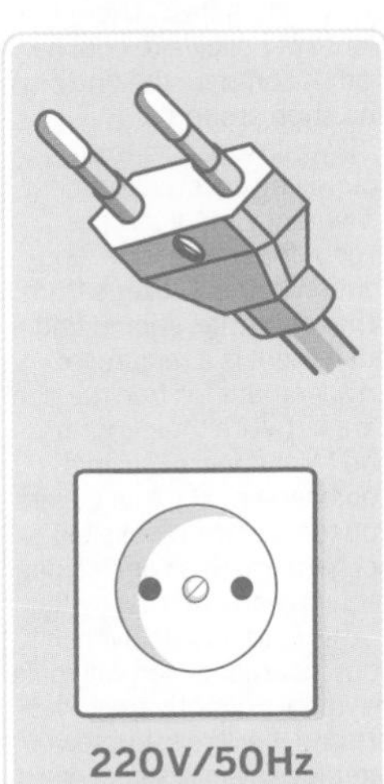

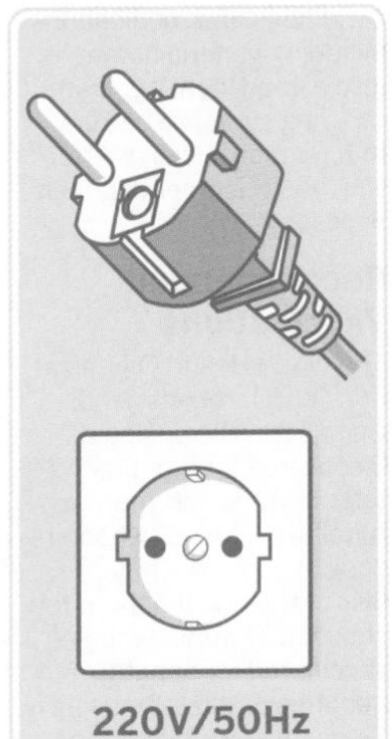

Embassies & Consulates

For a full list of foreign missions in Montenegro, see www.mip.gov.me. The following are all in Podgorica, unless otherwise stated:

Albanian Embassy (Map p100; ☎020-667 380; www.mfa.gov.al; Stanka Dragojevića 14)

Bosnia & Hercegovinian Embassy (Map p100; ☎020-618 105; www.mvp.gov.ba; Atinska 58)

Croatian Embassy & Consulate (www.mvep.hr) Podgorica (☎020-269 760; Vladimira Ćetkovića 2) Kotor (Map p46; ☎032-323 127; Trg od oružja bb)

French Embassy (Map p100; ☎020-655 348; Atinska 35)

German Embassy (Map p100; ☎020-441 000; www.auswaertiges-amt.de; Hercegovačka 10)

Serbian Embassy & Consulate Podgorica (Map p100; ☎020-667 305; www.podgorica.mfa.gov.rs; Hercegovačka 18) Herceg Novi (Map p36; ☎031-350 320; www.hercegnovi.mfa.gov.rs; Njegoševa 40)

UK Embassy (☎020-618 010; www.ukinmontenegro.fco.gov.uk; Ulcinjska 8)

USA Embassy (Map p100; ☎020-410 500; http://podgorica.usembassy.gov; Ljubljanska bb)

The following countries are represented from offices in nearby countries:

Australian Embassy (☎00-381-11-330 3400; www.serbia.embassy.gov.au; Vladimira Popovića 38-40, Novi Beograd, Belgrade, Serbia)

Canadian Embassy (☎00-381-11-306 3000; www.canada.rs; Kneza Miloša 75, Belgrade, Serbia)

Irish Embassy (☎00-361-301 4960; www.dfa.ie; Szabadsag ter 7, Bank Center, Gránit Tower, Budapest, Hungary)

The Netherlands Embassy (☎00-381-11-202 3900; www.nlembassy.rs; Simina 29, Belgrade, Serbia)

Food

See The Montenegrin Kitchen (p154) for information about local cuisine.

If you're ordering fish by the kilogram, a standard portion is around 200g to 250g; ask for a rough price before you choose a fish if you're unsure.

EATING PRICE RANGES

The price indicators used in this book are based on the cost of the cheapest dish on the menu which could be considered a main meal, regardless of whether it is labelled as a main.

€ up to €5

€€ €5 to €8

€€€ over €9

Gay & Lesbian Travellers

Where's the party? The answer's nowhere. Although homosexuality was decriminalised in 1977 and discrimination outlawed in 2010, you won't find a single gay or lesbian venue in Montenegro. Don't be fooled by all the men walking arm-in-arm, or hand-in-hand in the Albanian areas. Attitudes to homosexuality remain hostile and life for gay people is extremely difficult, exacerbated by the fact that most people are expected to live at home until they're married. In recent years there have been high-profile incidents of violence against gay activists, including the brutal beating in the centre of Podgorica in 2012 of three young men who were associated with an anti-homophobia video.

Many gay men resort to online connections (try www.gayromeo.com) or take their chances at a handful of cruisy beaches. These include Jaz Beach near Budva (far left-hand side) and below the ruins of Ratac near Bar. Lesbians will find it even harder to access the local community.

Health

Quality health care is readily available in Montenegro and pharmacists can give valuable advice and sell over-the-counter medication for minor illnesses. The standard of dental care is also good.

Before You Go

A little planning before departure, particularly for pre-existing illnesses, will save trouble later. See your dentist before a long trip. Carry a spare pair of contact lenses and glasses, and take your optical prescription with you. Bring medications in their original, labelled, containers. A letter from your physician describing your medical conditions and medications, including generic names, is also a good idea. If you are carrying syringes, be sure to have a physician's letter with you documenting their necessity.

Recommended Vaccinations

The World Health Organization (WHO) recommends that all travellers should be covered for diphtheria, tetanus, measles, mumps, rubella, pertussis (whooping cough) and polio, regardless of their destination. You should also consider being vaccinated for hepatitis A, hepatitis B and tetanus. Since most vaccines don't produce immunity until at least two weeks after they're given, visit a physician at least six weeks before departure.

Tick-borne encephalitis is spread by tick bites and is thought to exist in forested areas of Montenegro. It is a serious infection of the brain and vaccination is advised for those in risk areas who are unable to avoid tick bites (such as campers and hikers).

The US Center for Disease Control recommends a rabies vaccination for long-term travellers and 'wildlife professionals, researchers, veterinarians, or adventure travelers visiting areas where bats, carnivores, and other mammals are commonly found'.

Sea Urchins

Watch out for sea urchins around rocky beaches; if you get some of their needles embedded in your skin, olive oil will help to loosen them. If they are not removed, they could become infected. As a precaution wear rubber shoes while walking on the rocks and take care while bathing.

Snake Bites

To avoid getting bitten by snakes, do not walk barefoot or stick your hands into holes or cracks. Half of those bitten by venomous snakes are not actually injected with poison (envenomed). If bitten by a snake, do not panic. Immobilise the bitten limb with a splint (eg a stick) and apply a bandage over the site firmly, similar to a bandage over a sprain. Do not apply a tourniquet, or cut or suck the bite. Get medical help as soon as possible so that antivenom can be administered if necessary.

Tap Water

As a general rule, tap water is drinkable in Montenegro but there can be problems. For instance it's advisable not to drink the water in Herceg Novi in May as they close off and the clean the pipes from the main reservoir (in Croatia) and revert to a local reservoir. Bottled water is cheap and readily available.

Insurance

A watertight travel insurance policy covering theft, loss and medical problems is recommended. While theft isn't a huge problem, rental cars are sometimes targeted by opportunists and Montenegro's roads aren't the world's safest. There are plenty of policies to choose from – compare the fine print and shop around.

If you're an EU citizen, you will be covered for most emergency medical care except for emergency repatriation home. Citizens from other countries should find out if there is a reciprocal arrangement for free medical care between their country and Montenegro. Strongly consider a policy that covers you for the worst possible scenario, such as an accident requiring an emergency flight home. Find out in advance if your insurance plan will make payments directly to providers or if it will reimburse you later for any overseas health expenditures. The former option is generally preferable, especially if your finances are limited.

Some policies specifically exclude designated 'dangerous activities' such as scuba-diving, parasailing, paragliding, white-water rafting, skiing and even hiking. If you plan on doing any of these things (a distinct possibility in Montenegro), make sure the policy you choose covers you fully and includes ambulances and emergency medical evacuation.

If you need to make a claim, ensure you obtain and keep all relevant documentation. This may involve a police report in case of theft and invoices for medical expenses incurred. Some policies ask you to call back (reverse charges) to a centre in your home country where an immediate assessment of your problem is made.

Worldwide travel insurance is available at www.lonelyplanet.com/travel_services. You can buy, extend and claim online any time – even if you're already on the road.

Internet Access

Most accommodation providers (excluding private accommodation) now offer free wireless connections, although they often don't penetrate to every part of the building and may be limited to the reception area. Many bars and cafes also offer wireless. One of the sweeteners of the Porto Montenegro project for residents of Tivat is free wireless access throughout the town. Most towns also have an internet cafe; hourly rates start from around 50c.

In the reviews in this book, the internet symbol is used for places that have a computer linked to the internet for guests to use. Places that have a wireless connection are marked with the wireless symbol. Note that the symbols don't imply that the service is free, but in most cases it will be.

Legal Matters

It may seem obvious, but while you are in Montenegro you're covered by Montenegrin law and these laws may differ from those in your home country.

- If you're arrested, you have the right to contact your country's embassy or consulate and arresting officers have a responsibility to help you to do so. They're also required to immediately notify you of the charges you're facing in a language you understand and to inform you that you're not required to give any statement. You have the right to a defence counsel of your own choosing during any interrogation.
- A lower court can choose to detain you for three months pending trial, while a higher court can extend this for a further three months. Minors may not be held for more than 60 days.
- The Montenegrin constitution enshrines a right to a fair and public trial with a defence, legal aid if required and a presumption of innocence.
- Montenegro has outlawed the death penalty but if you're caught with drugs you may face a lengthy stint in a local jail.
- You are required to register with local police within 24 hours of arriving in Montenegro and whenever you change address. Accommodation providers usually do this on your behalf (which is the reason you're asked to hand over your passport when you arrive at a hotel).
- In the past there were incidences of traffic police asking for money upfront for alleged violations, although we are not aware of this being a problem at present. If this happens to you, ask for a full explanation of the situation from the officer and, if it's not forthcoming, ask to speak to your embassy.

Maps

Unless you're planning on doing a lot of driving on back roads, you shouldn't need to buy a road map *(auto karta)*. Sheet maps are available from bookshops and some tourist offices. Intersistem Kartografija publishes a Montenegro road map (1:370,000).

Detailed maps for hikers exploring the Lovćen, Durmitor or Bjelasica mountains are available from national park visitor centres and tourist offices in the vicinity.

Money

- Montenegro uses the euro (€) and all prices quoted in this book are in that currency, unless otherwise stated. See p17 for exchange rates.
- You'll find banks with ATMs in all the main towns, most of which accept Visa, MasterCard, Maestro and Cirrus. ATMs tend to dish out big notes which can be hard to break.
- Don't rely on restaurants, shops or smaller hotels accepting credit cards.
- Tipping isn't expected although it's common to round up to the nearest euro.

Opening Hours

Business hours in Montenegro are a relative concept. Even if hours are posted on the doors of museums or shops, don't be surprised if they're not heeded. Many tourist-orientated businesses, including hotels, close their doors completely from November to March.

Post offices In large towns are usually open from 7am to 8pm Monday to Friday, and sometimes on Saturday also. In smaller towns they may close mid-afternoon, or close at noon and reopen at 5pm.

Banks Generally open from 8am to 5pm Monday to Friday and until noon on Saturday.

Shops In busy areas shops open around 8am or 9am and close at a similar time in the evening. Sometimes they'll close for a few hours in the late afternoon.

Restaurants Open around 8am and close around 11pm or midnight, while cafe-bars may stay open until 2am or 3am.

Post

Every town has a post office that locals use for paying their bills, so you should be prepared for horrendous queues. Parcels should be taken unsealed for inspection. You can receive mail, addressed poste restante, in all towns for a small charge. International postal services are slow.

Public Holidays

New Year's Day 1 and 2 January

Orthodox Christmas 6, 7 and 8 January

Orthodox Good Friday & Easter Monday Date varies, usually April/May

Labour Day 1 May

Independence Day 21 May

Statehood Day 13 July

Safe Travel

- Montenegro's towns are generally safe places. You'll see children playing unsupervised on the streets and young women walking alone at night and hitchhiking (not that we necessarily recommend these things).
- The roads can be treacherous. They're generally in good condition but many are narrow and have sheer drops on one side. The main hazard is from other motorists, who have no qualms about overtaking on blind corners while talking on their mobile phones or stopping in the middle of the road without warning. There's plenty of random tooting – don't let it faze you. It's best to keep your cool and stick to the speed limit as the traffic police are everywhere.
- Chances are you'll see some snakes if you're poking around ruins during summer. Montenegro has two types of venomous vipers but they'll try their best to keep out of your way. If bitten, you will have time to head to a medical centre for the antivenom, but you should head there immediately. Water snakes are harmless.
- Check with the police before photographing any official building they're guarding.
- Since Montenegro is in an active seismic zone, earthquakes strike from time to time. The last major one that caused a loss of life was in 1979.

Telephone

- The international access prefix is 00 or + from a mobile phone.
- Press the *i* button on public phones for dialling commands in English.
- Mobile numbers start with 06.
- Local SIM cards are a good idea if you're planning a longer stay. The main providers (T-Mobile, M:tel and Telenor) have storefronts in most towns. Many shopping centres have terminals where you can top-up your prepay account. Mobile calls are expensive in Montenegro but the main providers offer heavily discounted rates to calls within their network, so it's not uncommon for businesses to advertise three different mobile numbers on different networks.

EMERGENCY NUMBERS

- **Ambulance** (☎124)
- **Fire service** (☎123)
- **Police** (☎122)

Time

- Montenegro is in the Central Europe time zone (an hour ahead of GMT).
- Clocks go forward by an hour for daylight saving at the end of March and return to normal at the end of October.
- Outside the daylight-saving period, when it's midday in Montenegro it will be 3am in Los Angeles, 6am in New York, 11am in London, 9pm in Sydney and 11pm in Auckland.
- Montenegrins use the 24-hour clock, so hours are usually listed as '9–17' rather than '9am–5pm'.

Tourist Information

Official tourist offices (usually labelled *turistička organizacija*) are hit and miss. Some have wonderfully helpful English-speaking staff, regular opening hours and a good supply of free material, while others have none of the above. Thankfully the National Tourist Office is more switched on and its website (www.montenegro.travel) is a great resource for travellers. It doesn't have a public office but you can dial 1300 at any time to receive tourist information from multilingual staff.

Travellers With Disabilities

The mobility-impaired will find the cobbled lanes and numerous stairways extremely challenging. There are very few specific facilities for either travellers or residents with disabilities. Some of the top-end hotels have wheelchair-accessible rooms.

Visas

Visas are not required for citizens of most European countries, Turkey, Israel, Singapore, South Korea, Israel, Australia, New Zealand, Canada and the USA. In most cases this allows a stay of up to 90 days. If your country is not covered by a visa waiver, you will need a valid passport, verified letter of invitation, return ticket, proof of sufficient funds and proof of medical cover in order to obtain a visa.

Women Travellers

Other than a cursory interest shown by men towards solo women travellers, travelling is hassle-free and easy. In Muslim areas some women wear a headscarf but most adopt European fashions.

Transport

GETTING THERE & AWAY

Whether you choose to fly, train, ferry or drive, it's not difficult to get to Montenegro these days. New routes are continually being added to the busy timetable at the country's two airports, although at present no low-cost carriers are represented. It's sometimes cheaper and more convenient to make your way from neighbouring countries, especially Croatia. Dubrovnik's airport is very close to the border and the Adriatic's most beautiful city makes an impressive starting point to a Montenegro holiday. Flights, tours and rail tickets can be booked online at www.lonelyplanet.com/bookings.

Entering the Country

Entering Montenegro doesn't pose any particular bureaucratic challenges. In fact, the country's dead keen to shuffle tourists in. Unfortunately, Croatia seems less happy to let them go, if the long waits at their side of the Adriatic highway checkpoint are any indication; it pays to allow an hour. The main crossing from Serbia at Dobrakovo can also be slow at peak times.

Passport

Make sure that your passport has at least six months left on it. You'll need a visa if you're not from one of the many countries with a visa-waiver arrangement. There are no particular nationalities or stamps in your passport that will deny you entry. Make sure that your passport is stamped when you enter the country or else there may difficulties when you leave.

Air

Airports & Airlines

Montenegro's largest and most modern airport is immediately south of the capital **Podgorica** (TGD; ☎020-444 244; www.montenegroairports.com). The entire south of the country and everywhere as far north as Kolašin is within 100km of this airport. If you're wondering about the airport code, the TGD is a hangover from Podgorica's previous name Titograd. Locals sometimes call it Golubovci airport as it's close to a village with that name. The airport's safety record is blemished only by a small plane skidding while landing in snowy conditions in 2005; there were no serious injuries.

The second international airport at **Tivat** (TIV; ☎032-670 930; www.montenegroairports.com) is well positioned for holidaymakers heading to the Bay of Kotor or Budva and now welcomes over half a million passengers annually. Despite its mountainous surrounds and a runway that ends only 100m from the

CLIMATE CHANGE & TRAVEL

Every form of transport that relies on carbon-based fuel generates CO_2, the main cause of human-induced climate change. Modern travel is dependent on aeroplanes, which might use less fuel per per person than most cars but travel much greater distances. The altitude at which aircraft emit gases (including CO_2) and particles also contributes to their climate change impact. Many websites offer 'carbon calculators' that allow people to estimate the carbon emissions generated by their journey and, for those who wish to do so, to offset the impact of the greenhouse gases emitted with contributions to portfolios of climate-friendly initiatives throughout the world. Lonely Planet offsets the carbon footprint of all staff and author travel.

water, there has never been an accident here.

Montenegro's de facto third airport is actually in neighbouring Croatia. **Dubrovnik airport** (DBV; ☎+385-20-773 100; www.airport-dubrovnik.hr) is a modern facility only 17km from the border and the closest airport to Herceg Novi. Commonly referred to locally as Čilipi airport, it's used by over 1.3 million travellers annually.

The word for airport in Montenegrin is *aerodrom* (аеродром). This was also used in Croatia until independence but in a fit of French-style linguistic nationalism the official Croatian term has been changed to a direct translation of the words for 'air' and 'port', *zračna luka* – a potential trap for English speakers.

Montenegro Airlines is the national carrier, running a small fleet of 102- to 116-seater planes. Apart from the skid at Podgorica airport mentioned above, its safety record has been unsullied during its 10 years of operation. It has code-share agreements with Adria, Austrian and JAT Airways.

AIRLINES FLYING TO/ FROM MONTENEGRO & DUBROVNIK

Literally dozens of airlines fly into Montenegro or neighbouring Dubrovnik from all over Europe. Some of them only operate in the busy summer months or reduce their services substantially at other times.

Adria Airlines (Map p100; www.adria.si) Flies between Ljubljana and Podgorica.

Aer Lingus (www.aerlingus.com) Flies between Dublin and Dubrovnik, from April to October only.

Austrian Airlines (www.austrian.com) Flies on their offshoot Tyrolean from Vienna to Podgorica and Dubrovnik.

British Airways (www.britishairways.com) Flies between London Gatwick and Dubrovnik.

Condor (www.condor.com) Flies between Frankfurt and Dubrovnik.

Croatia Airlines (Map p100; www.croatiaairlines.com) Flies from Zagreb to Podgorica; and from Frankfurt, Munich, Paris, Rome, Zagreb and Zurich to Dubrovnik.

easyJet (www.easyjet.com) Bargain flights to Dubrovnik from Berlin, Edinburgh, Geneva, London (Gatwick and Stansted), Lyon, Milan, Paris and Rome.

Eurolot (www.eurolot.com) Flies from Gdansk and Poznan to Dubrovnik.

Finnair (www.finnair.com) Seasonal flights from Helsinki to Dubrovnik.

germanwings (www.germanwings.com) Flies from Cologne/Bonn, Hanover and Stuttgart to Dubrovnik.

Jat Airways (www.jat.com) Flies from Belgrade to Podgorica and Tivat.

Jet2.com (www.jet2.com) Flies to Dubrovnik from Belfast (April to September), East Midlands, Newcastle (both May to September), Edinburgh, Leeds (both April to October) and Manchester (April to November).

Jetairfly (www.jetairfly.com) Flies between Brussels and Dubrovnik, from May to September.

Lufthansa (www.lufthansa.com) Flies between Munich and Dubrovnik.

Monarch Airlines (www.monarch.co.uk) Cheap flights to Dubrovnik from Birmingham, London Gatwick and Manchester from May to September.

Montenegro Airlines (www.montenegroairlines.com) Flies from Belgrade and Moscow to Tivat. Also from Belgrade, Frankfurt, Ljubljana, Moscow, Niš, Paris, Rome, Vienna and Zurich to Podgorica.

Moskovia Airlines (www.ak3r.ru) Flies from Moscow to Tivat.

Norwegian Air Shuttle (www.norwegian.no) Seasonal flights from Bergen, Copenhagen, London Gatwick, Oslo, Stavanger, Stockholm and Trondheim to Dubrovnik.

Rossiya Airlines (www.rossiya-airlines.ru) Flies from St Petersburg to Tivat.

S7 Airlines (www.s7.ru) Flies from Moscow to Tivat.

SAS (www.flysas.com) Flies from Copenhagen, Oslo and Stockholm to Dubrovnik.

Thomas Cook Airlines (www.thomascookairlines.com) Flies from Brussels to Tivat and Dubrovnik, from April to October.

Thomson (www.thomson.co.uk) Flies to Dubrovnik from Birmingham, London Gatwick and Manchester.

TUIfly (www.tuifly.com) Flies to Dubrovnik from Cologne/Bonn, Hanover and Stuttgart.

Turkish Airlines (www.turkishairlines.com) Flies between Istanbul and Podgorica.

Vueling (www.vueling.com) Seasonal flights between Barcelona and Dubrovnik.

Land

Montenegro may be a wee slip of a thing but it borders five other states: Croatia, Bosnia and Hercegovina (BiH), Serbia, Kosovo and Albania. You can easily enter Montenegro by land from any of its neighbours.

Bicycle

There are no problems bringing a bicycle into the country. There are not many cyclists here so road-users are not cycle savvy – and remember that there's a *monte* (mountain) in the country's name for a reason.

If you want to bring your own bike, most airlines allow you to put a bicycle in the hold for a fee. You can either take it apart and pack all the pieces in a bike bag or box, or simply wheel it to the check-in desk, where it should be treated as a piece of check-in luggage. You may have to remove the pedals and turn the handlebars sideways so that it takes up less space in the aircraft's hold; check all this with the airline before you pay for your ticket. If your bicycle and other luggage exceed your weight allowance, ask about alternatives or you may find yourself being charged a small ransom for excess baggage.

Bus

There's a well-developed bus network linking Montenegro with the major cities of the former Yugoslavia and onwards to Western Europe and Turkey. At the border, guards will often enter the bus and collect passports, checking the photos as they go. Once they're happy with them they return them to the bus conductor who will return them as the driver speeds off. Make sure you get yours back and that it's been stamped.

Routes include the following:

Belgrade (Serbia) to Rožaje (€14, seven daily), Pljevlja (€18, three daily), Podgorica (€27, frequent), Nikšić (€26, every second day), Budva (€26, 15 daily), Petrovac (€29, five daily), Ulcinj (€33, four daily), Tivat (€28, daily), Kotor (€32, seven daily) and Herceg Novi (€33, seven daily). Allow 10 hours to Podgorica and 13 hours to Herceg Novi.

Dubrovnik (Croatia) to Herceg Novi (€10, two daily), Kotor (€14, two daily), Petrovac (€18, daily) and Podgorica (€19, daily). Allow two hours to Herceg Novi.

Peć (Kosovo) to Rožaje (€5, two daily) and Plav (€8, daily). Allow two hours to Rožaje; longer if there's snow.

Priština (Kosovo) to Rožaje (€10, daily), Podgorica (€17, daily) and Ulcinj (€18, six daily). Allow eight hours to Ulcinj.

Sarajevo (BiH) to Pljevlja (€9, daily), Nikšić (€15.50, three daily), Podgorica (€19, six daily), Budva (€22, four daily), Herceg Novi (€24, two daily) and Ulcinj (€26, daily). Allow seven hours to Herceg Novi.

Shkodra (Albania) to Ulcinj (€6, two daily); allow 90 minutes.

Trebinje (BiH) to Nikšić (€6.50, 1¾ hours, three daily).

Car & Motorcycle

Crossing into Montenegro with a private or hire car won't pose any problems as long as you have all of your papers in order. You must have vehicle registration/ownership documents and a locally valid insurance policy such as European Green Card vehicle insurance. Be sure to check your hire car insurance cover as some Western European companies will not cover you for travel in Montenegro.

From the major border crossings with Croatia, Serbia, Kosovo and Albania you won't have to drive more than 25km to find a petrol station or assistance with mechanical repairs. From the Bosnian crossings don't expect to find anything before Nikšić.

There have been incidences of attacks on cars with Montenegrin plates in Croatia (particularly around Dubrovnik) and on cars with Croatian plates in Montenegro (particularly around the Bay of Kotor). These are usually limited to minor vandalism, such as cars being keyed while parked on the road. The author of this book has experienced this first hand, with his Montenegrin-registered car spat upon by youths in Dubrovnik and his Croatian-registered car spat upon by youths in Herceg Novi. However, in the course of several weeks researching every nook of Montenegro for this book, the Herceg Novi incident was the only such problem encountered.

Train

Montenegro's main train line starts at Bar and heads north through the middle of Montenegro and into Serbia. At least two trains head between Bar and Belgrade daily (€21, 11 hours) with one continuing on to Novi Sad and Subotica. You'll find timetables on the website of Montenegro Railways (www.zpcg.me). From Belgrade it's possible to connect to destinations throughout Europe; see the Serbian Railways website (www.serbianrailways.com) for timetables.

- Montenegro can be included as part of the **Eurail** (www.eurail.com) Select Pass, which offers varying days of rail travel over a two-month period in three, four or five neighbouring countries; for the purposes of this pass, Montenegro and Serbia are counted as one country. Adult prices range from €348 (five days, three countries) to €766 (15 days, five countries). There are youth discounts for those 25 years old and younger.
- **InterRail** (www.interrailnet.com) passes can only be used by European residents of more than six months' standing. The Global Pass allows unlimited train travel in 30 countries (including Montenegro) during a set period of time. Some are valid over a continuous period, while others are more flexible. Prices depend on age and class; youth passes for those younger than 25 are cheaper than adult passes, and child passes are 50% less than adult. For some examples of prices, a Global Pass valid for five days of 2nd-class travel in a 10-day period costs €267/175 per adult/youth, or €638/422 for one continuous month. Terms, conditions and occasional surcharges may apply on certain trains.

- The Balkan Flexipass from **Rail Europe** (www.raileurope.com) covers rail travel in Montenegro, BiH, Serbia, Macedonia, Bulgaria, Greece, Romania and Turkey. It covers travel in 1st class only, and costs from US$255 for five days' travel in one month to US$536 for 15 days' travel in one month. Discounted passes are available for both youth and seniors.
- If you plan to travel extensively by train, it is worth getting hold of the Thomas Cook European Rail Timetable, which gives a complete listing of train and ferry schedules, reservation information and indicates where supplements apply. It's updated monthly and available from Thomas Cook outlets and can be ordered online via www.thomascookpublishing.com.

Border Crossings

ALBANIA

There are two main crossings: Sukobin (between Shkodra and Ulcinj) and Hani i Hotit (between Shkodra and Podgorica). If you're paddling about on Lake Skadar, remember that the border runs through the lake and be careful not to cross it. Because of problems with trafficking (of cigarettes, drugs and women), the Montenegro police patrol the lake. The same caution should be applied while hiking in the Prokletije Mountains.

BOSNIA & HERCEGOVINA

There are two main crossings: Dolovi (between Trebinje and Nikšić) and Šćepan Polje. Other more remote crossings are marked on some maps but these may only be open to local traffic (if they are open at all) and we've heard of travellers being turned back at some crossings.

CROATIA

Expect delays at the Debeli Brijeg checkpoint on the Adriatic highway (between Herceg Novi and Dubrovnik). You can avoid them by taking a detour down the Prevlaka Peninsula to the Kobila border post. It's been suggested to us that this crossing is only for locals, but we haven't experienced or heard of any problems crossing here. To reach it from the Croatian side, turn right off the highway a few kilometres before the main border crossing and pass through Pločice and Vitaljina. The road rejoins the highway on the Montenegro side just before Igalo.

KOSOVO

There's only one crossing, Kulina, on the road between Rožaje and Pe ć.

SERBIA

The busiest crossing is Dobrakovo (north of Bijelo Polje), followed by Dračenovac (northeast of Rožaje) and Ranče (east of Pljevlja). The train crosses at Dobrakovo.

Sea

Montenegro Lines (☎030-303 469; www.montenegrolines.net) has boats from Bar to Bari at least twice weekly from May to September (deck ticket €44 to €48, cabin €56 to €210, 10 hours); and from Bar to Ancona at least weekly from July to August (€51 to €60, cabin €70 to €230, 16 hours). Cars cost €68 to €90, but are free for bookings for four cabin passengers.

GETTING AROUND

Bicycle

Cyclists are a rare species even in the cities and there are no special bike lanes on the roads. Don't expect drivers to be considerate; wherever possible, try to get off the main roads. The wearing of helmets is not compulsory.

However, the outlook for cyclists isn't as grim as it sounds. The National Tourist Office has developed a series of wilderness mountain-biking trails, making a two-wheeled tour of Montenegro an excellent proposition. As most of the country is mountainous, you'll have to be exceedingly fit to attempt it.

The key to a successful bike trip is to travel light, and don't overdo it on the first few days. Even for the shortest and most basic trip it's worth carrying the tools necessary for repairing a puncture. You might want to consider packing spare brake and gear cables, spanners, Allen keys, spare spokes and strong adhesive tape. At the risk of stating the obvious, none of the above are much use unless you know what to do with them. Maintenance is also important: check over your bike thoroughly each morning and again at night when the day's touring is over. Take a good lock and always use it when you leave your bike unattended.

A seasoned cyclist can average about 80km a day, but this depends on the terrain and how much weight is being carried. Again, don't overdo it – there's no point burning yourself out during the initial stages.

FLIGHT-FREE TRAVEL

If you fancy a guilt-free, low-carbon journey from London to Montenegro, log on to www.seat61.com and click on Montenegro on the side navigation. You'll find detailed instructions on how to get from London to Belgrade by train and then connect through to Montenegro, including departure times, fares and travel-pass information.

Boat

There are no regular ferries within Montenegro, but taxi boats are common during summer. They can be hailed from the shore for a short trip along the coast or to one of the islands. They're harder to find outside the high season; look for them at the marinas. Some boats advertise set cruises, but normally they operate on an ad hoc basis.

Bus

The local bus network is extensive and reliable. Buses are usually comfortable and air-conditioned, and rarely full. It's not difficult to find information on services and prices from bus stations. Most have timetables displayed, although they're not always up to date. As with many service-industry types in Montenegro, some station staff are more helpful than others. Where English isn't spoken they'll usually write down prices and times of the bus for you.

It's a bit cheaper to buy your ticket on the bus rather than at the station, but a station-bought ticket theoretically guarantees you a seat. Reservations are only worthwhile a) for international buses, b) at holiday times, and c) where long-distance journeys are infrequent. Luggage carried below is charged at €1 per piece.

Smoking is forbidden on buses and this rule is generally enforced. The standard of driving is no better or worse than that of anyone else on the roads.

Car & Motorcycle

Independent travel by car or motorcycle is an ideal way to gad about and discover the country; some of the drives are breathtakingly beautiful. Traffic police are everywhere, so stick to speed limits and carry an International Driving Permit.

Allow more time than you'd expect for the distances involved as the terrain will slow you down. You'll rarely get up to 60km/hr on the Bay of Kotor road, for instance. The standard of roads is generally fair with conditions worsening in rural areas, especially in winter and after bad weather. A particularly notorious road is the Podgorica–Belgrade highway through the Morača Canyon, which is often made dangerous by bad conditions and high traffic. It's a good idea to drive defensively and treat everyone else on the road as a lunatic – when they get behind the wheel, many of them are. That said, no matter how much they toot at you or overtake on blind corners, you should avoid confrontation.

The only toll in Montenegro is the Sozina tunnel between Lake Skadar and the sea (€2.50 per car).

Automobile Associations

The **Automobile Association of Montenegro** (Auto Moto Savez Crne Gore; ☎roadside assistance 9807; www.amscg.org) offers roadside assistance, towing and repairs. The UK **Automobile Association** (www.theaa.com) has excellent information on its website, with specific driving advice for Montenegro.

Bring Your Own Vehicle

As long as you have registration/ownership papers with you and valid insurance cover, there should be no problem driving your car into Montenegro. If your vehicle has obvious signs of damage the border guards should provide you with a certificate that must be produced upon leaving to prove that the damage didn't occur inside the country.

Driver's Licence

It's recommended that you arrange an International Driving Permit from your home country before the trip. Although many rental companies will hire out a car based on your foreign driver's licence, there's no assurance that the traffic police will accept it and it doesn't pay to give them any excuse to fine you.

Fuel & Spare Parts

Filling up is no problem in any medium-sized town but don't leave it until the last drop. There are few late-night petrol stations. Diesel, unleaded 95 and 98 octane are easy to find. Spare parts for major makes will be no problem in cities, and mechanics are everywhere for simple repairs.

Hire

It's easy to hire a car in the bigger towns. Budva, in particular, has many options. The major European car-hire companies are in various centres including airports, but local alternatives are often cheaper. If you're flying into Dubrovnik, it will be more convenient to arrange to collect your car at the airport, but this will need to be balanced against the (minor) risk of vandalism of cars with Croatian plates in Montenegro (see p170).

Alamo (☎020-445 555; www.alamo.com) Pick up from Podgorica, Podgorica Airport or Dubrovnik Airport.

Avis (www.avisworld.com) Pick up from Podgorica, Tivat or Dubrovnik airports, or Budva.

Europcar (☎020-653 141; www.europcar.com) Pick up from Podgorica, Tivat or Dubrovnik airports.

Hertz (☎020-441 555; www.hertz.me) Pick up from Podgorica or Podgorica, Tivat or Dubrovnik airports.

In Montenegro (☎031-345 700; www.inmontenegro.com) Pick up from Herceg Novi, Tivat Airport and Podgorica Airport.

Meridian Rentacar (☎020-234 944; www.meridian-rentacar.com) A reliable local option with offices in Budva, Bar, Podgorica and Podgorica Airport; one-day hire starts from €30.

National (☎020-445 555; www.roksped.com) Pick up from Podgorica, Podgorica Airport or Dubrovnik Airport.

Sixt (☎033-453 100; www.sixt.com) Pick up from Herceg Novi, Tivat, Budva, Podgorica or Podgorica, Tivat or Dubrovnik airports.

Insurance

Third-party insurance is compulsory and you'll need to be able to prove you have it in order to bring a car into Montenegro. You should get your insurer to issue a Green Card (which may cost extra), an internationally recognised proof of insurance, and check that it lists all the countries you intend to visit. You'll need this in the event of an accident outside the country where the vehicle is insured. The European Accident Statement (known as the 'Constat Amiable' in France) is available from your insurance company and is copied so that each party at an accident can record information for insurance purposes. The Association of British Insurers (www.abi.org.uk) has more details. Never sign accident statements you cannot understand or read – insist on a translation and sign that only if it's acceptable.

Some insurance packages (particularly those covering rental cars) do not include all European countries and Montenegro is often one of those excluded – make sure you check this before you rent your car. When you're renting a car, ensure you check all aspects of the insurance offered, including the excess (you may wish to pay extra to reduce it) and rules regarding where you may or may not drive it (on dirt roads, for example).

Parking

Local parking habits are quite carefree, so it's possible you can be blocked in by someone double-parking next to you. Sometimes parking that looks illegal (eg on footpaths) is actually permitted.

Road Rules

- As in the rest of continental Europe, people drive on the right-hand side of the road and overtake on the left. Keep right except when overtaking, and use your indicators for any change of lane and when pulling away from the kerb.
- School buses can't be overtaken when they stop for passengers to board or alight.
- Vehicles entering a roundabout have right of way.
- Standard international road signs are used.
- By law you must wear a seatbelt (including in the back seat if fitted), drive with dipped headlights on (even during the day) and wear a helmet on a motorbike.
- Children's car seats aren't compulsory but kids under 12 and intoxicated passengers are not allowed in the front seat.
- Using a mobile phone while driving is prohibited.
- Driving barefoot is a no-no.
- Penalties for drink-driving are severe and could result in jail time. The legal limit is 0.05% of alcohol in your bloodstream. Police can issue an on-the-spot fine but cannot collect payment.
- Standard speed limits are 50km/h in built-up areas, 80km/h outside built-up areas and 100km/h on certain roads. Often the limit will change several times on a single stretch of the road because of mountainous conditions. Speeding 30km over the limit could lead to your driver's licence being temporarily confiscated.
- Cars must carry a set of replacement bulbs, first-aid kit, warning triangle and a reflective jacket.
- If you're involved in an accident resulting in major injury or material damage to your or another vehicle, you're legally obliged to report it to the police.

Hitching

Hitching is never entirely safe but it is a common practice in Montenegro. Wherever you are, there's always a risk when you catch a ride with strangers. It's safer to travel in pairs and to let someone know your plans. Once you've flagged down a vehicle, it's safer if you sit next to a door you can open. Ask the driver where they're going before you say where you are going. Trust your instincts if you feel uncomfortable about getting in, and get out at the first sign of trouble. You can find more pointers and info on ride sharing at www.hitchhikers.org.

Local Transport

Most Montenegrin towns, even Podgorica, are small enough to be travelled by foot. Podgorica is the only city to have a useful bus network, costing 80c per trip. Taxis are easily found in most towns. If they're not metered, agree on a fare in advance. Some Budva taxis have their meters set at extortionate rates, so ask to be let out if you suspect something's amiss.

Train

Montenegro Railways (Željeznica Crne Gore; www.zpcg.me) has services heading north from Bar and crossing the country before going into Serbia; useful stops include Virpazar, Podgorica, Kolašin, and Mojkovac. A second line heads northwest from Podgorica to Danilovgrad and Nikšić.

The trains are old and can be hot in summer, but they're priced accordingly and the route through the mountains is spectacular. In January 2006 a failure in the breaking system caused a train to derail in the Morača Canyon, killing 43 people and injuring hundreds. In November 2012 two people were killed when a train crashed into a repair trolley.

Language

Montenegrin belongs to the western group of the South Slavic language family. It is very similar to other languages in this group (Serbian, Croatian and Bosnian), and there are only slight variations in pronunciation and vocabulary between them.

Both Latin and Cyrillic alphabets are used in Montenegro. It's worth familiarising yourself with the latter in case you come across it on menus, timetables or street signs – see the box on the following page.

If you read our coloured pronunciation guides as if they were English, you'll be understood. The stressed syllables are indicated with italics – in most cases the stress falls on the first syllable in a word.

Some Montenegrin words have masculine and feminine forms, indicated after the relevant phrases in this chapter by 'm' and 'f'. Polite ('pol') and informal ('inf') alternatives are also included where necessary.

BASICS

Hello.	*Zdravo.*	*zdra*·vo
Goodbye.	*Do viđenja.*	do vi·*je*·nya
Yes.	*Da.*	da
No.	*Ne.*	ne
Please.	*Molim.*	*mo*·leem
Thank you.	*Hvala.*	*hva*·la
You're welcome.	*Nema na čemu.*	*ne*·ma na *che*·moo
Excuse me.	*Oprostite.*	o·*pro*·stee·te
Sorry.	*Žao mi je.*	*zha*·o mee ye

WANT MORE?

For in-depth language information and handy phrases, check out Lonely Planet's phrasebooks series. You'll find it at **shop.lonelyplanet.com**, or you can buy Lonely Planet's iPhone phrasebooks at the Apple App Store.

How are you?
Kako ste/si? (pol/inf) — *ka*·ko ste/see

Fine. And you?
Dobro. — *do*·bro
A vi/ti? (pol/inf) — a vee/tee

My name is ...
Zovem se ... — *zo*·vem se ...

What's your name?
Kako se zovete/zoveš? (pol/inf) — *ka*·ko se *zo*·ve·te/*zo*·vesh

Do you speak (English)?
Govorite/Govoriš li (engleski)? (pol/inf) — *go*·vo·ree·te/*go*·vo·reesh lee (*en*·gle·skee)

I (don't) understand.
(Ne) Razumijem. — (ne) ra·*zoo*·mee·yem

ACCOMMODATION

Do you have a room available?
Imate li slobodnih soba? — ee·ma·te lee *slo*·bod·neeh *so*·ba

Is breakfast included?
Da li je doručak uključen? — da lee ye *do*·roo·chak *ook*·lyoo·chen

How much is it (per night/per person)?
Koliko košta (za noć/po osobi)? — ko·*lee*·ko *kosh*·ta (za noch/po *o*·so·bee)

Do you have a ... room?	*Imate li ... sobu?*	ee·ma·te lee ... *so*·boo
single	*jednokrevetnu*	*yed*·no·kre·vet·noo
double	*dvokrevetnu*	*dvo*·kre·vet·noo

air-con	*klima-uređaj*	klee·ma·oo·re·jai
bathroom	*kupatilo*	koo·pa·tee·lo
bed	*krevet*	kre·vet
campsite	*kamp*	kamp
cot	*dječji krevet*	dyech·yee kre·vet
guesthouse	*privatni smještaj*	pree·vat·nee smyesh·tai
hotel	*hotel*	ho·tel
wi-fi	*bežični internet*	be·zheech·nee een·ter·net
window	*prozor*	pro·zor
youth hostel	*omladinsko prenoćište*	om·la·deen·sko pre·no·cheesh·te

DIRECTIONS

Where is ...?
Gdje je ...? gdye ye ...

What's the address?
Koja je adresa? ko·ya ye a·dre·sa

Can you show me (on the map)?
Možete li da mi pokažete (na mapi)? mo·zhe·te lee da mee po·ka·zhe·te (na ma·pee)

at the corner	*na uglu*	na oo·gloo
at the traffic lights	*na semaforu*	na se·ma·fo·roo
behind	*iza*	ee·za
in front of	*ispred*	ees·pred
far (from)	*daleko (od)*	da·le·ko (od)
left	*lijevo*	lee·ye·vo
near	*blizu*	blee·zoo
next to	*pored*	po·red
opposite	*nasuprot*	na·soo·prot
right	*desno*	de·sno
straight ahead	*pravo naprijed*	pra·vo na·pree·yed

EATING & DRINKING

What would you recommend?
Šta biste preporučili? shta bee·ste pre·po·roo·chee·lee

I'm a vegetarian.
Ja sam vegetarijanac/vegetarijanka. (m/f) ya sam ve·ge·ta·ree·ya·nats/ve·ge·ta·ree·yan·ka

That was delicious!
To je bilo izvrsno! to ye bee·lo eez·vr·sno

Please bring the menu/bill.
Molim vas donesite jelovnik/račun. mo·leem vas do·ne·see·te ye·lov·neek/ra·choon

CYRILLIC ALPHABET

In 2009 two new letters – indicated in the following list with an asterisk (*) – were introduced to the Montenegrin alphabet.

А а	a	short as the 'u' in 'cut'; long as in 'father'
Б б	b	as in 'but'
В в	v	as in 'van'
Г г	g	as in 'go'
Д д	d	as in 'dog'
Ђ ђ	j	as in 'joke'
Е е	e	short as in 'bet'; long as in 'there'
Ж ж	zh	as the 's' in 'measure'
З з	z	as in 'zoo'
*** З́ з́**		soft zh
И и	i	short as in 'bit'; long as in 'marine'
Ј ј	y	as in 'young'
К к	k	as in 'kind'
Л л	l	as in 'lamp'
Љ љ	ly	as the 'lli' in 'million'
М м	m	as in 'mat'
Н н	n	as in 'not'
Њ њ	ny	as in 'canyon'
О о	o	short as in 'hot'; long as in 'for'
П п	p	as in 'pick'
Р р	r	as in 'rub' (but rolled)
С с	s	as in 'sing'
*** С́ с́**		soft sh
Т т	t	as in 'ten'
Ћ ћ	ch	as in 'check'
У у	u	short as in 'put'; long as in 'rule'
Ф ф	f	as in 'fan'
Х х	h	as in 'hot'
Ц ц	ts	as in 'cats'
Ч ч	ch	as in 'change'
Џ џ	j	as in 'judge'
Ш ш	sh	as in 'shop'

I'd like a table for ...	*Htio/Htjela bih sto za ...* (m/f)	htee·o/htye·la beeh sto za ...
(eight) o'clock	*(osam) sati*	(o·sam) sa·tee
(two) people	*(dvoje) ljudi*	(dvo·ye) lyoo·dee

I don't eat ...	*Ne jedem ...*	ne ye·dem ...
fish	*ribu*	ree·boo
meat	*meso*	me·so
nuts	*orahe*	o·ra·he

Signs

Izlaz	Exit
Muški	Men
Otvoreno	Open
Ulaz	Entrance
Zabranjeno	Prohibited
Toaleti/WC	Toilets
Zatvoreno	Closed
Ženski	Women

Key Words

bar	*bar*	bar
bottle	*boca*	*bo*·tsa
breakfast	*doručak*	*do*·roo·chak
cafe	*kafić*	*ka*·feech
cold	*hladno*	*hlad*·no
dinner	*večera*	*ve*·che·ra
fork	*viljuška*	*vee*·lyoosh·ka
glass	*čaša*	*cha*·sha
knife	*nož*	nozh
lunch	*ručak*	*roo*·chak
plate	*tanjir*	*ta*·nyeer
restaurant	*restoran*	re·*sto*·ran
spoon	*kašika*	*ka*·shee·ka
warm	*toplo*	*top*·lo

Meat & Fish

beef	*govedina*	*go*·ve·di·na
carp	*šaran*	*sha*·ran
chicken	*piletina*	*pi*·le·ti·na
cod	*bakalar*	ba·*ka*·lar
crabs	*račići*	*ra*·chi·chi
hake	*oslić*	o·slich
ham	*šunka*	*shun*·ka
lamb	*jagnjetina*	*yag*·nye·ti·na
lobster	*jastog*	*ya*·stog
mussels	*dagnje*	*dag*·nye
oysters	*školjke*	*shkoly*·ke
pork	*svinjetina*	*svi*·nye·ti·na
prawns	*škampi*	*shkam*·pi
salmon	*losos*	*lo*·sos
sausage	*kobasica*	ko·*ba*·si·tsa
squid	*lignje*	*lig*·nye
trout	*pastrmka*	*pas*·trm·ka
turkey	*ćuretina*	*chu*·re·ti·na
veal	*teletina*	*te*·le·ti·na

Fruit & Vegetables

apple	*jabuka*	*ya*·bu·ka
apricot	*kajsija*	*kai*·si·ya
banana	*banana*	ba·*na*·na
beans	*pasulj*	*pa*·suly
beetroot	*cvekla*	*tsve*·kla
cabbage	*kupus*	*ku*·pus
capsicum	*paprika*	*pa*·pri·ka
carrot	*šargarepa*	shar·ga·*re*·pa
cauliflower	*karfiol*	kar·*fi*·ol
cherry	*višnja*	*vish*·nya
cucumber	*krastavac*	*kra*·sta·vats
fig	*smokva*	*smok*·va
grapes	*grožđe*	*grozh*·je
lemon	*limun*	*li*·mun
lettuce	*zelena salata*	*ze*·le·na sa·*la*·ta
melon	*dinja*	*di*·nya
mushrooms	*pečurke*	*pe*·chur·ke
olives	*masline*	*mas*·li·ne
onion	*crni luk*	*tsr*·ni luk
orange	*pomorandža*	po·*mo*·ran·ja
peach	*breskva*	*bres*·kva
pear	*kruška*	*kru*·shka
peas	*grašak*	*gra*·shak
plum	*šljiva*	*shlyi*·va
potato	*krompir*	*krom*·pir
spinach	*spanać*	*spa*·nach
strawberry	*jagoda*	*ya*·go·da
tomato	*paradajz*	pa·ra·*daiz*
watermelon	*lubenica*	lu·*be*·ni·tsa

Other

bread	*hljeb*	hlyeb
cheese	*sir*	seer
egg	*jaje*	*ya*·ye
honey	*med*	med
pepper	*biber*	*bee*·ber
rice	*pirinač*	*pee*·ree·nach
salt	*so*	so
sugar	*šećer*	*she*·cher

Drinks

beer	*pivo*	*pee*·vo
coffee	*kafa*	*ka*·fa
(fruit) juice	*(voćni) sok*	(*voch*·nee) sok
milk	*mljeko*	*mlye*·ko

tea	*čaj*	chai
(mineral) water	*(mineralna) voda*	(*mee*·ne·ral·na) *vo*·da
(red/white) wine	*(crno/bijelo) vino*	(*tsr*·no/*bye*·lo) *vee*·no

EMERGENCIES

Help!
Upomoć! oo·po·moch

Leave me alone!
Ostavite me na miru! o·sta·vee·te me na *mee*·roo

I'm lost.
Izgubio/ Izgubila sam se. (m/f) eez·*goo*·bee·o/ eez·*goo*·bee·la sam se

Call a doctor!
Zovite ljekara! *zo*·vee·te lye·*ka*·ra

Call the police!
Zovite policiju! *zo*·vee·te po·*lee*·tsee·yoo

I'm ill.
Ja sam bolestan/ bolesna. (m/f) ya sam *bo*·le·stan/ *bo*·le·sna

I'm allergic to ...
Ja sam alergičan/ alergična na ... (m/f) ya sam a·*ler*·gee·chan/ a·*ler*·geech·na na ...

Where are the toilets?
Gdje su toaleti? gdye soo to·a·*le*·tee

SHOPPING & SERVICES

I'd like to buy ...
Želim da kupim ... *zhe*·leem da *koo*·peem ...

I'm just looking.
Samo razgledam. *sa*·mo *raz*·gle·dam

May I look at it?
Mogu li da pogledam? *mo*·goo lee da *po*·gle·dam

How much is it?
Koliko košta? ko·*lee*·ko *kosh*·ta

That's too expensive.
To je preskupo. to ye *pre*·skoo·po

Do you have something cheaper?
Imate li nešto jeftinije? *ee*·ma·te lee *nesh*·to yef·*tee*·nee·ye

There's a mistake in the bill.
Neka je greška na računu. *ne*·ka ye *gresh*·ka na ra·*choo*·noo

Question Words

How?	*Kako?*	*ka*·ko
What?	*Šta?*	shta
When?	*Kada?*	*ka*·da
Where?	*Gdje?*	gdye
Who?	*Ko?*	ko
Why?	*Zašto?*	*za*·shto

bank	*banka*	*ban*·ka
market	*pijaca*	*pee*·ya·tsa
post office	*pošta*	*posh*·ta
tourist office	*turistički biro*	too·*ree*·steech·kee *bee*·ro

TIME & DATES

What time is it?
Koliko je sati? ko·*lee*·ko ye *sa*·tee

It's (10) o'clock.
(Deset) je sati. (*de*·set) ye *sa*·tee

Half past (10).
(Deset) i po. (*de*·set) ee po

morning	*jutro*	*yoo*·tro
afternoon	*poslijepodne*	*po*·slee·ye·*pod*·ne
evening	*veče*	*ve*·che
yesterday	*juče*	*yoo*·che
today	*danas*	*da*·nas
tomorrow	*sjutra*	*syoo*·tra

Monday	*ponedjeljak*	po·*ne*·dye·lyak
Tuesday	*utorak*	*oo*·to·rak
Wednesday	*srijeda*	sree·*ye*·da
Thursday	*četvrtak*	chet·*vr*·tak
Friday	*petak*	*pe*·tak
Saturday	*subota*	*soo*·bo·ta
Sunday	*nedjelja*	*ne*·dye·lya

January	*januar*	*ya*·noo·ar
February	*februar*	*feb*·roo·ar
March	*mart*	mart
April	*april*	*ap*·reel
May	*maj*	mai
June	*jun*	yoon
July	*jul*	yool
August	*avgust*	*av*·goost
September	*septembar*	*sep*·tem·bar
October	*oktobar*	*ok*·to·bar
November	*novembar*	*no*·vem·bar
December	*decembar*	*de*·tsem·bar

TRANSPORT

Public Transport

boat	*brod*	brod
bus	*autobus*	a·oo·*to*·boos
plane	*avion*	a·vee·on
train	*voz*	voz

Numbers

1	*jedan*	*ye*·dan
2	*dva*	dva
3	*tri*	tree
4	*četiri*	*che*·tee·ree
5	*pet*	pet
6	*šest*	shest
7	*sedam*	*se*·dam
8	*osam*	*o*·sam
9	*devet*	*de*·vet
10	*deset*	*de*·set
20	*dvadeset*	*dva*·de·set
30	*trideset*	*tree*·de·set
40	*četrdeset*	che·tr·*de*·set
50	*pedeset*	pe·*de*·set
60	*šezdeset*	shez·*de*·set
70	*sedamdeset*	se·dam·*de*·set
80	*osamdeset*	o·sam·*de*·set
90	*devedeset*	de·ve·*de*·set
100	*sto*	sto
1000	*hiljadu*	*hee*·lya·doo

I want to go to (Dubrovnik).
Htio/Htjela bih da idem u (Dubrovnik). (m/f) — *htee*·o/*htye*·la beeh da *ee*·dem oo (*doo*·brov·neek)

Does it stop at (Budva)?
Staje li u (Budvi)? — *sta*·ye lee oo (*bood*·vee)

What time does it leave?
U koliko sati kreće? — oo ko·*lee*·ko *sa*·tee *kre*·che

What time does it get to (Podgorica)?
U koliko sati stiže u (Podgoricu)? — oo ko·*lee*·ko *sa*·tee *stee*·zhe oo (*pod*·go·ree·tsoo)

Could you tell me when we get to (Cetinje)?
Možete li mi reći kada stignemo do (Cetinja)? — *mo*·zhe·te lee mee *re*·chee *ka*·da *steeg*·ne·mo do (*tse*·tee·nya)

I'd like to get off at (Kotor).
Želim da izađem u (Kotoru). — *zhe*·leem da *ee*·za·jem oo (*ko*·to·roo)

A ... ticket.	*Jednu ... kartu.*	*yed*·noo ... *kar*·too
1st-class	*prvo-razrednu*	pr·vo·*raz*·red·noo
2nd-class	*drugo-razrednu*	*droo*·go·*raz*·red·noo
one-way	*jedno smjernu-*	*yed*·no·smyer·noo
return	*povratnu*	*po*·vrat·noo

first	*prvi*	*pr*·vee
last	*poslednji*	*pos*·led·nyee

aisle seat	*sjedište do prolaza*	*sye*·deesh·te do *pro*·la·za
platform	*peron*	*pe*·ron
ticket office	*blagajna*	*bla*·gai·na
timetable	*red vožnje*	red *vozh*·nye
station	*stanica*	*sta*·nee·tsa
window seat	*sjedište do prozora*	*sye*·deesh·te do *pro*·zo·ra

Driving & Cycling

I'd like to hire a ...	*Htio/Htjela bih da iznajmim ...* (m/f)	*htee*·o/*htye*·la beeh da eez·nai·meem ...
4WD	*džip*	jeep
bicycle	*bicikl*	bee·*tsee*·kl
car	*auto*	*a*·oo·to
motorcycle	*motocikl*	mo·to·*tsee*·kl

bicycle pump	*pumpa za bicikl*	*poom*·pa za bee·*tsee*·kl
child seat	*sjedište za dijete*	*sye*·deesh·te za dee·*ye*·te
diesel	*dizel gorivo*	*dee*·zel *go*·ree·vo
helmet	*kaciga*	*ka*·tsee·ga
mechanic	*auto-mehaničar*	*a*·oo·to·me·*ha*·nee·char
petrol	*benzin*	*ben*·zeen
service station	*benziska stanica*	*ben*·zeen·ska *sta*·nee·tsa

Is this the road to (Herceg Novi)?
Je li ovo put za (Herceg Novi)? — ye lee *o*·vo poot za (*her*·tseg *no*·vee)

(How long) Can I park here?
(Koliko dugo) Mogu ovdje da parkiram? — (ko·*lee*·ko *doo*·go) *mo*·goo *ov*·dye da *par*·kee·ram

The car/motorbike has broken down (at Bar).
Automobil/Motocikl se pokvario (u Baru). — a·oo·to·*mo*·beel/mo·to·*tsee*·kl se pok·*va*·ree·o (oo *ba*·roo)

I need a mechanic.
Treba mi automehaničar. — *tre*·ba mee a·oo·to·me·*ha*·nee·char

I have a flat tyre.
Imam probušenu gumu. — ee·mam *pro*·boo·she·noo *goo*·moo

I've run out of petrol.
Nestalo mi je benzina. — *ne*·sta·lo mee ye ben·*zee*·na

I've lost the keys.
Izgubio/Izgubila sam ključeve. (m/f) — eez·*goo*·bee·o/eez·*goo*·bee·la sam *klyoo*·che·ve

GLOSSARY

aerodrom – airport
autocamp – camping ground for tents and caravans
Avars – Eastern European people who waged war against Byzantium from the 6th to 9th centuries

bb – in an address the letters 'bb' following a street name (eg Jadranski Put bb) stand for *bez broja* (without number), indicating that the building has no street number
Bokelj – inhabitant of Boka Kotorska (Bay of Kotor)
Bosniak – Slavic Muslim, not necessarily from Bosnia
burek – heavy pastry stuffed with meat or cheese

čaršija – old market area
Cattaro – Venetian name for Kotor
ćevapčići – small spicy beef or pork sausages
čojstvo i junaštvo – literally 'humanity and bravery' (ie the concept of chivalry present in Montenegrin culture)
crkva – church
Crna Gora – Montenegrin name for Montenegro (literally 'black mountain')

Dom kulture – cultural centre
Dom zdravlja – medical centre
donji (m), donja (f) – lower
Duklja – early Serbian state considered a precursor of Montenegro
džamija –mosque

galerija – gallery
garderoba – left-luggage office
Glagolitic – ancient Slavic alphabet (precursor of the Cyrillic alphabet) created by Greek missionaries Cyril and Methodius
gora – mountain
gornji (m), gornja (f) – upper
gorske oči – literally 'mountain eyes'; name for glacial lakes in mountainous regions
grad – city
guslar – singer/composer of epic poetry accompanied by the *gusle*
gusle – one-stringed folk instrument

hajduk – Balkan outlaw during the period of Ottoman rule
hammam – Turkish bathhouse
Hitna pomoć – emergency clinic

Illyrians – ancient inhabitants of the Adriatic coast, defeated by the Romans in the 2nd century BC
ispod sača – (meat) roasted under a metal lid covered with hot coals

jezero – lake

karst – highly porous limestone and dolomitic rock
katun – traditional shepherds' mountain hut
klapa – a traditional form of unaccompanied singing from Dalmatia
klima – air conditioning
kolo – lively Slavic round dance in which men and women alternate in the circle
konoba – the traditional term for a small, intimate dining spot, often located in a cellar; now applies to a wide variety of restaurants; usually a simple, family-run establishment
kula – a blocky tower-like house built for defence

mali (m), mala (f) – little
manastir – monastery
most – bridge
muzej – museum

novi (m), nova (f) – new

obala – waterfront
oro – traditional Montenegrin circle dance
ostrvo – island

palačinke – pancakes
Partisans – communist-led WWII resistance fighters
pivo – beer
plaža – beach
polje – field
pršut – smoke-dried ham
put – path; road; trail

rakija – fruit brandy
ražnjići – small chunks of pork grilled on a skewer
restoran – restaurant
rijeka – river
rruga – Albanian word for 'street' (used in Ulcinj street names)

šetalište – walkway
sladoled – ice cream
sobe (pl) – rooms (available for hire)
stara maslina – literally 'old olive', a famous 2000-year-old tree in Bar
stari (m), stara (f) – old
Stari Grad – Old Town
stećci – mysterious carved stone monuments from the Middle Ages found throughout northern Montenegro
sveti (m), sveta (f) – saint

trg – square
turbofolk – version of Serbian music, a mix of folk and pop

ulica – street

veliki (m), velika (f) – large
vladika – bishop-prince
vrh – peak; summit

Zakonik – legal code (historic term)
Zdravstvena stanica – medical centre or emergency clinic
Zeta – early Serbian state considered a precursor of Montenegro
zimmer – German word for 'rooms' (available for hire)

Behind the Scenes

SEND US YOUR FEEDBACK

We love to hear from travellers – your comments keep us on our toes and help make our books better. Our well-travelled team reads every word on what you loved or loathed about this book. Although we cannot reply individually to postal submissions, we always guarantee that your feedback goes straight to the appropriate authors, in time for the next edition. Each person who sends us information is thanked in the next edition – the most useful submissions are rewarded with a selection of digital PDF chapters.

Visit **lonelyplanet.com/contact** to submit your updates and suggestions or to ask for help. Our award-winning website also features inspirational travel stories, news and discussions.

Note: We may edit, reproduce and incorporate your comments in Lonely Planet products such as guidebooks, websites and digital products, so let us know if you don't want your comments reproduced or your name acknowledged. For a copy of our privacy policy visit lonelyplanet.com/privacy.

OUR READERS

Many thanks to the travellers who used the last edition and wrote to us with helpful hints, useful advice and interesting anecdotes:
Bo Ahren, Drita Busatlic, Neil Clipperton, Antoinette Daley, Jennifer Delany, Carol Fisher, James Gardiner, Richard Gault, Gerrit Glas, Kay Harrison, Heather Holt, Garfield Lam, Diana Maddison, Ignacio Morejon, John Newton, Andrea Palazzi, Aude Richon, Sarah A Smith, Vic Sofras, Angus Stewart, Suzanne Stuijfzand, Ciska Tillema, Daniel Torocsik, Maurice & Karin Van Dael, Marie-Jose Zondag

AUTHOR THANKS

Peter Dragičević

Many thanks to all the wonderful people who helped me on the ground in Montenegro, especially Ivica Erdelja, Hayley Wright and Jack Delf, Emma and Ben Heywood, Krstinja Petranović, Danica Ćeranić and Matthew Lane. Also, I owe a debt of gratitude to James and Lorraine Hedderman, Tim Benzie and Kerri Tyler for their contributions before and after the journey.

Vesna Marić

Massive thanks to Rafael, Frida and my mother, as well as to Sanja, Jon, and beautiful Irian, in Dubrovnik.

ACKNOWLEDGMENTS

Climate map data adapted from Peel MC, Finlayson BL & McMahon TA (2007) 'Updated World Map of the Köppen-Geiger Climate Classification', Hydrology and Earth System Sciences, 11, 1633–44.

Extract (p152) from Euro Neuro © Rambo Amadeus 2012. Used by permission of the publisher.

Cover photograph: Kastio fortress, Petrovac, Johanna Huber/4Corners ©

THIS BOOK

This 2nd edition of Lonely Planet's *Montenegro* guidebook was researched and written by Peter Dragičević. Vesna Marić wrote the Dubrovnik (Croatia) chapter. The previous edition was also written by Peter Dragičević and Vesna Marić; the History chapter was written by Will Gourlay.

This guidebook was commissioned in Lonely Planet's London office, and produced by the following:

Commissioning Editors Korina Miller, Joanna Cooke, Dora Whitaker, James Smart
Coordinating Editors Nigel Chin, Andrea Dobbin
Coordinating Cartographer Mark Griffiths
Coordinating Layout Designer Joseph Spanti
Managing Editors Barbara Delissen, Annelies Mertens
Senior Editor Catherine Naghten
Managing Cartographers Alison Lyall, Anthony Phelan
Managing Layout Designer Chris Girdler
Assisting Editors Holly Alexander, Luna Soo
Cover Research Naomi Parker
Internal Image Research Aude Vauconsant
Language Content Branislava Vladisavljević
Thanks to Ryan Evans, Larissa Frost, Jouve India, Trent Paton, Kirsten Rawlings, Raphael Richards, Gerard Walker

Index

Map Pages **000**
Photo Pages **000**

D

E

F

Map Pages **000**
Photo Pages **000**

V

W

Y

Z

Map Legend

Sights

- Beach
- Bird Sanctuary
- Buddhist
- Castle/Palace
- Christian
- Confucian
- Hindu
- Islamic
- Jain
- Jewish
- Monument
- Museum/Gallery/Historic Building
- Ruin
- Sento Hot Baths
- Shinto
- Sikh
- Taoist
- Winery/Vineyard
- Zoo
- Other Sight

Activities, Courses & Tours

- Bodysurfing
- Diving/Snorkelling
- Canoeing/Kayaking
- Course/Tour
- Skiing
- Snorkelling
- Surfing
- Swimming/Pool
- Walking
- Windsurfing
- Other Activity

Sleeping

- Sleeping
- Camping

Eating

- Eating

Drinking & Nightlife

- Drinking & Nightlife
- Cafe

Entertainment

- Entertainment

Shopping

- Shopping

Information

- Bank
- Embassy/Consulate
- Hospital/Medical
- Internet
- Police
- Post Office
- Telephone
- Toilet
- Tourist Information
- Other Information

Geographic

- Beach
- Hut/Shelter
- Lighthouse
- Lookout
- Mountain/Volcano
- Oasis
- Park
- Pass
- Picnic Area
- Waterfall

Population

- Capital (National)
- Capital (State/Province)
- City/Large Town
- Town/Village

Transport

- Airport
- Border crossing
- Bus
- Cable car/Funicular
- Cycling
- Ferry
- Metro station
- Monorail
- Parking
- Petrol station
- Subway station
- Taxi
- Train station/Railway
- Tram
- Underground station
- Other Transport

Note: Not all symbols displayed above appear on the maps in this book

Routes

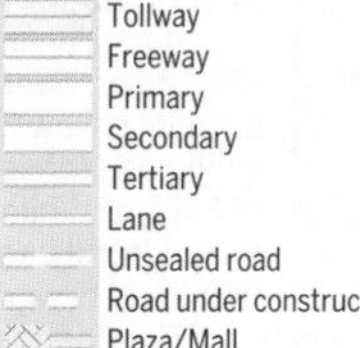

- Tollway
- Freeway
- Primary
- Secondary
- Tertiary
- Lane
- Unsealed road
- Road under construction
- Plaza/Mall
- Steps
- Tunnel
- Pedestrian overpass
- Walking Tour
- Walking Tour detour
- Path/Walking Trail

Boundaries

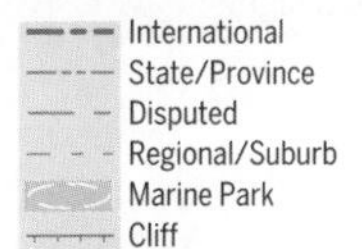

- International
- State/Province
- Disputed
- Regional/Suburb
- Marine Park
- Cliff
- Wall

Hydrography

- River, Creek
- Intermittent River
- Canal
- Water
- Dry/Salt/Intermittent La
- Reef

Areas

- Airport/Runway
- Beach/Desert
- Cemetery (Christian)
- Cemetery (Other)
- Glacier
- Mudflat
- Park/Forest
- Sight (Building)
- Sportsground
- Swamp/Mangrove

OUR STORY

A beat-up old car, a few dollars in the pocket and a sense of adventure. In 1972 that's all Tony and Maureen Wheeler needed for the trip of a lifetime – across Europe and Asia overland to Australia. It took several months, and at the end – broke but inspired – they sat at their kitchen table writing and stapling together their first travel guide, *Across Asia on the Cheap*. Within a week they'd sold 1500 copies. Lonely Planet was born.

Today, Lonely Planet has offices in Melbourne, London and Oakland, with more than 600 staff and writers. We share Tony's belief that 'a great guidebook should do three things: inform, educate and amuse'.

OUR WRITERS

Peter Dragičević

Coordinating Author; Bay of Kotor, Adriatic Coast, Central Montenegro, Northern Mountains After a dozen years working for newspapers and magazines in both his native New Zealand and Australia, Peter finally gave in to Kiwi wanderlust, giving up staff jobs to chase his typically antipodean diverse roots around much of Europe. While it was family ties that first drew him to the Balkans, it's the history, natural beauty, convoluted politics, cheap *rakija* and, most importantly, the intriguing people, that keep bringing him back. He wrote the very first edition of this book when the country was freshly independent and has contributed to literally dozens of other Lonely Planet titles, including four successive editions of the *Eastern Europe* guide.

Contributing Writer

Vesna Marić wrote the Dubrovnik (Croatia) chapter. Vesna was born in Bosnia and Hercegovina while it was still a part of Yugoslavia, and she has never been able to see Croatia as a foreign country. A lifetime lover of Dalmatia's beaches, pine trees, food and wine, she found researching this chapter a true delight.

Published by Lonely Planet Publications Pty Ltd
ABN 36 005 607 983
2nd edition – June 2013
ISBN 978 1 74179 602 5

10 9 8 7 6 5 4 3 2
Printed in Singapore